The
Expanded
Campus

Dyckman W. Vermilye, EDITOR

1972

CURRENT ISSUES IN HIGHER EDUCATION

ASSOCIATE EDITOR, *Joseph Axelrod*

THE
EXPANDED
CAMPUS

Jossey-Bass Inc., Publishers
San Francisco · Washington · London · 1972

THE EXPANDED CAMPUS
Dyckman W. Vermilye, Editor

Library of Congress Catalogue Card Number LC 72-6043

International Standard Book Number ISBN 0-87589-143-8

Manufactured in the United States of America

JACKET DESIGN BY WILLI BAUM

FIRST EDITION

Code 7228

THE JOSSEY-BASS SERIES IN HIGHER EDUCATION

 A publication of the

AMERICAN ASSOCIATION FOR HIGHER EDUCATION
National Center for Higher Education
One Dupont Circle, Northwest
Washington, D.C. 20036

DYCKMAN W. VERMILYE, *Executive Director*

The American Association for Higher Education, AAHE,
promotes higher education and provides a national
voice for individual members. AAHE, founded in 1870,
is the only national higher education organization
open to faculty members, administrators, graduate
students, and trustees without regard to rank, discipline,
or type or size of institution. AAHE is dedicated to
the professional development of college and university
educators, to the achievement of their educational
objectives, and to the improvement of conditions
of service.

45863

Preface

The financial worries of higher education have not blown away, but they do not appear to be the obsession they were a few years ago. This is not to say colleges are better off financially. In some quarters, notably in the private sector, a real threat to survival exists. But even there the initial shock of curtailed prosperity has given way to a shirt-sleeve, belt-tightening determination to make do with what's at hand.

Efforts in this direction might be expected to weaken efforts in other directions—particularly service to society—but if the chapters in *The Expanded Campus* are any indication, this weakening has not occurred. The new austerity seems to have sharpened rather than dulled the sense of social commitment among institutions. Perhaps, coupled with all the other challenges colleges have had to face the past few years, having to hustle to make ends meet has burned off fat and toned muscles grown sluggish with complacency. Whatever the reasons, higher education seems more sensitive than ever to the needs of society and more determined to meet them. The prevailing mood is summed up in the title of Samuel Gould's contribution to this volume: "Less Talk, More Action."

The campus is expanding, not just physically and numerically but ideologically. Colleges and universities are trying to reach out to new students in new ways. The idea of universal higher education—or higher education for almost anybody who wants it—is far from a reality, but it is no longer just a dream. The doors are opening. The gap between action and intention is closing. The first trials have been run and the first errors made. Colleges and universities, whose standards and traditions people have always been expected to adjust to, are trying to learn to adjust to people. And they are finding it is not an easy adjustment to make.

For one thing, there is all this diversity to contend with. It is so much easier to fit the people into the mold than to fit the mold to the people. It is easier because those who do not fit either do not get in or get in and do not last long. Viewed this way, college is synonymous with test. Those who do not pass are failures; the burden is on them. Now, increasingly, the burden is on the colleges as centers of teaching and learning, and students are the test.

For colleges and universities today, the heart of the challenge is the recognition and accommodation of personhood—the personhood of women, blacks, young, old, rich, poor, gifted, and plodding —in whatever form it touches academic life. This challenge runs through nearly all the twenty-five chapters in *The Expanded Campus* from the deft summary of, and reactions to, the work of the Carnegie Commission to Ivan Illich's eloquently searing critique of education as a bureaucracy designed to perpetuate the established order of people and things. While it is appropriate to call for less talk, more action, it is comforting to note that, in any event, the action has begun. This book is about some of the things institutions have learned as a result.

My special thanks to K. Patricia Cross, who served as chairman of the Twenty-Seventh National Conference on Higher Education, helped shape the sessions from which *The Expanded Campus* was drawn, and assisted in the editorial selection process.

Washington, D.C.   DYCKMAN W. VERMILYE
September 1972

Contents

Contributors

STEPHEN K. BAILEY, chairman, Policy Institute, Syracuse University Research Corporation

LAURA BORNHOLDT, vice-president, The Danforth Foundation

JOHN A. CENTRA, research psychologist, Educational Testing Service

KING V. CHEEK, JR., president, Morgan State College

SHIRLEY CHISHOLM, U. S. Representative from New York

ARLAND F. CHRIST-JANER, president, College Entrance Examination Board

E. D. DURYEA, professor, Department of Higher Education, State University of New York at Buffalo

ROBERT S. FISK, professor of educational studies, State University of New York at Buffalo

GEORGE FRANCIS, professor and chairman, Department of Man-Environment Studies, University of Waterloo, Ontario

SAMUEL B. GOULD, chairman, Commission on Non-Traditional Study

ROBERT G. HARRIS, president, Johnson County Community College

IVAN ILLICH, director, Center for Intercultural Documentation, Cuernavaca, Mexico

MORRIS KEETON, academic vice-president, Antioch College

CLARK KERR, chairman, Carnegie Commission on Higher Education

JANE LICHTMAN, director, American Association for Higher Education Free University Project

JAMES L. MILLER, JR., professor of higher education, Center for the Study of Higher Education, University of Michigan

FLORENCE MOOG, professor, Department of Biology, Washington University

EZRA A. NAUGHTON, associate secretary, American Association of University Professors, and director, Project for Developing Institutions

JOHN F. NOONAN, professor of English and chairman, Liberal Studies Program, Findlay College

GARY H. QUEHL, executive director, College Center of the Finger Lakes

PAUL C. REINERT, president, Saint Louis University

RICHARD C. RICHARDSON, JR., president, Northampton County Area Community College

BERNICE SANDLER, executive associate, Association of American Colleges

SHELDON ELLIOT STEINBACH, staff associate, American Council on Education

DAVID E. SWEET, president, Minnesota Metropolitan State College

ALAN WOLFE, professor of sociology, Richmond College of the City University of New York

The
Expanded
Campus

PART ONE

The Carnegie Commission: Point and Counterpoint

The Carnegie Commission on Higher Education has undertaken the most comprehensive study of higher education ever done. The work of the Commission is now more than two-thirds completed, and it is therefore appropriate for educators to speculate in a preliminary way about the impact the Commission is likely to have.

The opening chapter by Clark Kerr reviews the work of the Commission and the recommendations it has made. "Policy Concerns for the Future" defines the seven policy areas that have been of special concern to the Commission and analyzes the major problems within each area. Kerr's goal is "to demonstrate the roles policy can play in shaping the future of higher education."

Of the chapters that follow, two are favorable to the Commission approach and philosophy: "A Reaction to the Commission Recommendations," by Richard Richardson, and "Pluralism and Diversity in Higher Education," by Paul Reinert. The third essay is unfavorable. "The Carnegie Commission: Voice of the Establish-

ment," by Alan Wolfe, expresses the view that Commission accomplishments will contribute little to a solution of the basic problem confronting higher education because the Commission "has defined the problem incorrectly" in the first place.

According to Wolfe, a reader of the Commission reports would never suspect that the fundamental crisis in higher education "is systemic, involving our whole political and economic system," and he criticizes the Commission for its "failure to be theoretical, to place things in their political context, to examine causes, to be historical."

Richardson, however, agrees with "much that the Commission has said," and he commends the Commission particularly for its sensitivity to articulation problems between the community college and the four-year college. But some aspects of the work of the Commission cause Richardson serious concern. He believes, for example, that Commission recommendations "often unsuccessfully seek to chart bold new directions while at the same time preserving all of the established practices."

For Reinert, too, there are some areas of dissatisfaction. His fundamental dispute with the Commission lies in its willingness "to sacrifice the principle of pluralism and diversity in higher education" as it pursues another important goal, the principle of equality of opportunity. But Reinert makes clear that he, like Richardson, supports the bulk of the Commission recommendations.

The four chapters of Part One provide a surprisingly complete—although, admittedly, preliminary—view of responses to the Commission. The reader will come away from them with a comprehensive picture of the way the Commission has approached its task, the directions it has taken, and its accomplishments to date. The chapters also demonstrate how three knowledgeable and outspoken educators have found both satisfaction and disappointment in the work of the Commission. But the reader will realize from these chapters that the Commission agenda has been monumental in scope and that the potential impact of its recommendations has great significance for higher education.

JOSEPH AXELROD

🙰 1 🙰

Policy Concerns
for the Future

Clark Kerr

🙰🙰🙰🙰🙰🙰🙰🙰🙰🙰🙰🙰

During the 1960s, American higher education faced growing pressures from within and without. As a result, the late 1960s ushered in a period of intensive reassessment, a period in which faults in the existing system as well as certain new directions became more visible, a period of transition to respond to new clienteles and to the needs of a rapidly changing society.

In this period of transition, inevitably, task forces and commissions arose under various auspices to examine the goals and structure of higher education in its rapidly changing context. In 1968 the President asked Wilbur Cohen, Secretary of Health, Education and Welfare, to prepare a long-range plan for federal finan-

3

cial support for higher education. Again, in 1970, a special presidentially appointed task force under the chairmanship of James Hester was asked to report on federal priorities in higher education. In 1969, the American Academy of Arts and Sciences appointed a group under the chairmanship of Martin Meyerson to suggest and develop new possibilities for defining the missions of universities and the means of carrying them out. And about the same time, then Secretary of HEW, Robert Finch, appointed a task force chaired by Frank Newman to appraise and propose needed changes in higher education. This task force has now been reorganized somewhat to develop more specific recommendations growing out of its proposals. In specific response to turbulence on campus, President Nixon appointed a special committee under the chairmanship of William Scranton to look into the causes of unrest on America's campuses. At the national level several other commissions, including many working under the auspices of particular higher education associations, examined specific aspects of higher education. The 1960s also gave rise to numerous state commissions created to study particularly questions concerning the status of private higher education, the need for coordination and control at the state level, and development of future plans to meet the state's demands for postsecondary education.

The proliferation of commissions and task forces in a period of transition is to be expected; what is somewhat less expected is that commissions operating under quite different auspices and with substantially different membership characteristics, funding patterns, and methods of operation should have so many significant areas of agreement on both the weaknesses in the present system and the measures to remedy those weaknesses.

The work of the Carnegie Commission has been aided by the work of these many other groups studying higher education. Whether in the future the Carnegie Commission will be looked upon as one of the more influential commissions studying higher education in the 1960s and 1970s is difficult to predict, but it will probably be viewed as having undertaken the most comprehensive survey of higher education not only in American history but in the history of any nation.

The very breadth of scope predisposes the Carnegie Commission to a measure of impact on at least some areas of higher education. But as our publications are completed with little logical sequence, readers may find it difficult to perceive the central thrusts of the Commission. Hopefully, our final report in 1973 will supply the unifying themes, but in the meantime I have been asked by the American Association for Higher Education to give some notion of the Carnegie Commission's view of higher education as we now see it, what the relative certainties and uncertainties are for the period ahead to 2000, and what aspects of higher education might be subject to policy control to develop a higher education system more suited to our present and changing needs. This view from the perspective of the Carnegie Commission is being given at a time when the work of the Commission is about two-thirds completed, when nearly half of our research reports have been published, and when eleven of our estimated eighteen Commission reports have been issued. Through our series of profiles, of which eight have already been issued and ten more are in process, we have tried to provide new descriptive and analytical material on the several types of institutions and significant functions that comprise American higher education. Through a series of essays by foreign observers, we are gaining international perspective on American higher education. And through more than sixty-five individual research projects on particular aspects of higher education, of which thirty have been completed, we are seeking the necessary information to guide policy recommendations.

Our studies to date have led us to identify several relative certainties about higher education that confront us over the next few decades. First of all we know the general magnitude of the numbers of students that must be served. In the 1970s places must be found for an additional three million students. This is the same additional number we accommodated in the 1960s, but it represents a smaller proportional gain. The addition of three million students in the 1960s constituted a 100 per cent growth, while the same addition in the 1970s will only result in a 50 per cent growth. In the 1980s, we face some years in which the absolute numbers will go down in peacetime and in prosperity (if in fact we have peace and prosperity) for the first time in more than 335 years since the founding of Harvard. There will be a reduction in some years and no net increase over the decade. In 1990, in fact, there may be slightly fewer students in our traditional colleges and universities than it now appears there will be in 1980. This will be a traumatic experience for colleges and universities that have been geared for decades to growth and for the last two decades to particularly rapid growth.

It is likely that there will be one further spurt in enrollment in the 1990s, when the grandchildren of the GIs enroll. But after that period, higher education will be growing at a slower rate than it has historically. Since 1870, we have doubled the number of students in college every twelve to fifteen years. If we were to continue that doubling, beginning with 1970, we would have sixteen million students in 1985; we would have thirty-two million students in the year 2000; we would have sixty-four million students in the year 2015. But this continued rate of growth is absolutely impossible and will never again occur in higher education. In the past we have grown at a much faster rate than has American society. In the future, the higher education growth rate is much more likely to parallel that of society.

The second relative certainty with which we enter the next few decades concerns the general magnitude of the costs of higher education. The cost of higher education has grown enormously over the last few decades. Part of this growth can be attributed to the increase in numbers of students, but a part must also be attributed to rising costs per student. A study made for us by the Brookings Institution shows that since 1930 cost per student per year has gone up at a rate which is a combination of the general rate of inflation plus 3 per cent. At the present time, our institutions of higher education have expenditures of about twenty billion dollars. Even if there were no general inflation, given the anticipated increase in the number of students and the 3 per cent per year increase in costs, we can anticipate an expenditure of $40 billion in 1980, of $60 billion in 1990, and $100 billion in the year 2000. Not only are absolute costs rising, they are becoming a larger proportion of our gross national product. And as the cost threatens to push toward 3 per cent of our gross national product, further increases are meeting increased resistance, particularly at a time when the nation's many other priorities—the renovation of our cities, the adequate financing of early, elementary, and secondary education, growing welfare costs, and the preservation of our physical environment— must also be met.

Third, we now have what is probably the best and most complete information ever available on the attitudes of students and faculty members. These findings emerge from a study sponsored by the Carnegie Commission in which seventy thousand undergraduates, thirty thousand graduates, and sixty thousand faculty members were surveyed. While we cannot be certain that these attitudes will continue throughout the twentieth century, certainly they must be a factor in policy determinations in the immediate future, and the findings on attitudes point to clearly needed reforms and adjustments in the next few decades. Although the overall level of general satisfaction seems to be relatively high, with only 12 per cent of undergraduates in all types of institutions indicating they were dissatisfied or very dissatisfied with the education they were getting at their colleges, and an additional 22 per cent indicating they are on the fence, there were relatively higher levels of criticism on specific aspects of the educational process.

Ninety-six per cent of the students favor an open access system. Though such a system exists in some states and areas, we have far to go to achieve it across the nation. Students also are overwhelmingly in favor of putting the emphasis on teaching effectiveness rather than on publications as the major criterion for hiring and promoting faculty members. Ninety-five per cent of the students surveyed indicated this preference, and 86 per cent of the faculty agreed with this preference. Ninety per cent of the students believed that course work should be more relevant to contemporary life and problems.

Other findings suggest further need for reassessment of present structures and programs. Sixty-seven per cent of the students feel that colleges should have a responsibility for helping solve the social problems of society and not just through research; 62 per cent believe that colleges should be governed primarily by faculty and students; 59 per cent believe that all grades should be abolished; 53 per cent feel that all courses should be elective; 48 per cent believe that every student should be required to undertake a year of national service. There is more dissatisfaction among graduate students (23 per cent) but the general trend of opinions suggests similar changes.

And finally, we know that our college graduates if educated in the traditional college and university program will have increasing difficulties obtaining positions upon graduation. Job markets for Ph.D.s in many fields are rapidly becoming buyers' markets and the average holder of a baccalaureate degree will no longer be able to command the premiums in the job market which he was once able to command now that an ever greater percentage of our young people are attending colleges and universities.

Thus, in seeking policy development for the period ahead in higher education, we have some relatively certain findings to guide us. More difficult to assess will be the impact of many important uncertainties. First is the attitude of the public toward higher education. Will we be able to avoid the "collision course" between the campus and society which some, including David Riesman, have predicted? The campus is increasing its demands on society through requests for greater financial support and for freedom from control by society at the same time that campus elements are urging the campus to take a more active role in attacking and changing society. It is difficult to predict at this time whether the crisis of public confidence which has intensified the growing financial stringency in higher education will continue. But there are some signs of growing public support. Many states have added to their commitment of funds to public higher education new commitments for funds to private institutions. The federal government is now considering higher education legislation which would substantially increase the availability of federal funds for students and institutional aid. In the legislative halls of the nation one finds continued deep seated support for higher education, but coupled with a growing desire for new types of accountability to the public for the manner in which higher education spends its resources.

A second and important uncertainty relates to the long-range potential impact of the sensate concerns of students. In the survey of attitudes mentioned earlier, 83 per cent of the students believed that more attention should be given by our colleges and universities to the emotional development of the student. Fifty-three per cent felt that colleges should provide more opportunities for students to engage in creative activity, particularly the creative arts. There are other evidences of some turning away from the cognitive aspects of higher education and a movement toward experiential satisfaction. The strength of this movement is difficult to assess at this time.

Third, there are also signs of a growing politicization of academic life.

A fourth factor is the technological revolution that seems to be waiting in the wings. Computers are becoming more useful and more readily available. The video cassette may turn every living room in the nation into a classroom. And computers and/or television may provide access to virtually unlimited information in regional or network-linked library and learning resource storage systems. How soon technology will show its mark on the structure and delivery of higher education is difficult to know. How much technology will become a substitute for present systems and how much it will simply augment existing systems is also difficult to predict.

The uncertainties of higher education today lead some people to ignore the certainties and to urge that we make only minimal plans for the future. But the development of· our colleges and universities is much too important to leave to fate or chance. We cannot afford to refuse to identify important objectives and effective ways of reaching them just because we are afraid we might upset some mystical natural evolution of our institutions and our society. We cannot hesitate to select a policy only because our choice might conflict with some ultimate, dark, and as yet unknown eventuality.

The Carnegie Commission was established because it seemed clear that American higher education could not prosper on a "wait and see" basis. That philosophy ignores present realities and encourages preservation of myths and wishful thinking. It leads to unwarranted duplication of effort and to wasteful uses of resources that are in short supply.

The future can be determined by principles as well as by events, by men and women no less than by the mere passage of time. But if men and women, guided by principles, are to make sound decisions, they must have available the results of an orderly examination of important information and experience in higher education and reliable definitions of those principles that have proved useful in the past and may be promising for the future.

Perhaps the clearest way to demonstrate the roles policy can play in shaping the future of higher education is to review briefly seven policy areas that have been of special concern to us. In each case, I outline some of the circumstances that have created the problems to be solved and indicate what the Commission has said about them thus far. In some instances, I will suggest aspects of the problems that remain to be considered.

One policy concern of the Commission is as old as our nation itself. It involves applying the principle of *social justice* to higher education. It commands priority so long as we strive to achieve the dream of our nation's founders that all men should be guaranteed equal opportunities to seek and enjoy the benefits of the democratic society they created. In our very first report, *Quality and Equality: New Levels of Federal Responsibility for Higher Education*,[1] we noted the historic role educational institutions have played in building our society. We also presented in that report ways the federal government could alleviate the financial barriers to higher education that confront many young people from low-income families. We urged the federal government to strengthen and expand current educational opportunity grants, providing $1,000 to undergraduates and $2,000 to graduate students found to be in financial need. We urged that the federal work-study program be continued and expanded and that institutions be given federal funds for scholarships to be awarded to students with financial need. We recommended that certain federal incentives be employed to encourage states, local governments, and private philanthropy to continue and increase their contributions to student assistance. We urged that student assistance be instituted to reward various forms of national service provided by youth. To further eliminate financial barriers to educational opportunity, we recommended creation of a National Student Loan Bank from which students could obtain loans to be paid back out of their earnings after leaving college. The total first-year expenditures for such programs would be about $2.4 billion. They would increase to about $5 billion within ten years. Through such measures, we believe that all economic barriers to education could be eliminated by 1976, the two-hundredth anniversary of the Declaration of Independence.

We have recommended that federal funds given to students should be considered an entitlement, similar to that given to G.I.s.

[1] The Carnegie Commission reports are published by McGraw-Hill.

Students should receive the assistance we recommended regardless of where they reside or which institutions they choose to attend. Moreover, the students' entitlements should be accompanied by federal grants—cost of education supplements—paid directly to the institutions in which they enroll. We estimate that such grants to institutions would total about $1 billion in the first year in which they were made and should increase to about $3.6 billion by 1980.

Unlike other proposals for giving financial assistance to institutions—particularly those based on across-the-board support tied to enrollment or degrees awarded—the proposals of the Commission are rooted deeply in the principle of social justice. They extend educational opportunity to those who would be deprived of it without federal assistance or if there were not enough college doors open to them. This form of support is clearly appropriate to the federal government because it serves the cause of equality of opportunity for all people that is so deeply imbedded in our national purpose.

The second report of the Commission, *A Chance to Learn: An Action Agenda for Equal Opportunity in Higher Education,* reiterated our proposals for increased financial aid to students, again underscoring the importance of the financial barrier to educational opportunity for many Americans. It also pointed out, however, that educational opportunity in America is unequally available for other reasons—including ethnic origin, location of higher education facilities, age, and quality of early schooling. In response to these inequities, we have made recommendations concerning the improvement of the education in elementary and secondary schools that is available to children who live in disadvantaged or ethnically segregated neighborhoods. In this and subsequent reports we have also stressed the importance of having some kind of higher education available within commuting distance of 95 per cent of the people in the country, as a means of improving accessibility of institutions to prospective students.

To overcome inequalities of educational opportunity that are the result of age, we recommended, both in our second report and in a subsequent report, *Less Time, More Options: Education Beyond the High School,* that there be greater flexibility in the patterns of college attendance, so that people could attend throughout their lifetimes.

To assure that educational opportunities would remain open at available institutions, we recommended that each state plan to provide universal access to its total system—though not necessarily to each of its institutions. We also proposed programs to help people who did not have adequate college preparation to adjust to education at the postsecondary level. By the year 2000, opportunities can and must be totally free of all limitations imposed by ethnic grouping, geographic location, age, or prior schooling.

We are currently considering another item on the agenda for improving social justice—the equal participation of women in higher education. Thoughtful observers have long acknowledged that women have not enjoyed the same degree and quality of participation in higher education that have been available to men. Evidence that the time has come for important changes has pressed itself on the national consciousness and conscience with increasing impact. Our Commission now has the question under study and we hope to offer a statement and recommendations on it before very long.

A second concern that requires study and policy formation involves the question of whether American higher education is producing the *trained manpower* the nation needs. In the past, our record has been generally good. Our colleges and universities deserve a large share of the credit for providing the skill and leadership the American nation has needed for its dynamic growth. But we now have information indicating that we may be in trouble on two manpower fronts. The first is that we are geared up to train many more teachers than we are going to need. The U. S. Department of Labor and the Bureau of the Census estimate that if our colleges continue to produce teachers at the current rate, we will, by the end of the 1970s, have produced one, two, or even three million more teachers than can be placed in the American school system. Primary level registrations are already down; high school registrations are going down; and higher education enrollment in the 1980s, as an average, will be absolutely level. In health services, on the other hand, we face serious shortages. During the present decade, through either private or public auspices, there will be some form of health insurance, we assume, available to all Americans. The resulting demand for health service will be much greater than anything we have seen before—even during the years when Medicare was introduced. We need at least a million more people trained in the health manpower fields than we are now prepared to train.

Before the end of the current academic year, the Commission hopes to have completed a fairly comprehensive review of the relationship between the nation's manpower needs and higher education. We have already given considerable attention to the problems of training health service manpower. With the help of leaders in this field from all over the country, we have compiled data and experiences that have been highly instructive. Particularly important was a study on *Financing Medical Education* done for the Commission by Rashi Fein of the Harvard Medical School and Gerald Weber of the Brookings Institution. It will probably be a classic in its field for a long time to come. We were also helped considerably by an analysis of *Trends and Projections of Physicians in the United States* made by Mark S. Blumberg, who is now a planning advisor for Kaiser Foundation Health Plan. The Commission's own report on this subject, *Higher Education and the Nation's Health: Policies for Medical and Dental Education*, recommends that the number of medical school entrants be significantly increased, that all university health science centers consider developing training programs for physicians' and dentists' associates and assistants, and that the instruction programs leading to the M.D. and D.D.S. degrees be accelerated so that they might take three years instead of four beyond the B.A. degree. Beyond these measures for increasing the supply of health care personnel, we recommend that health manpower research programs in the Department of Health, Education and Welfare be strengthened and expanded.

Of all the reports issued by the Commission thus far, this one on medical education has been the most completely accepted. Almost all of its recommendations that require federal implementation are reflected in legislation that was passed by Congress during the current session and signed into law by the President.

A third area of policy concern is broadly described by the phrase *academic reform*. One of the consequences of rapid growth in higher education in this country, with its increasing diversity of institutions and its increasing accessibility to students from more varied sectors in our society, has been an erosion of consensus about what constitutes a good education. Between the two World Wars, colleges in this country were known the world over for their general education for undergraduates—for the idea that a core of knowledge in several subject fields could be taught in ways adequate to the needs of an "educated" man or woman. Today, if I were to pick one real disaster area in higher education, it would be general education. The failure of general education in America has been described with great insight in essays written for the Commission by such informed foreign observers as Sir Eric Ashby of Great Britain and Joseph Ben-David of the Hebrew University of Jerusalem. They attribute the failure mainly to the fact that there is no longer agreement in America on what ought to be taught to college undergraduates. Other factors are the unwillingness of many first-rank professors to teach undergraduate courses and a lack of consensus about the kind of person an "educated" man or woman ought to be. A consequence of the failure of general education is that at some institutions there are no longer any requirements at all, and students are allowed to take virtually any courses they want.

Another concern subject to policy influence involves the general structure of the college experience. In many respects it has changed very little since the mid-nineteenth century. Until very recently, four years was almost inevitably the norm required for earning a bachelor's degree, and these years were usually spent uninterruptedly beginning three months after graduation from high school. The modes of instruction, including lectures, discussion groups, and seminars, have varied little from institution to institution. Testing, grading, and certification for accomplishment were greatly standardized.

Effecting change in such matters has proved to be extremely difficult. Few guilds remain as strong as the academic guild and few other guilds have been as unreceptive to altering their ways of doing things. These observations were confirmed for the Commission in Dwight Ladd's down-to-earth review of the efforts of many institutions to effect significant academic change through self-studies conducted by their own faculties. His book, *Change in Educational Policy,* is sobering reading for anyone disposed to regard the task of institutional reform as involving no more than putting the influence of distinguished and respected colleagues behind rational solutions to identifiable problems.

Despite these difficulties, I believe the Commission is now having significant influence on efforts to achieve desirable changes.

Stephen Spurr's study for us on *Academic Degree Structures,* and Alden Dunham's "Radical Recommendation" in his profile of the nation's state colleges and regional universities, helped to crystallize the Commission's recommendations in its report *Less Time, More Options* that (1) a degree or some other form of credit be made available to students every two years during their college careers; (2) the time required to earn a degree be shortened by one year for the B.A. and by one to two additional years for the Ph.D. and M.D.; and (3) two new degrees, the Master of Philosophy and the Doctor of Arts, be widely accepted throughout our colleges and universities. The latter degree would recognize training to a level comparable to that of the Ph.D., but would be designed to prepare people primarily to engage in teaching rather than research.

This same report, in many ways the most controversial of the reports we have issued thus far, generally urges greater flexibility in higher learning. It recommends that more opportunities be created for students to "stop-out" at appropriate points in their educational career for work experience, national service, travel, or some other alternative activity. We also urge expansion of opportunities for students to pursue education while they hold part-time or full-time jobs or to alternate periods of employment with periods of education. To reduce the pressure on young people to enter college immediately after graduating from high school, we recommend that, after high school graduation, every person in the United States have two years of postsecondary education put "in the bank" for them for use at any time during their lives.

But many unanswered questions of academic policy remain. How do we define the basic core of undergraduate education? What kind of flexibility and alternatives are desirable in development of a general curriculum? What styles of instruction are to be encouraged? What are the roles of the emerging technologies in the teaching and learning process? How should academic achievement be evaluated and certified? What are the most desirable academic environments for students at different stages in their education? How do we reward good teaching? These and other tough questions are now being considered by the Commission.

Easily as difficult as questions involving academic reform are those that concern *governance*. There has been an almost invariable sequence of battles affecting the distribution of power in higher education. The first contests were between the trustees of institutions and the agencies that chartered their colleges. One development in this contest has been the addition of lay alumni to the board of trustees of church-related colleges in an effort to dilute the influence of the clergy. The second contest occurred when presidents demanded and, to a considerable extent, won from trustees greater authority in administrative matters. The third contest was between the faculties of many institutions and their presidents. The result was considerable new power for faculties. The fourth one, now in progress, and with an outcome still to be decided, is between students and everyone else. Many institutions have experienced all four contests. And they have learned that after each one the powers of contending forces may be altered but no segment has yet lost as much power as it has gained in previous redistributions of authority.

One result of these contests is that there is no clear-cut vertical power structure on most American campuses. Instead, there tend to be elaborate veto systems through which every important policy must be filtered before it can be enacted. In this state of affairs—which is absolutely bewildering to students of political or business organizations—many questions must be answered if we are going to plan effectively for the future. Three of them are of special importance today. The first is the degree to which students are to be granted participation in decision-making. The second is how much autonomy our systems of education are to have from state and federal government and from the growing number of coordinating agencies being created to plan educational development at state and local levels. This question will acquire increasing importance as government financial support for all institutions—public and private—becomes more commonplace. Finally, when it becomes necessary for someone to act promptly to meet an emergency, how can he break through the relatively cumbersome governmental procedures of the average campus? We have begun to formulate answers to questions of this kind and hope to issue a report on our conclusions in the near future.

A fifth area of major policy involves the number and *variety of institutions* that ought to be available as we enter the twenty-first century. We do not believe we will need more new Ph.D. granting universities. Higher education and our society cannot absorb all the Ph.D.s we are graduating now, and existing institutions have the capacity to produce all of the Ph.D.s we will need in the foreseeable future. But our report *New Students and New Places: Policies for the Future Growth and Development of American Higher Education,* issued in October 1971, recommends that between 175 and 235 new community colleges be built by 1980 with between 80 and 125 of them located in metropolitan areas with populations of half a million or more. We also recommend that between 80 and 105 new comprehensive colleges be built by 1980 and that between 60 and 70 of these be in large metropolitan areas.

To preserve the diversity of institutions that has been a hallmark of American higher education, we must assist the private colleges in their fight for survival. In many respects, private institutions have been those hardest hit by the hard times now confronting higher education. The problem is particularly acute for some of the smallest of these institutions. The nature of the challenges facing about five hundred of these colleges has just been outlined for us in a profile by Alexander Astin and Calvin Lee. They say that many of them are plagued by inefficient size, apparent ceilings on tuition charges, and inadequate recognition for their educational contributions. Our report on *The Capitol and the Campus: State Responsibility for Postsecondary Education* urges the states to contribute or increase support of private colleges and universities, noting that "their graduates and the graduates of public institutions benefit society equally, that they provide diversity, innovative opportunities, models of interest in the individual student, and standards of autonomy useful to all higher education." Specifically, we support state subsidy of tuition costs at private colleges for students who cannot meet them. We also favor state support for special endeavors, such as medical schools, and assistance through grants or loans for construction. Of course, the financial aid we have urged the federal government to provide should also be given without differentiation between public and private institutions.

The colleges founded for Negroes constitute a rather special group of institutions, though they are only a small part of the total resources of the country employed to meet increasing student demand. These institutions are unique in terms of their history and will continue for the foreseeable future to have certain missions that other institutions cannot serve as well as they can. They are the subject of a Commission profile entitled *Between Two Worlds,* written by Frank Bowles and Frank DeCosta, which is one of the most thorough historical and descriptive profiles of these institutions yet written. It clearly describes the problems of transition faced by these colleges as they lose their roles as the only institutions giving higher education to blacks in a segregated society and are led to compete with all other institutions in the country not only for financial support but also for students and faculty members. In our own Commission report on them, *From Isolation to Mainstream: Problems of the Colleges Founded for Negroes,* we stress the past contributions of these institutions, note the role they will play in providing educational opportunity for students in the coming years, encourage them to double their enrollments, reaching an aggregate of three hundred thousand by the year 2000, and then propose special federal expenditures of some $41 million annually through the 1970s to assist them with their problems of transition. These funds would be in addition to the approximately $315 million in federal financing to which these institutions would be entitled under other Commission recommendations. In all, the Commission urges federal expenditures for black institutions that are more than five times as great as the amount of funds actually expended on them in 1968–1969. At a time when many were doubting the continued vitality of the black colleges, we concluded that they should be viewed as a "national asset."

A sixth area of the Commission's interest that is susceptible to analysis and policy recommendations relates to the probability that *much of the higher education available in the future will be carried on externally to that available on the nation's traditional campuses.* We in higher education often ignore the fact that considerable postsecondary education is already available in some seven thousand private, trade, and technical schools and in hundreds of apprenticeship programs, adult public schools, and correspondence schools that are not now regarded as part of the nation's higher education system. The Carnegie Commission has already urged that these institutions be taken into consideration in future planning of higher education facilities at state and local levels.

In addition to these existing facilities, however, new kinds of programs within traditional colleges and totally new kinds of externally based institutions are being established. It is still difficult to anticipate the full impact of such extended education programs, but a few results now seem highly probable. The first is that extended learning will encourage people over a wide range of ages and in many walks of life, people not served well by existing colleges and universities, to take advantage of greater access to postsecondary education of considerable variety. Second, as has been the case in Great Britain, these programs will also attract many students who would normally go to traditional colleges. The reason for this is that individuals' tastes and needs for different kinds of education vary. Certain young people will prefer the alternative systems. Third, these institutions will probably become the proving ground for some of the emerging instructional technologies. To the degree that they are successful in these endeavors, they will accelerate the use of such technologies within traditional institutions.

The Commission is already on record as advocating further experiments with degrees-by-examinations, open university-type programs, and increased opportunities for people to obtain higher education throughout their lifetimes. In future reports we intend to elaborate on these proposals and place the traditional systems of higher education more realistically within the full context of educational opportunities available in our country.

The seventh—and last—policy concern I want to discuss is the whole question of where the responsibility lies for *financing* higher education. It is quite possible that Earl Cheit's report on *The New Depression in Higher Education* did as much as any single prior effort to open the eyes of the public and of policymakers throughout the country to the serious financial problems facing colleges and universities in 1971. By analyzing specific institutions and recording the experience and expectations of presidents and administrators across the country, Cheit demonstrated that the financial problems were pervasive. Seventy-one per cent of the institutions in his sample were either headed for financial difficulty or in financial difficulty. And the financial problems he encountered afflicted institutions across the board, public and private, large and small. Moreover, he found the fundamental problem to be universal —costs are rising faster than income.

The obvious question suggested by these findings is "Where is the additional money going to come from to close the gap?" We look naturally to the federal government for funds, partly out of habit but also because it collects the largest portion of the tax dollar in the country. We also look to the federal government with some justifiable reservations. The experience of nations that have become heavily dependent upon national subsidies for their higher education has generally not been good. They have found that regardless of how they try to avoid it, national centralized support invites controls that significantly threaten institutional independence. This is one reason why the Carnegie Commission has consistently urged that, although federal support for higher education should increase from about one-fifth of total institutional support to about one-quarter, it should not become the basic component of financial support. Moreover, we have urged that federal funding, whenever possible, should support endeavors that are clearly in the national interest. Thus, as I mentioned previously, we believe that both student assistance and aid to institutions which is tied to educational opportunity grants are appropriate forms of help. Funds thus provided obviously advance the principle of social justice, a national concern. We similarly urge continued federal support of research, medical education, and other special programs that are clearly in the national interest.

In our report on *The Capitol and the Campus,* we recommend that the major responsibility for maintaining, expanding, and improving postsecondary education in the United States should reside in the state governments in cooperation with local governments and private institutions. We believe that the state share of funding for higher education, like the federal share, should be about one-quarter of the total expenditures.

That leaves half of the total expenditures to be provided by the private sector through fees and tuition and gifts and grants. By far the largest portion of the total amount from the private sector will be in the form of tuition and fees. If tuitions must continue to increase, adequate loan funds must also be available for students from low- or modest-income families if we are not to abandon the principle of equal opportunity. To provide this support the Commission favors creation of a National Student Loan Bank, a private nonprofit corporation financed by the sale of governmentally guaranteed bonds.

Predictions and prescriptions are much easier to make when we have fairly clear trends and definite information about what affects those trends. In higher education, the many uncertainties make predictions hazardous at the present time. Nonetheless, we must make our best efforts to develop wise policy to meet existing and future needs. It is hoped that the work of the Carnegie Commission, which is but one of many groups currently studying higher education, will be a meaningful addition to the ongoing discussions on the future of American higher education.

A Reaction to the Commission Recommendations

Richard C. Richardson, Jr.

I agree with much of what the Carnegie Commission has said. Certainly not all students should attend college, although access should be universal. The concept of the comprehensive community college as opposed to the more restrictive forms of two-year institutions does deserve our endorsement. The Commission has been particularly perceptive in its comments on articulation between two- and four-year institutions, particularly as these relate to current practice. One state university has established an upper-division institution ostensibly to serve the needs of students transferring from community colleges. At the same time, the financial aid policies of the school prohibit assistance to upper-division students who have not been enrolled in the university at least one semester as a full-time student. When the Commission observes that one-third of entering freshmen receive financial aid their initial semester compared with only 14 per cent of transfer students, they have done a great deal to focus attention on this problem.

I like the idea of providing more options, of the concept of stopping out, of tailoring the length of educational experience required for a specific objective to the ability of the individual seeking that objective. Equally important is the emphasis upon service and work experience as a corollary of education. While this is not a new idea, new emphasis on it can help to destroy some of our traditional notions about the importance of the institutional cocoon.

The idea that employers should assume more responsibility for screening their own talent, relying less on college credentials, may encourage some institutions to take the initiative in restructuring higher education more as an experience in personal growth and less as a test of who can jump over what hurdles in order to obtain what job. I also like the emphasis on career-ladder concepts and the less rigid stratification of occupations providing for more career mobility.

Any attempt to be objective about the work of the Commission must recognize its significant contributions as well as the constructive influence of the magnitude and visibility of this work during a period of great uncertainty in higher education.

There are also aspects of Commission work which cause me serious concern. Evident throughout are attempts to compromise serious differences of opinion through choice of recommendations and through qualifying these recommendations. While I recognize the practical necessity of such action when dealing with widely divergent interests and concerns, the results often unsuccessfully seek to chart bold new directions while at the same time preserving all of the established practices. Perhaps the greatest problem of this aspect of the effort, in addition to the confusion it causes about what the recommendations actually mean, is the appearance of consensus about issues when none, in fact, actually exists.

I mentioned a number of the things I liked about Commis-

sion reports. In the same report where many of these recommendations occur, much of the impact is tarnished by the emphasis on
degrees. The concept that higher education should be divided into
two-year periods, at the end of which each individual would receive
either one of the traditional credentials or a new credential—such
as the Doctor of Arts or Master of Philosophy degrees—represents
almost an anachronism in terms of much of the rest of what the
reports say. I would argue that we should be more concerned about
competencies and their relationship to the real world as opposed to
the academic world than we should be about credentials and the
length of time it takes to acquire such credentials. I am particularly
concerned about the emphasis placed on new degrees such as the
Doctor of Arts. I do not believe that the problem of preparing
faculty for community colleges, for example, will be solved by
establishing new names for old practices. Produce a Ph.D. who is
truly concerned about teaching and about students, and who is
interested in lower-division instruction, and you will not have to find
a new label in order to secure his ready acceptance by community
colleges.

Another source of concern is the recurring theme of the
importance of quality and standards, which are never adequately
defined, as well as the assumptions about the self-validating nature
of the degrees offered by our institutions. We find these statements:
"Each college should maintain the qualifications for its degrees,
recognizing that these qualifications are quite diverse," and "the
Quality of the academic degree should not, under any circumstances, be reduced."[1] Great emphasis is also placed on the foundation year for students who are not prepared to do the standard
work expected of students admitted to college in the past. The
implicit assumption behind the entire discussion of the foundation
year seems to be that existing practices will be retained virtually
intact and that they will determine standards of quality and excellence. Wider access is to be provided through a transitional program which will in some undefined manner fit nontraditional
students to traditional programs. This assumption—that in one or
perhaps even two years students can, through changing the pace of

---

[1] Carnegie Commission on Higher Education, *A Chance to Learn:
An Action Agenda for Equal Opportunity in Higher Education*. New York:
McGraw-Hill, 1970, p. 3 and p. 14.

their learning, compensate for deficiencies which may range up to six years or more as measured by standard tests and which have been accumulated during a period of twelve years or longer—is completely unrealistic, as those of us in community colleges who have been struggling with this problem for more than ten years can readily attest.

There are other instances where the Commission does not appear to understand fully the problems we face in working with students who learn less rapidly than do those traditionally served by higher education—or who learn in a different way. Unless we propose to restructure radically the nature of higher education (which obviously is not envisioned in the reports), we can never expect improvements at the public school level, even if stimulated by the assistance of institutions of higher education, to solve the problems of making our current approaches to higher education equally good for all who now seek their benefits when these approaches were designed originally for a small select group.

While I am certain that many of my colleagues would not share this point of view, I do feel that charging no tuition or low tuition in community colleges represents an unrealistic approach at a time when resources are extremely limited for all forms of higher education. When such a recommendation by the Commission is combined with a statement emphasizing the necessity for some substantial degree of local support as a concomitant of meaningful local policymaking responsibility, we find once again the attempt to reconcile conflicting facts. If students should pay a defined part of the costs of their education in public four-year colleges and universities in proportion to their ability to pay, I see no good reason for not initiating similar practices in two-year colleges, provided that the option is there to provide free education to those who cannot afford to pay. With regard to the financing of higher education, we must reach some kind of consensus. Either the first two years should be free, in which case they ought to be free or underwritten in all institutions, or a comparable policy of assessing costs should be devised. By isolating two-year colleges as the free segment of higher education, we are making some doubtful assumptions about the nature of their responsibility to low-income groups in comparison with the responsibilities of other types of institutions. In addition, we are making community colleges the focus of the rightful concern of private institutions about the extent to which free public higher education can be provided without impairing the ability of private higher education to continue to fulfill its significant and essential role. The assumption that people will not attend two-year colleges unless a substantial concession is made in the form of cost reductions is no longer valid in most parts of the nation. Neither we nor our students require this special and somewhat dubious concession.

Although there is a widely held belief that local support is required in order for community colleges to be responsive to the local community, I question some Commission conclusions in this regard. We have no hard evidence at this point to support the essential nature of local contributions. Neither can I accept the assertion that community colleges can establish their identity as institutions of higher education only if they have their own local governing boards. There is likewise no evidence to suggest that locally made decisions will always be better than decisions reached at the state level. The emphasis placed upon local autonomy, while desirable from the standpoint of those of us who currently enjoy it, does great disservice to states such as Virginia, Massachusetts, Minnesota, and Colorado where strong state systems have been established and are providing excellent community college services.

In summary, while there are many things I like about the work of the Carnegie Commission, and while I think that all of higher education is indebted to the body of information developed through its efforts, I must express concern about certain assumptions regarding governance and financing, particularly as these relate to differential tuitions and to the importance of local contribution and its relationship to the governance process. I am equally concerned about the attempt to straddle the need for change and the desire to preserve that which already exists; this problem is reflected in the emphasis on standards and quality, which are presumed to be self-validating concepts, as well as in the extensive support for credentialing and the assumptions made about the effectiveness of titles such as the Master of Philosophy and the Doctor of Arts degrees as an approach to improving college teaching. I am perhaps most concerned about the lack of understanding of the needs of nontraditional students as this is revealed in insufficient emphasis on changing admissions practices, in the assumption that the foundation year, combined with changes in the public schools, will solve the problems of students who learn less rapidly or in different ways, and in the implication that our major effort should be to adjust students to existing programs rather than to change programs to fit the needs of students.

The Commission, under the able leadership of Clark Kerr, has identified significant issues and suggested directions in which solutions may lie. Ten years from now we will be better able to evaluate the effectiveness of these solutions. In the interim we must act. As we shape priorities and commit resources in response to pragmatic concerns, the work of the Commission can provide one important source of insight and perspective.

3

The Carnegie Commission: Voice of the Establishment

Alan Wolfe

A criticism I have written of the Carnegie Commission appeared in the May/June 1971 issue of *Social Policy*. The same problems I report in that article still hold now, a year later. These problems do not refer so much to the actual content of the reports as to the assumptions underlying them. So long as these assumptions are maintained—and they still seem to be tenaciously held—there is not much that I can expect from this Commission. Since it has defined the problem incorrectly, it is hard to expect the proposed solutions to solve the problem. Three assumptions of the Commission seem to me to be particularly troublesome.

First, the Commission takes what I would call a subjective approach to the so-called crisis surrounding higher education. By this I mean that they define the problem not in terms of an objective condition about higher education that is wrong but in terms of what people think is wrong. To illustrate, there have always been tremendous problems facing higher education in this country, a perpetual state of crisis. But so long as nobody objects, there is no Carnegie Commission. Only when students and junior faculty occupy buildings and refuse to accept the system handed to them do those in power in the United States proclaim the existence of a "problem." The crisis, then, is not that our schools are bad, for they have always been bad, but that people are now aware that they are bad. What the Commission wishes to reform, it seems, is not higher education but people's attitudes toward higher education.

This subjective definition of the situation is most clear in one of the products of the Carnegie Corporation, Charles Silberman's *Crisis in the Classroom*. It also pervades the work of some of the Commissioners, for example Kenneth Keniston's recent book *Youth and Dissent*. One can also find it in Clark Kerr's chapter in the present volume where he cites survey data reflecting people's attitudes toward education as prima facie evidence that things need changing. People's attitudes are an important aspect of any problem, but to make them the only aspect, or even the primary one, ignores the real objective factors that have created the situation in higher education in the United States, factors to which I shall return shortly.

Second, there is a selective definition of terms which runs throughout these reports. In Kerr's chapter we are told, very briefly, that "there are also signs of a growing politicization of academic life." I must confess that I cannot understand this use of the word *political*. American universities have always been highly political, serving the needs of corporate capitalism, providing research and manpower for fighting foreign wars, reinforcing class and caste segregation in the United States, and doing countless other things which uphold the status quo. Attacks on these functions by student radicals and faculty have, if anything, led to a depoliticization of the university, as I have argued elsewhere. Only a selective definition, which holds that attacks on the status quo are political while activities which uphold it are not, permits statements like the one just quoted. Until we clear up confusion of this sort, we again will not have defined the problem correctly.

But these are minor issues. The third—and most significant —problem facing the Commission is its failure to be theoretical, to place things in their political context, to examine causes, to be historical—in short, to comprehensively analyze what is wrong with higher education. The Commission accepts the present political and economic system as a given and only seeks to tamper with its least essential operations. It never questions whether corporate capitalism will permit a humane educational system and it never examines the reasons for the enormous problems which exist. It is as if higher education just appeared out of nowhere and the Commission wants only to make sure it continues without attack, from the Left or the Right. Given the close corporate connections and ruling-class ties of the Commissioners, it is no wonder they never lay the blame for the problems with capitalism itself or go into great detail about who is responsible for the system's failures. But so long as this bias is present, the issues discussed will only be tangential ones and the remedies suggested will only be temporary. This point can be illustrated by examining the seven policy areas which Kerr lists as constituting the essential work of the Commission.

The first policy area concerns social justice. The Commission and Kerr argue that equality of admissions to college must be guaranteed. That of course is a valid goal. But merely stating it does not take us very far. Why have colleges been exclusionary in the past? Surely it is because America exemplifies a class system in which certain groups have traditionally been excluded from the rewards offered by the establishment, despite the success of a few token individuals who have "made" it. One cannot, it seems to me, argue that all should have the chance to go to college—and the Commission does not want everyone to go but merely to have the chance—without looking at the broader society and its manifest inequalities and forms of stratification. But such an examination might lead to social criticism, to attacks on vested interests and power, and this the Commission never seems to want to do.

My own students would never have gone to college thirty years ago. They are predominantly Catholic, working-class students from South Brooklyn and Staten Island. Now they are in college. But the society in which they grew up played an important part in their precollege education, and many of them cannot obtain what they should from higher education because of the viciousness of that society. They learned a great deal from authoritarian families, from rigid bureaucracies, from unemployment and hunger, from horrid schools, from neighborhoods that encourage the worst in people. I am glad they can now go to college, but that is not enough. We must work to create a society in which everyone will be equally prepared to learn from college, and that can only be done outside the college itself, through a change in the society at large.

Kerr's second policy area concerns the training of manpower. He points out that we have too many teachers, too few health workers. Again, the reasons for the imbalance are not analyzed. But we know why. The health field has been dominated by an arrogant group of profit-seeking, elitist professionals who have consistently followed policies of self-interest which, in fact, encouraged shortages of health workers. Unless the Commission thus deals with causes, it cannot expect results. At some point, vested interests must be confronted and responsibility pointed out.

Interestingly enough, it is in this area of training manpower that the university takes on an explicitly political function. The Carnegie Commission reveals in its discussion of this problem its fondness for the contemporary political and economic arrangements that govern this country. In doing so, they ignore questions like these: What kinds of jobs exist? Why is work in America demeaning? What is the relationship between social class and type of work? Why do students resent having their education channel them into a job which they are not sure they want? How can a student use his or her job to serve people's needs, rather than to oppress them? Education must do more than job training; it must raise broad issues and assume a critical role.

This aspect of education, which is relegated to a minor place in the Commission's work, is addressed slightly in the third area of policy that Kerr discusses—academic reform. Kerr laments (perhaps too strong a term for such a dispassionate account) the failure of programs of general education. I lament them too. Helping students to liberate themselves through studying the many traditions which have existed in this world is an essential task of any university. Yet since our colleges are presently designed for job training, general, critical education is sacrificed. Once again, we must seek causes. To imply that the blame somehow lies in our national character, which Kerr does by citing two non-American authorities, does not advance us in understanding why American undergraduate education has been such a failure.

Fourth, Kerr and the Commission deal with the structure of the college experience. They make extensive proposals involving time. I have little to say about these proposals, since they seem, again, to be tinkering rather than dealing with basics. It matters little whether people are miseducated in three years or four; the problem is to genuinely educate them, however long it takes. And that Kerr defines this area as one of the most "controversial" indicates how muddled is the thinking of many people about what is wrong with higher education. I am continually amazed that so much discussion can be given to a question like the academic calendar without ever addressing, in basic ways, the question of what ought to happen during the college years.

Governance is part of this policy area. Because the governance of our colleges and universities has been seeped in unrepresentative traditions and archaic practices, this issue has been the target of students' most insistent demands. The problem is to create a humane institution that people will feel they are part of and not something that has been imposed on them by an illegitimate system. To do that means to recognize how inequitable is the distribution of power in most universities. Yet, when Kerr addresses this problem he applies to the university David Riesman's analysis of power in American society and lets it go at that. Riesman maintains that power in America is concentrated in the hands of veto groups that block each other's wishes and prevent any one group from holding too much power. But this is a poor analogy for Kerr to use. Riesman is simply wrong in his analysis. Veto groups may exist at a middle-level of power, but the Vietnam war indicates that somebody has enormous power in this country somewhere.

The same is true of the universities. I have very little power to shape an educational system that would satisfy my needs, and my students have even less. Each time we have tried to assume power we have been denounced as acting illegally or immorally. Nor are we even a veto group. There is a hierarchical system of power in American universities in which some have a great deal and others have almost none. That fact must be recognized if we are going to deal adequately with governance.

The fifth policy area discussed by Kerr is the variety of institutions which exist in this country to service the needs of higher education. Kerr calls this diversity a "hallmark." It is more than that. It reflects the same class system that pervades all of American society. Elite schools service the elite, and community colleges the masses, with others in between. Different kinds of institutions exist mainly because different classes exist. Perhaps diversity of that sort should not be preserved, as Kerr argues. Perhaps it should be abolished. A diversity which reinforces stratification and oppression is not even diversity, ultimately, but rigidity. Breaking down the class barriers of our educational system might then be a first step toward ensuring true diversity.

In short, Kerr's analysis in this area again ignores causes. Take the case of the formerly all-black colleges. Kerr tells us they are unique and serve a vital need. But he does not describe their uniqueness or show what needs they serve. He romanticizes them. He avoids mentioning, in his discussion of their development, the viciousness of segregation and regional exploitation. One would never suspect, from his statement, why they have suffered and suffered so enormously. Perhaps we can now make them, as Kerr suggests, a "national asset," but to do that requires that we first deal explicitly with the racism that was responsible for their existence in the first place. But this kind of analysis never enters adequately into the Commission's studies and profiles.

Sixth, there are the external degree programs and other forms of off-campus study. So long as these programs make education available for those who otherwise would not obtain it, they are worth developing. But the Commission should recommend that we avoid another form of segregation which may develop—the wealthiest students at residential colleges, the less wealthy at commuter colleges, while poorer students would study off campus altogether.

Finally, Kerr deals with the financing of education in America. The money for these reforms has to come from somewhere, but Kerr is wary of asking the federal government for too much, preferring to increase the federal component moderately while still relying on private sources. He is afraid that the government, if it pays, will also seek to exercise control. That is a valid fear; it should be broadened. Whoever pays wants to exercise control, including private centers of power. The Carnegie Corporation itself is paying and it wishes to exercise control. I for one would be less afraid of government domination of our educational system than the corporate domination that has paralyzed us for so long and made our universities appendages of the corporate order. But, because of selective definition, once again, Kerr does not seem to recognize private power as seeking to control, but only public power. It may be true that I have very little say in what my government does, but I have even less say in what the private sector is up to. The problem of control thus remains, whoever pays the bills.

The essence of what I have been saying is that the cause of our educational problems lies outside our educational system. We are in the mess we are in because the capitalist system has concentrated power in a few hands, led to rigid class stratification, required our universities to perform antieducational functions, encouraged mystification and parochialism, promoted imperialism, exacerbated racism and sexism, destroyed community, distorted values, ruined our environment, and forced us to work toward competitive, narrowly defined goals. Given that system, it is no wonder that a meaningful education is so difficult to obtain in this country. In short, the crisis we face is systemic, involving our whole political and economic system. When one of the leading educational commissions examines a single part of our complex society without taking into account its relationships with the whole, we have clear evidence, once and for all, of the poor quality of higher education in this society.

Kerr says that he has learned from experience. We who were on the other side of the barricades in Berkeley in 1964 (I speak figuratively here as I was actually in Philadelphia at the time) have learned from our experience as well. When we abolish the repressive society that faces us at every turn, then we will be able to talk about what a real education is all about.

4

Pluralism and Diversity in Higher Education

Paul C. Reinert

Clark Kerr's excellent chapter is an impressive summary of the certainties and uncertainties in higher education which the Commission has discovered and an analysis of the seven major concerns with which their reports have grappled. I have read all of the Commission's reports as well as some of their unpublished materials, and I support the bulk of their recommendations. But each one of us reads from a background of his own priorities and prejudices, and I would like to explain my fundamental dispute with the general

35

stance of the Commission. Among its seven concerns, let me concentrate on two: the first, the application of the principle of social
justice to higher education, and the fifth, the availability of a
number and a variety of institutions. My contention is that both of
these should be top priorities in our national philosophy. All of us
are and must be committed to equality of opportunity, to equal
access to higher education; but equally important must be our
commitment to the principle of choice, to the free, unhampered
ability of the individual to choose the kind of higher education he
prefers. It seems to me the Commission is willing to sacrifice the
second of these priorities in order to guarantee the first. Or to put
it in another way, the Commission wants to make sure that our
system of higher education is an effective instrument for social
change but in doing so seems willing to let that system lose one of
its essential, intrinsic characteristics—its pluralism and diversity.

Let me be more specific. The Commission opposes direct
institutional aid from the federal government. For reasons that have
some validity, it recommends that such aid must be attached to the
number of low-income students enrolled. Yet this recommendation
ignores several considerations that militate directly against the other
priority of preserving a public-private, pluralistic system.

In order to offer quality education without the state subsidy
paid for students in public institutions, a private institution would
take a financial loss on each needy student in spite of the opportunity grant and five hundred dollars from the federal government
proposed by the Commission. The same can be said regarding the
proposed two-hundred-dollar supplement for middle-income students receiving subsidized federal loans. For private institutions,
already overburdened with their own financial aid programs for
low-income students, this form of governmental aid can only be an
incentive to worsen their fiscal plight.

The goal should not be to fulfill any self-serving desire for
continued existence on the part of private institutions but to preserve
pluralism in higher education—a national asset that faces imminent
extinction. What is the cause of this danger of extinction? The
Commission seems to fear that it would be a "nationalization" of
the private sector, generated by direct governmental support. I sub-
mit it will be bankruptcy, not nationalization, that kills pluralism
in this country. And I think this conclusion is documented in the

Commission's own publications, especially *The New Depression in Higher Education* and *The Invisible Colleges*.[1]

The Commission pushes hard for continued and growing state responsibility for financing higher education, both public and private. I endorse that principle wholeheartedly. But the Commission closes its eyes to the real situation. As a practical recommendation to private institutions in some twenty states, including Missouri, this answer is a very sad joke. At the present rate it will be years before some states actually assume their responsibilities. The tax system in many states, the unwarranted disenchantment with higher education among some state legislators, and the open hostility and anti-intellectualism on the part of others does not augur well for increased support even in an indirect form through state student-aid programs. Direct institutional aid to the private sector is non-existent in all but a very few states; it may never be realized in some states. Moreover, the fear that the possibility of direct assistance by the federal government might cause states to hold off funding has a hollow ring to administrators in many areas. Federal legislation could easily include provisions that would compel states to keep their support of higher education at a reasonable level. Here, again, it seems to me that many of the points in the Commission's own publications, including *The Capitol and the Campus* and *State Officials and Higher Education,* negate the possibility of preserving pluralism in higher education unless other forms of assistance are implemented, at least for the immediate future.

The Commission appears strangely myopic about the kind of student mix which will result from the implementation of its recommendations. Through no desire on their part, the day is approaching when private colleges and universities will constitute isolated colonies of the very wealthy and a minimal number of the very needy supported largely by the tuition of the wealthy and by too many and too large loans from the federal government. If the middle American is the forgotten American, then the middle-income student is surely the forgotten student. In terms of student distribution, the total impact of the Commission's recommendations would be (a) not to increase the number of low-income students in private institutions since, even with the piggyback federal aid

---

[1] Commission reports are published by McGraw-Hill.

proposed, the major financial burden will fall on the institution itself; (b) to decrease the number of middle-income students in the private sector, at least in those states that de facto will not live up to their responsibilities to provide equal opportunity for their residents to attend the institution of their choice; and (c) to reserve the private sector for the wealthy or near-wealthy who have sufficient means to meet the inevitably increasing tuition rates or who have enough future security to justify borrowing from governmental or private sources.

Kerr states, in Chapter One, that "the Carnegie Commission was established because it seemed clear that American higher education could not prosper on a 'wait and see' basis." Yet it seems to me that in regard to the private sector of American higher education, with the exception of a few prestigious institutions, this is the attitude that prevails. Let's wait and see how many and which private colleges and universities either close or merge into the public system and then decide what to do about the survivors. Last summer when I discussed this problem all over the country with legislators, business executives, and opinion-makers in the communications industries, I was appalled at the number of intelligent citizens who subscribe, at least implicitly, to this "survival of the fittest" philosophy. If a college, private or public, has lost its reason for existence, it should close. But I am not convinced that only the weak, unjustifiable private institutions will be closing in the next three to five years. The real issue is whether we who represent higher education are doing all that can be done to preserve the diversity and pluralism in higher education, for it is one of the most precious yet fragile possessions in our heritage.

PART TWO

Women and Blacks
in Higher Education

❧❧❧❧❧❧❧❧❧❧

As in society at large, the two groups most discriminated against
in higher education are women and blacks. Part Two contains two
chapters which deal with women and two chapters which deal with
black students.

     Ezra Naughton and King Cheek, both writing about blacks,
emphasize the concept of pluralism and its meaning in the American experience. Both men believe that the answer for blacks lies
not in integration but in pluralism, as it has for other minority
groups. Cheek's chapter, "The Black College in a Multiracial
Society," argues that black colleges, now in danger of extinction,
must be saved—not just for their own sakes, but for the sake of
America and its future. Naughton's chapter, "What You See Is
What You Get: Black Student/White Campus," takes its title from
an oft-repeated line of Flip Wilson's character Geraldine. Naughton

tells us that Geraldine knows her needs, has a sense of direction, is herself. Black students in white colleges have not been able, in the past, to be themselves—and they must, Naughton asserts, because "for them to be what they are is now their only hope of survival."

Bernice Sandler, in "Equity for Women in Higher Education," proceeds analytically and logically to show why and how colleges and universities must change their structures if they are to accommodate the female half of the population. Historically, she points out, higher education was designed for students who were young, single, and male. Faculty members were to provide appropriate models for these students and were envisioned as somewhat older and preferably married, but also male. Sandler offers dozens of statistical and qualitative examples to illustrate how the traditional pattern operates on our campuses. She shows, for example, that a married woman is paid less than her male counterpart because, since she is married, her needs are said to be less; but the unmarried woman, also, is paid less, and that practice is justified with the statement that her needs are less because she is not married. Readers of this chapter may be startled by the statistics which demonstrate that women's positions in the academic world have not improved but deteriorated in recent years. Sandler concludes her chapter with a warning to male chauvinists: the hands that have rocked the cradle can—and will—rock the boat.

Of the four authors represented in Part Two, three are black and two are women. This peculiar arithmetic reminds us that about half of every minority group in this country consists of women. When Shirley Chisholm, author of "Of Course Women Dare," first announced that she was a candidate for a seat in the United States Congress, she encountered heavy resistance. It came from males and from those she calls "brain-washed 'Uncle Tom' females." Their advice to her was: Go back to teaching and leave politics to men. The thesis of Chisholm's chapter is profound, and it should be kept in mind as the other chapters of Part Two are read. The struggle, Chisholm reminds us, is not against racism or sexism per se. The struggle is against antihumanism.

JOSEPH AXELROD

5

Of Course
Women Dare

Shirley Chisholm

Do women dare to take an active part in society, and in particular do they dare to take a part in the present social revolution? I find this question as insulting as "Are you, as a black person, willing to fight for your rights?" America has been sufficiently sensitized to the answer that black people are willing to both fight and die for their rights to make the question asinine and superfluous. But America is not yet sufficiently aware that such a question applied to women is equally asinine and superfluous.

I am both black and a woman. I therefore have a good vantage point from which to view at least two elements of what is becoming a social revolution: the American Black Revolution and

41

the Women's Liberation Movement. But being a black woman is also a horrible disadvantage because America, as a nation, is both racist and antifeminist. Racism and antifeminism are two of the prime traditions of this country.

For any individual, challenging social traditions is a giant step, for there are no social traditions which do not have corresponding social sanctions, the sole purpose of which is to protect the sanctity of the traditions. Thus, when we ask the question "Do women dare?" we are not asking whether women are capable of a break with tradition; we are asking "Are they capable of bearing the sanctions that will be placed upon them?"

Coupling this idea with a hypothesis presented by some social thinkers and philosophers—that in any given society the most active groups are those nearest to the particular freedom they desire —it does not surprise me that those women most active and vocal on the issue of freedom for women are young, white, and middle-class; nor is it too surprising that there are not more from that group involved in the Women's Liberation Movement.

There certainly are reasons why more women are not involved. Few, if any, Americans are free of the psychological wounds imposed by racism and anti-feminism. A few months ago while testifying before the Office of Federal Contract Compliance, I noted that antifeminism, like every form of discrimination, is destructive both to those who perpetrate it and to their victims; that males with their antifeminism maim both themselves and their women.

Eldridge Cleaver[1] points out how America's racial and sexual stereotypes are supposed to work. Whether or not his insight is correct, it bears close examination. In the chapter "The Primeval Mitosis," he describes the four major roles: there is the white female who is considered to be "Ultra-Feminine" because "she is required to possess and project an image that is in sharp contrast to . . ." the white male's image as the "Omnipotent Administrator . . . all brain and no body." The black female is seen as "Subfeminine" or "Amazon" by virtue of her assignment to the lowly household chores and those corresponding jobs of a tedious nature. And the black male has the role of the "Supermasculine Menial . . . all

[1] E. Cleaver, *Soul on Ice*. New York: Dell, 1968, pp. 179–182.

body and no brain" because he is expected to supply society with its source of brute power.

What these roles and the strange interplay between them have meant to America Cleaver points out quite well. What he does not say and what I think must be said is that because of the bizarre aspects of the roles and the influence that nontraditional contact between them has on the general society, blacks and whites, males and females must operate almost independently of each other in order to escape from the quicksands of psychological slavery. Each—black male and black female, white female and white male— must escape first from his own historical trap before he can be truly effective in helping to free his companions.

Therein lies one of the major reasons that there are not more women involved in the Women's Liberation Movement. Women cannot, for the most part, operate independently of males because they often do not have sufficient economic freedom. In 1966 the median income of women who worked full-time for the whole year was less than the median earnings of males who worked full-time for the whole year. In fact, white women workers made less than black male workers and, of course, black women workers made the least of all.

Whether this discrimination is intentional or not, women are paid less than men for the same work, no matter what their chosen field. Employment for women is regulated still more in terms of the jobs that are available to them. This is almost as true for white women as it is for black women. When it becomes time for a young high school girl to think about preparing for her career, her counselors, whether they be male or female, will think first of her so-called natural career—housewife and mother—and begin to program her for a field with which marriage and children will not unduly interfere.

The situation is exactly the same for the young black or Puerto Rican who is advised by the racist counselor to prepare for service-oriented occupations because he does not even consider their entering the professions. The response of the average young lady is precisely the same as that of most young blacks or Puerto Ricans —tacit agreement—because the odds do seem to be stacked against them. This discrimination is not happening as much as it once did to young members of minority groups, but only because they have been radicalized and the country is becoming sensitized to its racist attitudes and the damage they do.

Women must rebel—they must react to the traditional stereotyped education mapped out for them by society. Their education and training is programmed and planned for them from the moment the doctor says "Mr. Jones, it's a beautiful baby girl," and Mr. Jones begins deleting mentally the things that she might have been and adds the things that society says she *must* be.

That young woman will be wrapped in a pink blanket (pink because that is the color of her caste) and the unequal segregation of the sexes will have begun. Small wonder that the young girl sitting across the desk from her counselor will not be able to say "No" to educational, economic, and social slavery. She has been a psychological slave and programmed as such since the moment of her birth.

In May 1970 I introduced legislation concerning equal employment opportunities for women. At that time I pointed out that there were three and one-half million more women than men in America but women held only 2 per cent of the managerial positions; that no women sit on the AFL-CIO Council or the Supreme Court; that only two women had ever held Cabinet rank; and that there were at that time only two women of ambassadorial rank in the diplomatic corps. I stated then, as I do now, that this situation is outrageous. In my speech on the House floor that day I said:

> *It is true that part of the problem has been that women have not been aggressive in demanding their rights. This was also true of the black population for many years. They submitted to oppression and even cooperated with it. Women have done the same thing. But now there is an awareness of this situation, particularly among the younger segment of the population. As in the field of equal rights for blacks, Spanish-Americans, the Indians, and other groups, laws will not change such deep-seated problems overnight. But they can be used to provide protection for those who are most abused and begin the process of evolutionary change by compelling the insensitive majority to reexamine its unconscious attitudes.*

The law cannot do it for us. We must do it ourselves. Women in this country must become revolutionaries. We must refuse to accept the old—traditional—roles and stereotypes. We must reject the Greek philosopher's thought: It is thy place, women, to hold thy peace and keep within doors. We must reject the view of St. Paul: Let the woman learn in silence. And we must reject Nietzsche's statement that when a woman inclines to learning, there is something wrong with her sex apparatus.

But more than merely rejecting, we must replace those thoughts and the concepts that they symbolize with positive values based on female experience. Women must come to realize that the superficial symbolisms surrounding us are negative only when we ourselves perceive and accept them as negative. We must begin to replace the old negative thoughts about our femininity with positive thoughts and positive actions affirming it and more. But we must also remember that these efforts will be breaking with tradition and we must prepare ourselves educationally, economically, and psychologically to be able to accept and bear the sanctions that society will immediately impose on us.

I am a politician. I detest the word only because of the connotations that cling like slime to it in our society, but for want of another term I must use it. I have been in politics for twenty years, and in that time I have learned a few things about the role of women in politics. I found that women are the backbone of America's political organizations. They are the letter-writers, the envelope-stuffers, the telephone-answerers; they are the campaign workers and organizers. Many are speech writers, and as a group they have the largest number of potential voters. Yet they are rarely the standard-bearers or elected officials. Perhaps in America, more than in any other country, the inherent truth of the old bromide "The power behind the throne is a woman" is readily apparent.

There are only ten United States Representatives who are women. There is only one Senator, and there are no Cabinet members who are women. There are no women on the Supreme Court and only a small percentage of women judges at the federal court level who might be candidates. (At the state level the picture is somewhat brighter for women, just as the North presents to the black American a somewhat more appealing surface than does the

South.) One of the reasons why there are relatively few women standard-bearers on the American political scene is the attitude toward women candidates that is held by political bosses. A few years ago a politician remarked to me about a potential young female candidate: "Why invest all the time and effort to build up the gal into a household name when she's pretty sure to drop out of the game to have a couple of kids at just about the time we're ready to run her for mayor?"

I have pointed out time and again that the harshest discrimination I have encountered in the political arena is antifeminism —both from males and from brainwashed "Uncle Tom" females. When I first announced that I was running for the United States Congress in 1970, both males and females advised me, as they had when I ran for the New York State Assembly, to go back to teaching, a woman's vocation, and leave the politics to men.

The device used to limit competition is to assign different roles to different groups within society. White males have assigned to themselves such roles as President of the United States, corporate executives, industrialists, doctors, lawyers, and professors at our universities. They have assigned to white women roles such as housewife, secretary, PTA chairman, and schoolteacher. Black women can now be schoolteachers too, but they are most prominently assigned to domestic roles—maid, cook, waitress, and babysitter. Black men are thought to be good porters, bus drivers, and sanitation men.

These are roles which have been engrained into the minds of all of us; and any attempt on the part of the other three groups to rise above their particular roles is looked upon with apprehension by the white males who form the establishment. All too often the potential for full intellectual development and goal realization on the part of minorities and women is suppressed by denying these groups the appropriate job training and educational opportunity necessary to assume a role which white males consider to be their domain.

I do not mean to suggest that there is anything degrading about work as a domestic or a clerical worker or a teacher or any other job that is honest and satisfying. Hard work at any occupation can be fulfilling and rewarding. But I do object to assigning certain roles to particular groups on the basis of sex and color when there is no generic reason. And I resent the efforts of white males to limit competition for the more prestigious and higher-paying occupations.

Blacks, Spanish-speaking Americans, and Indians have long objected to the exclusiveness of the establishment. Today, women are voicing their objections too; and statistics tell us why. Among all employed women, 82 per cent are clerical, sales, factory, and farm workers or in service occupations. Six per cent are medical and health workers, college teachers, or other professional and technical workers. Just 5 per cent of American women are managers, officials, or proprietors.

If women are, as the Department of Labor has concluded, more reliable and are absent from their jobs less frequently than men, what is the reason for their preponderant employment at the lower-level positions and pay scales? Quite simply, it is discrimination.

Women are sick and tired of being told "See how far you've come. You've come a long way, Baby." If that is so, then why, among ten thousand civil service employees in jobs paying $26,000 a year or better, are there only about 150 women? If it is true, then why are fewer than 1 per cent of federal policymaking positions held by women?

The truth is that the top policymaking positions within the American establishment remain in the hands of white males who are not responsive to the needs of the poor, minorities, or women. Nor can these men be called to account for their actions—for their failure to control inflation and unemployment, for their failure to respond to the call of consumers for better products at nonexorbitant prices—because regular citizens, such as you and I, have no power to control them or to replace them as long as they deny the great majority of Americans the opportunity to compete freely in our society.

Yet there is hope for oppressed groups if we unite and challenge the forces which now hold all the power in our country. This is an effort that requires these groups—minorities, women, consumers—to come together and demand representation in the high councils of the establishment; and it also asks us to forget about role-playing and allow all individuals to engage in work that is suited to their intellectual and physical abilities. New goals and new priorities—not only for this country but for all of mankind—must be set. We must confront people with their own humanity and their own inhumanity wherever we meet them—in the church, in the classroom, on the floors of Congress and the state legislatures, and on the streets. We must reject not only the stereotypes that others hold of us but also the stereotypes that we hold of ourselves.

We must not only work for integrated schools, churches, and marriages—the integration of black and white; we must also work for, fight for, the integration of male and female—human and human. As Fanon points out, the anti-Semitic was eventually the antifeminist.[2] All discrimination is eventually the same thing—antihumanism.

[2] F. Fanon, *Black Skin—White Masks*. Translated by C. L. Markmann. New York: Grove, 1967.

6

What You See Is What You Get: Black Student/ White Campus

Ezra A. Naughton

When the 1960s began, relatively few black students were attending traditionally white colleges and universities. But by the end of the decade, the number of blacks enrolled on white campuses had increased substantially: according to some reports, half of the 492,000 black students enrolled in all institutions of higher education in the United States were attending traditionally white colleges and universities. This trend probably will continue.

In the discussion which follows, I point to some issues and practices relating to this "black surge" which undoubtedly will influence profoundly the character of many traditionally white colleges and universities, if not the character of American higher education itself.

I have not sought here for objectivity at the expense of opinion. This is not a research paper in the sense that there is no point of view. One disadvantage of the research approach to the problems of black Americans is that often researchers fail to keep uppermost in their minds that they are dealing with the problems of individual human beings. Kovel succinctly stated this view: "Reform has always floundered in its goal of helping the black person, by and large ignoring him in his actuality and concentrating instead on the evils to which he has been exposed. In this way American culture has managed to expose the black to a succession of different evils by a succession of different reforms."[1]

Historically, blacks have been almost entirely excluded from traditionally white institutions. Yet as early as 1826 Edward Jones and John Russwurm graduated two weeks apart from Amherst and Bowdoin respectively and won the distinction of being the first blacks in this country to receive college degrees. It was not until 1870 that a black graduated from Harvard University, our nation's oldest institution of higher learning. Richard T. Greener took the A.B. degree there, and three years later, in 1873, during Reconstruction, Greener was appointed a professor of metaphysics at the University of South Carolina. By 1895, when Booker T. Washington was being hailed for his Atlanta Exposition Address, and one year before the fateful Supreme Court ruling in *Plessy* v. *Ferguson* was made, W. E. B. DuBois earned the Ph.D. at Harvard. At that time there probably were about 195 black college graduates in the United States. Of this number, however, almost 40 per cent were graduates of Oberlin alone.

In 1915, when Paul Robeson entered the 149-year-old Rutgers University on a state scholarship, he was the sole black on

---

[1] J. Kovel, *White Racism: A Psychohistory.* New York: Pantheon Books, 1970, p. 30.

the campus. The son of a former slave, Robeson was the third black to matriculate at Rutgers. As recently as a few years before the outbreak of World War II, blacks were not admitted to traditionally white institutions on a continuous basis or in any significant numbers. In the South, it was not until 1935—nearly three-quarters of a century after the passage of the Morrill Act—that at least one traditionally white institution, the University of Maryland, was opened to black students, when Donald Murray was ordered admitted to Maryland's Law School. On the other hand, in 1940 the University of West Virginia became the first white institution outside the North voluntarily to admit blacks to its graduate schools.

Before the 1960s, the relatively few black students enrolled in white institutions were generally regarded by the majority with an attitude that might be described as "benign toleration." For generations the black student on the white campus of necessity had to go his own way. Often he was unwanted and misunderstood. Almost always his unique needs and his potential for contributing to the campus community and the nation were overlooked or ignored. An article in the *Chronicle of Higher Education* noted, for example: "Until the civil rights revolution of the past decade, those committees [Rhodes Scholar Selection] saw the future leaders of America as almost exclusively white. The best evidence available indicates that, before 1960, only one black American ever became a Rhodes Scholar—Alain Locke, a 1907 Harvard graduate who was a leader of the Harlem Renaissance movement of the late 1920s."[2] Not a single Rhodes Scholar has come from a black institution, the author of the article also observed.

For obvious reasons the black student's education—or miseducation as some persons describe it—has generally denied him a genuine opportunity to derive some of the benefits of higher education in a pluralistic milieu. Pluralism is defined, by Yinger, as being in contrast with separation and segregation. Pluralism "means something quite different. Membership in distinctive ethnic, religious, or cultural groups is accepted and even applauded." Yinger states: "Pluralistic societies pride themselves on the freedom granted to diverse groups to preserve their different heritages, support

---

[2] L. Munford, "Rhodes Scholars No Longer All White." *Chronicle of Higher Education,* January 17, 1972, p. 8.

various religions, speak different languages, and develop independent associations. This freedom is qualified only by reinforcement of loyalty to the prevailing political and economic systems."[3]

Were it not for the present influx of blacks, American colleges and universities would remain the preserve principally of the white middle-class. In the past, admissions standards and policies, the racial composition of the faculty, the costs, the exclusivity of the system of fraternities and sororities, the campus atmosphere, and the factor of social expectancy conspired to keep the black student away from the white campus.

There are now signs of change. However, present and future efforts must go beyond providing access to higher education for the black student. They must clearly afford him opportunities to be successful. For black and other minority students "success" means more than the mere satisfactory completion of a course of study. Not that this concept of success does not apply to nonminority students as well. But in the present preoccupation with getting the black student onto the white campus we must be urgently concerned that through his attendance at or graduation from the white institution he does not emerge coolly intellectual. The white higher education experience must offer the minority student, as a matter of basic principle, insights that will enable him to be actively involved with the challenges he and his group face. He must be able still to relate to his people; he must be able still to understand their needs and aspirations. He must be eager to speak *with* them and share common cause.

Among the changes which stand in striking contrast to the pattern of the past, one significant development can be observed. Unlike previous generations of black students who had to brave the indifference, isolation, and challenge of the white campus, today's black is eagerly sought after and encouraged to enroll in the traditionally white institution. Bowles and DeCosta comment as follows:

> *The Negro students constitute, for most of the historically white colleges, a new social group making their entry into higher education. Unlike previous such groups—Jewish, Irish, Italian, Puerto Rican, Chinese, Japanese—which have pushed their way*

[3] J. M. Yinger, "Integration and Pluralism Viewed from Hawaii," *Antioch Review,* 1962, 22, 398.

into higher education inch by inch, Negroes, after years of exclu-
sion, have been sought, invited, recruited, and subsidized to enter.
They have come in sizable groups rather than in the slow trickle
by which the other new social groups began their entry to higher
education. They have been selected in unusual ways. The better
prepared among them could have entered the white colleges but
have chosen not to. The least well prepared have for the most part
entered on special waivers. The athletes have been recruited as
athletes—as, in effect, mercenaries rather than students. Some of
the students have come from schools which have failed, or perhaps
been unable, to prepare them for the kinds of colleges they have
entered. Some have come burdened with doubt and suspicion,
which carried over into college, and have been faced with the task
of reshaping their values, or they have come in violent protest,
forcing their carried-over values onto their colleges.[4]

Another relevant point which Bowles and DeCosta might have made
is that unlike yesterday's black student who was largely rejected by
whites, today's black student attempts to reverse the process and
currently many blacks often reject their white fellow students.

These new black students are enrolling in white colleges and
universities at a time when one of the observable salient characteristics of the black population in general is a keen self-assertiveness.
This posture, many blacks believe, will enable them to achieve an
identity that connotes racial and personal pride. Let me point out
that "black" is a self-chosen category; "Negro" is an imposed one.
And while Negro connotes, essentially, the individual or the group
as defined by whites, many Negroes are engaged in an ongoing
process of defining themselves as *blacks*. Contrary to the frequently
misinformed and misunderstood frames of reference of the white
institutions, in the present context of self-assertiveness being "black"
has meaning beyond such yardsticks as educational attainments or
the achieving of middle-class status.

Being "black" is, I think, a composite of attitudes: a way of
perceiving the self within the social order as well as a way of relating
to the "brothers" and "sisters" who are members of the race,
particularly in terms of a concern for the welfare of black men

---

[4] F. Bowles and F. DeCosta, *Between Two Worlds: A Profile of Negro
Higher Education.* New York: McGraw-Hill, 1971, p. 219.

everywhere. While in the past the black student may have been ashamed of himself because of the supposed personal stigma of blackness, today's black student generally takes pride in his heritage and insists upon being a person in his own right. The rhetoric as well as the evolving black esthetics of the present era are reminiscent of the lines from a poem by W. E. B. DuBois—a scholar of awesome intellectual depth and range—who sometimes used poetry to record ideas and feeling which he otherwise recorded so ably in prose. In "The Song of Smoke," a poem he first published in *The Horizon* in 1899, DuBois declared:

> I am the smoke king,
> I am black.
>
>   . . . . . .
>
> I will be as black as blackness can,
> The blacker the mantle the mightier the man.[5]

DuBois's words at the turn of the century and the later expressions of Marcus Garvey, James Baldwin, Eldridge Cleaver, Malcolm X, and many others resound today in the cry heard on the white campus—"Black is Beautiful!" In these three words are subsumed many of the feelings, aspirations, and hopes of the black student.

The experiences of blacks have shaped the contents of their culture, and the adaptations they have had to make brought about their unique perception of the world. While noting that he is not speaking of the "elite of various 'sets,' " Cruse maintains that "American Negroes (as distinct from West Indians) do not come out of the European tradition, know very little about it, and care less."[6]

I will not undertake to elaborate—even if I could—on the specific aspects of the "black experience" which comprise the cultural differences between black and white students. It is not surprising that the black student brings to the white campus different cultural patterns, given the history of racial segregation and discrimination in the United States. Another significant consideration, upon which many black students insist, pertains to their African cultural origins. Although the extent to which these cultural

---

[5] As found in *Freedomways*, 1965, 5(1), 92–93.
[6] H. Cruse, *The Crisis of the Negro Intellectual.* New York: William Morrow, 1967, p. 482.

patterns have persisted among blacks in the United States has not been ascertained, it cannot be disputed that there are differences.

Some intellectuals insist that there are no differences between blacks and whites except those which have an economic basis, and even blacks sometimes claim that they are "no different from anyone else." Paradoxically, such protestations are both true and false. They are true to the extent that blacks share whatever is common to mankind. On the other hand, the assumption is false if it is meant to suggest that blacks have no shared way of life significantly different from white Americans.

To consider for a moment the different perspectives of blacks and whites regarding approaches to thinking and learning, two recent reports entitled "Are There Two Kinds of Thinking?" and "Cognitive Styles and Social Order,"[7] based on studies conducted by researchers at the University of California at Riverside, advance the hypothesis that minority groups tend to concentrate their intellectual development in the direction of inductive interpretation of experience rather than on deductive processes. Considering the active campaigns to lure blacks who often come from the so-called ghetto areas of our cities to the white campus, the implications of this hypothesis have significance for the higher education of blacks, particularly in terms of renewal of the traditional curriculum.

In his presidential address, "Technical Education and Its Relation to Science and Literature," presented to the Mathematical Society in 1917, Whitehead declared that "firsthand knowledge is the ultimate basis of intellectual life . . . what the learned world has to offer is one secondhand scrap of information illustrating ideas derived from another secondhand scrap of information." Whitehead's view has poignant implications for the renewal of higher education through the enrolling of blacks in white colleges and universities as equal partners in a pluralistic society. Whitehead contended that "the secondhandedness of the learned world is the secret of its mediocrity." Through pluralism in higher education, it seems to me, many of the challenges in our society can be faced and many of the realities of the past and the present dealt with, finally making untrue Whitehead's implied indictment in his addi-

---

[7] Prepared under contract for the Office of Economic Opportunity, copies of these reports have been filed with the National Technical Information Service, U. S. Department of Commerce, Springfield, Virginia 22151.

tional comment, "[the learned world] is tame because it has never been scared by facts."[8]

A question seriously to be considered is whether what has long been regarded as "education" through socialization now calls for reexamination. It is clear (and is not this true of many white students also?) that the higher education establishment has not adequately worked for a significant segment of our society. In the case of blacks, their culture and even their existence has not been adequately reflected in the educational goals and objectives of our institutions. In fact, the black student consistently has been prevailed upon to abandon his language patterns, cultural traditions, and racial identity as a condition for partial acceptance by the larger society. If the traditionally white institution requires—even by implication—that the black student abandon his heritage, the potential values of pluralism in higher education will not be realized. A campus milieu to which blacks have been afforded access as members of a minority group, and in which their identity as blacks is accepted within pluralistic limits, enhances the entire educational enterprise. Jacob observed that "college can contribute to the growth of student values only when it penetrates the core of his life and confronts him with fresh and disturbing implications which are different from those he and his society have taken for granted."[9] The pace of change has invalidated the assumptions upon which the socialization model of higher education rests. In fact, toleration was then the rule for the black student in the white institution and access to those institutions was then severely restricted. Another factor which invalidates the socialization model stems from the complex nature of the contemporary society which higher education serves. Whose society—whose culture—should the student be socialized into? In short, should the black student be respected and appreciated for what he is and provided specific opportunities to enhance his black self, or should he deny his blackness, seeking to escape it? To adapt Logan Wilson's remark: The university truly must be for the black student, too. The black student must not only be *in* the university, he must also be *of* it.

    [8] A. N. Whitehead, *The Aims of Education and Other Essays*. New York: Macmillan, 1929, p. 79.

    [9] P. E. Jacob, *Changing Values in College: An Exploratory Study of the Impact of College Teaching*. New York: Harper & Row, 1957, p. 38.

Perhaps now as never before the white institution should pursue with candor, vigor, and insight the new vistas opened to it by virtue of its more diverse student population. White colleges and universities should seize this new situation as an opportunity for renewal.

I shall now deal with some specific issues and practices related to the black student on the white campus. I will consider recruiting and admissions, instruction, counseling and guidance, and campus life.

Many white colleges and universities have attempted to respond to the educational needs of blacks by establishing special instructional programs for them. Blacks are often recruited from urban ghettos and, in many instances, provided financial, academic, and counseling assistance as part of their program throughout their college careers. This pattern seems to be an effort to compensate for generations of overall disadvantages which blacks have experienced. To quote from Bowles and DeCosta again: "The colleges have been unprepared for the students. The students come from a background unknown to the colleges, and they do not have advisers or faculty members or even other students who are ready to talk to the new students, or programs to offer them, or even the privilege of entry into the group life of the college. And, it appears, there is no mediating apparatus in most colleges by which communication between the college and its new Negro students can be established. In other words, the black surge into higher education has found both parties unprepared."[10]

During the time I served on the faculty of a traditionally white institution, and again while preparing this chapter, I talked with black students who are enrolled in public as well as private white institutions. Many of them expressed feelings of meaninglessness, powerlessness, and alienation from the campus mainstream. One student said, for example, that he always had the feeling that he was fighting the college. Among students in special educational programs there was a feeling that it would be difficult for them to succeed in an institution where recruiting, admissions, and the "special" instructional programs hint at their inferiority. As one student put it, "They" (meaning the institution) "are trying to set

[10] Bowles and DeCosta, p. 219.

up a ghetto on the campus for me." Many of the students assisted by the programs are ambivalent, at best, over the assistance they receive. In other instances, students cited what might be described as the duplicity of the institution, considering the special circumstances under which they had entered. The Southern Regional Education Board observes that at times the "student feels wanted *before* he enrolls and is forgotten afterward."[11] This factor, when operative, leads to intense problems of adjustment for the black student.

Of course, I am aware that not all blacks in white institutions have been admitted under special provisions, nor are they the recipients of what one student contemptuously called "white money." I wish to advance the view, however, that it might be well for recruiters to stop romanticizing the ghetto and also seek to enroll blacks from other than the so-called ghetto circumstances who have a higher potential for survival while taking the regular curriculum. To open doors for the black student with limited ability only to have him go " 'round and 'round" is immoral.

Recruiting and admitting blacks to white campuses calls for on-going consideration of issues such as the role previous academic achievement should play. Similarly, with special reference to the private institution, should black enrollment be limited? And if so, what criteria should be employed in limiting their admission? Should an equal ratio be maintained between the number of black males and black females admitted? Is there relatively easy access from the white campus to a predominantly black community in the vicinity?

The problems of the black student become all the more acute when he must endure, in addition to his being physically away from home, the trauma of being away from home spiritually as well. Is it any wonder that increased enrollment of blacks in white institutions has often led to protests against what the student perceives as hypocrisy and paternalism? The college should examine how the black perceives the institution and explore whether what he perceives is what the institution intends him to perceive. It should also consider, and irrespective of what jurists might con-

[11] Southern Regional Education Board, *The College and Cultural Diversity: The Black Student on Campus, A Project Report.* Atlanta: Institute for Higher Educational Opportunity, 1971.

tend, whether institutional traditions—songs, symbols, and the like—represent an affront to the black student.

Another issue relating to recruitment is of great significance. Bayer and Boruch, writing in the American Council on Education's *Research Report,* note the following:

The recent legal and social stress on integration has prompted competition in the recruitment of black students. Not only do the Negro colleges compete for the same students, but the predominantly white institutions are increasingly competing, both among themselves and with the predominantly Negro institutions, for the same black students. This competition has been stimulated by major reevaluations of the recruitment policies among the predominantly white institutions. The instituting of major recruitment efforts by these schools has posed some additional problems for Negro institutions. The more able black students are likely to be lost by predominantly Negro institutions and recruited by predominantly white ones. [12]

With reference to curriculum and instruction, the black student on the white campus, in many instances, views these aspects of the educational program as being "racist." He frequently perceives them as inimical to his heritage, his people, and his sense of personal worth. Probably because of his perceptions of the curriculum and instruction, among other factors, the black student is often heard now espousing separatism. The rhetoric of separatism that has emerged is seen by many as a viable means of achieving pluralism. The black student apparently despairs that pluralism can be achieved in American higher education.

The tendency in higher education toward emphasizing cultural conformity can prove especially crippling for blacks and can create circumstances that will make "success" for the black student improbable indeed. In fact, seeking to inculcate in the black student an assiduous preoccupation with the perspectives and life style of whites might prepare him only for the best of all impossible worlds. Certainly such a preoccupation will tend to reduce his value as a

[12] A. E. Bayer and R. F. Boruch, "The Black Student in American Colleges," *Research Report,* 1969, 4(2), 3.

"leader" in his own cultural milieu. Above all, if education is to be most worthwhile, it seems to me, a great need that must be met for the black student—as for others—is helping him to establish a positive identity concept: he must, at least, have an opportunity to discover who *he* is.

It is now recognized, I think, that liberal education must not be limited to Western material. Black studies should form a part of the *basic* curriculum. As such, it has positive value for whites and can also reflect the institution's acceptance of the concept of pluralism in education. Through such studies, black and white students can critically consider, for example, the hypothesis that among the basic ingredients of the black experience the oral, aural, and kinesthetic elements are paramount. Some individuals, either out of genuine interest or malicious curiosity, often assert, "Blacks fought for the Black Studies Program but few of them enroll in the program." Such a view is beside the point. The black student fights on the white campus not so much for participation as for *recognition*.

In other words, as Thomas Pettigrew observed, although identity and participation are ineluctably intertwined in a pluralistic society, identity precedes participation.[13] This is true both for the institution and the individual. Institutional efforts must be directed first toward allowing the student to experience growth in his own identity, and, subsequently, awareness of his identity as a person in the pluralistic campus and general societies can also be experienced. On the contemporary scene, the black student's contribution to higher education might well be that his presence on the white campus and his focus upon the "validity" of the black experience can help to revitalize higher education by proclaiming the potential illumination of the interdepartmental and multicultural approaches to learning.

Despite the innovations which are clearly reflected by Black Studies programs, there still must be at the center of the education-in-action curriculum that ingredient to which Malcolm X once referred: books. Apart from their pragmatic and symbolic importance, books which honestly deal with the implications of the black experience are of incalculable value in promoting pluralism in higher education and in society at large. Malcolm X wrote:

[13] See Pettigrew's article in *Daedalus* (Summer 1971), 813.

I have often reflected upon the new vistas that reading opened to me. I knew right there in prison that reading had changed forever the course of my life. As I see it today, the ability to read awoke inside me some long dormant craving to be mentally alive. . . . My homemade education gave me, with every additional book that I read, a little bit more sensitivity to the deafness, dumbness, and blindness that was afflicting the black race in America. Not long ago, an English writer telephoned me from London, asking questions. One was "What's your alma mater?" I told him. "Books."[14]

Responses to black demands for change in higher education, although clearly warranted, must provide the black student an education which offers substance and quality.

By accepting the concept of cultural diversity in higher education, white institutions can gain considerable benefits when they cooperate with black institutions, especially those in the same geographic area. Examples of black-white institutional cooperation include consortia such as those involving Fisk and Vanderbilt Universities in Nashville, Howard University and the four principal white institutions in Washington, D. C., and Grambling College and Louisiana Institute of Technology.

Reform in instruction cannot focus only on the curriculum. In addition to providing access to college and providing tutorial assistance for black students when indicated, culturally diverse faculty members are crucial if pluralism in higher education is to be viable. Although assessments are often subjective, some pertinent questions relating to faculty must be asked: Does the composition of the faculty hint that the institution is racist? Can faculty members relate to the black student without being patronizing? Can they generally appreciate the black student's cultural differences as well as his quest for identity? Do faculty and administration comprehend that self-identity must first be established before the student's integration into the institution can occur? Also, what is the faculty's responsibility for modifying the curriculum and course content to reflect the pluralistic character of our society?

If the black student's access to the white institution is to be fruitful and if cultural diversity is to flourish, faculty and administra-

[14] Malcolm X, *Autobiography*. New York: Grove Press, 1964, p. 179.

tion must understand the difference between assimilation (loss of assured identity) and integration (freedom to move, relate, and interrelate while still retaining one's black identity). And there are other concerns: Is the institutional program such that the black student could return home without feeling superior to his community or being ostracized? What negative predictions for the academic success of the black student does the faculty make? How does the faculty view the black—from the ghetto or elsewhere— who elects to enroll in the white college or university? And ever so important, how does the black student regard himself for enrolling in a traditionally white institution?

Although blacks should be represented on the faculty of the white institution, they should also be visible in staff positions and jobs unrelated to institutional housekeeping and maintenance. Furthermore, administrators, department chairmen, and even white faculty members must be prepared to consider employing blacks who have human relations skills, quite apart from their academic credentials and their presumed or demonstrated expertise. Also, the advantages of having blacks at administrative levels, in addition to their presence in faculty and staff appointments, must be regarded as essential.

The black faculty member and administrator have important contributions to make to the education of all students—black or white. Based upon this potential to contribute to the total institution, administrators should not recruit and appoint only those faculty members who are deemed "safe" for the white environment and who are unlikely to rock the boat. The concept of cultural diversity should apply to faculty members as well as to students. Careful thought and attention must be given to appointing not only individuals who are best suited on the basis of credentials but— probably even more important within the context of the renewal of higher education and the attaining of pluralism—those who potentially can carry out the objectives of the institutional mission as it relates to the black and other minority students.

However, one caveat must be entered. The traditionally white colleges and universities recruiting faculty and staff should not raid personnel of black institutions, which can ill afford to have their faculties raided. Whites need to address themselves vigorously to the training of blacks at the graduate level, for the black colleges and universities as a class are not prepared to provide such training.

Perhaps the most critical factor affecting the success of black students is counseling and guidance. Black students frequently leave high school without clearly defined career goals. Besides, they often lack information about college in general. Once in the white institution, what they receive is not, some students report, what they had anticipated. Recruiting officers, faculty members, and administrators must consider the needs of the black student in such areas as educational planning, financial aid, health, testing, personal problems, and the like.

The lack of qualified black counselors on the white campus creates critical problems for the black student. Insensitivity to the needs of the student on the part of white counselors also hampers his adjustment and the likelihood of his success. I cannot state too emphatically that blacks must be involved at policy-making levels in the counseling activities of the white campus. The centralization and coordination of student personnel services with reference to the increased number of blacks are also needed.

The Southern Regional Education Board reports some institutional efforts to deal with counseling and guidance problems. Eckard College, for example, deals with the situation in this way: A Freshman Advisory Council, whose members reflect the ethnic backgrounds of their advisees, was organized to act as social advisers to new students. FACs live in the dormitories with their advisees and are generally available to provide tutorial assistance and other help. In addition, paid resident advisers, who are juniors or seniors at the institution, are responsible to the Dean of Students for the health and safety of those students in their houses. RAs assist the students with minor personal, racial, or academic problems, or else secure help for their advisees if the scope of the problem is beyond their capacity to handle. This latter function is critical, for the black student on the white campus may not know where to go or to whom to turn for help with his problems. Counseling services are provided by professional counselors, one black and one white, who provide such services as academic and psychological counseling and referral, career guidance, and encounter group experience.

The University of Maryland, in response to the need for

coordination, set up the office of Black Student Educational Services, which "serves as a clearinghouse, referral service, coordinating office and information exchange for matters concerning black students. Serving as a liaison between administration and students, the office director disseminates information, evaluates university services, determines community needs and serves as an advisor to the students and administration."[15]

At the University of South Florida, the disadvantaged student is identified by definition and upon admission assigned to an adviser who, even before the student comes to the campus, initiates a relationship with him by means of letter, telephone, or a personal visit. The adviser assists the student in applying for financial aid, planning his academic program, and the like. Key features of this program are that "the faculty members and the assisting students assigned to this service are volunteers who have indicated their interest in work with culturally disadvantaged students."

However, the Southern Regional Education Board reports:

Most colleges and universities fail at a critical point. For an ideal program of counseling minority students, the task ought to be shared by all faculty, administrators, and staff—housemothers, secretaries—who deal at all with students. To accomplish this end, training procedures on relationships with minority students must be provided at all levels. Even the maintenance staff must be provided with understandings which most of them do not have. Efforts in this direction were noticeably absent in the responses from institutions. Yet many instances of campus disruption might have been avoided had such training been provided, and it is known from SREB's junior college project that some dropouts of black students took place because of happenings which need not have occurred.[16]

Black students must be counseled concerning new occupations and careers which are developing and encouraged to enter the new fields. For example, considering the increasing significance of leisure and recreation activities, blacks might be encouraged to seek careers in park management. Also, they must be encouraged to go into older occupations which traditionally have been staffed only

[15] Southern Regional Education Board, p. 31.
[16] Southern Regional Education Board, p. 32.

by whites. In this category are careers related to communications, particularly television and journalism. Moreover, white administrators and faculty must take initiative in seeing that trained blacks are available to enter union-type occupations from which blacks have been excluded for several reasons, not the least of which has been the lament that "we can't find any qualified ones" in the field. White institutions can begin to set up programs to meet these occupational needs; if there is a supply, the demand will follow. Providing access to higher education is not enough, especially when access is motivated by institutional action based on complying with government decrees, securing federal or foundation grants, doing "the right thing," or—as it sometimes seems—destroying the viability of the traditionally black colleges and universities.

Success in higher education for the black student, in addition to his being able to offer skills the labor market needs and thereby improve the quality of his own life, must include his being able to appreciate his heritage, to relate to and identify with his people. Such outcomes of his access to higher education will make access truly worthwhile.

From what many black students report, it appears that campus life for them revolves around organizations such as the BSU—Black Student Union—and the like. This situation may be attributable to the feelings of alienation and isolation which they report and, given the articulation of these negative feelings, a relevant question appears to be: How effective can the teaching and learning processes or the developing of positive feelings about the self be in an environment from which the student feels detached? Harold Taylor's view that "the involvement of the student in the central life of the college is the key to the improvement of the quality of individual education" has special relevance and cannot be too strongly emphasized.

If the black student is to be successful, the white institution must encourage and support the BSU and similar organizations and include them among the legitimate and representative groups in the structure of campus life. The black must see himself as a partner within the institution. The structure of campus organizations, generally, should constructively reflect the need for black identity as well as the need for participation in the pluralistic society. The black student must be included as a member of committees for aid-ing other blacks with problems of adjustment, for example. He must be encouraged to participate in general campus life as well as to relate to the surrounding white community, if one exists.

The increased enrollment of blacks in white colleges and universities reflects the recognition of the pluralistic structure of our society. That American higher education will be changed by this there is little doubt. One change of importance which might result is a redefinition of what makes for student success. Indeed, it is apparent that success must no longer be defined only in terms of course accomplishments or even the attaining of riches or fame. In a society such as ours in which status is traditionally achieved rather than inherited, and one's self-esteem depends largely on personal achievement, it must come at last to be accepted that self-actualization is a significant basis for success in a pluralistic society.

Counseling the emerging University of Virginia, Thomas Jefferson wrote: "We cannot always do what is absolutely best. Those with whom we act, entertaining different views, have the power and the right of carrying them into practice. Truth advances and error recedes step by step only; and to do our fellow men the most good in our power, we must lead where we can, follow where we cannot, and still go with them, watching always the favorable moment for helping them another step."[17] The favorable moment for embracing pluralism in American higher education is now.

Perhaps the real meaning and importance for the black student when pluralism is accepted as fundamental for our colleges and universities can be seen through Flip Wilson's character Geraldine. She knows her needs; she has a sense of direction. And through it all she is *herself*. "What you see is what you get!" For blacks in white colleges and universities to be what you see has not in the past been possible. For them to be what they are is now their only hope of survival.

[17] Thomas Jefferson to Dr. Cooper, October 7, 1814. *Writings,* vol. XIV, p. 200. Monticello, 1905.

7

The Black College in
a Multiracial Society

King V. Cheek, Jr.

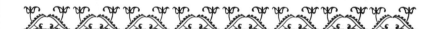

In only a few years America celebrates its bicentennial—
the two hundredth birthday of the Declaration of Independence.
More than one hundred years have passed since the Emancipation
Proclamation. Yet black Americans are still searching to fulfill the
dream of America as a land of opportunity.

The black colleges and universities, some of which were
founded over a century ago, have represented the one vehicle of
hope for black Americans. They have helped to give this nation
vitality and strength. We offer no apology or defense for these colleges. We do not need to prove their value. History has amply
demonstrated their worth. Why then do we question their future?

Put simply, black colleges are in imminent danger of extinction—of losing their racial identities. This fear is no paranoid illusion. It is real.

Bluefield State, West Virginia State, and Lincoln University in Missouri were once predominantly black. Now they are predominantly white. Other changes of the same kind are appearing on the horizon. Suggestions have been made that Morgan, Coppin, and Towson should merge and become a University of Metropolitan Baltimore. Many other examples, too numerous to mention, suggest that the trend is national and pervasive.

What is the explanation? Black colleges were founded at a special moment in history. The educational opportunities they provided for black Americans were not available in meaningful terms in the established colleges and universities. Although educational opportunity was the primary motive, these colleges were also established to perpetuate segregation as a way of life. In a real sense, they were responses to racism. The doctrine of "separate but equal" never became a reality. Neither was there a firm public commitment to make it so. Now that this policy has been replaced by integration, one wonders if this too is not a smokescreen for the accomplishment of other objectives.

We hear the rhetoric calling for an end to racial dualism in higher education. For reasons of efficiency and economy educators and legislators advocate the merger of separate black and white colleges that are located in the same area. The elimination of the racial identifiability of all institutions of higher learning appears to be the national goal. Thus, black Americans legitimately fear that integration, mergers, and reduction in status will, by deliberate design, destroy the identities of black colleges and universities.

The major question is whether the policy is consistent which promotes integration on one hand and preserves the racial identity of black colleges on the other. Many persons argue that the historical missions of black colleges are no longer relevant in today's world. Those who advance this argument are like ostriches who hide their heads in the sand believing they can escape the sad realities of life. Equal opportunity for black Americans never has been and is not now an accomplished goal. Black colleges have a special and unique mission to help America become the nation it was intended to be.

Black colleges *will* be saved. They will retain their identities

—not only for their sakes but for the sake of America and its future. This country will reach its zenith as a civilization only when full freedom and real equality of opportunity have been secured for all its citizens. The black college is indispensable to this quest.

Three interrelated arguments support the case for the survival and support of the black college. First, the black college, by appropriately interpreting the black experience and by revealing and analyzing the impact of racism, can free both black and white America from the bondage of psychological taboos and misconceptions. Second, the black college's mission is to guarantee that equality of opportunity for all Americans becomes a reality. And finally, the black college as a power base can provide the force, the vision, and the resources to promote needed change and to lift the quality of life within the black community.

The first argument is that the black college is peculiarly equipped to analyze and interpret the black experience and the impact of racism in America. America's first step to freedom consists in understanding the legacy of its past—in recognizing that racism is a fact. White Americans must begin with some perception of the black experience and its profound relevance to their own quest for their lost humanity. Only the naive reader would wonder why blacks have not moved in larger numbers into the mainstream as have other ethnic minorities. No other ethnic minority in America carries a badge of color which gives it visibility and identification and which is used to maintain its relationship to the past. All other immigrant groups were free to move into the mainstream of American life and to pursue the goals which were not and are not yet available to American blacks. White Americans must understand the historical and contemporary impact of the black presence in America. Black colleges can provide the prototypes for this enlightenment. Indeed, during the turbulent era of the sixties black students in black colleges formed the advance guard for the reawakening of America to the meaning of social and racial justice. It is appropriate to review this period in our history and the lessons we learned.

The black college campus and its students helped to give America hope and progress toward total freedom. Through their protests, black students exposed the sham and hypocrisy which was a part of America. They helped to place in bold relief the mockery of law-and-order slogans when they challenged the structure and practice of justice. They helped to reveal a little more of the reality of America and deepened our conviction that so long as any of our brothers and sisters are enslaved the rest of us are dehumanized by the conditions which permit their bondage. By refusing to scratch where they did not itch and to laugh when there was no humor, they brought candor and honesty to white and black relations. Out of their expressions came a deep concern for black institutions—for their roles in helping America understand its greatest dilemma and in devising strategies to overcome neglects of the past.

The psychological, spiritual, and social revolt which was born on these campuses still has not been thoroughly grasped. Reflecting for a moment on the climate and character of those times, we see that black Americans had reached the low point of tolerance and frustration. The pendulum had to swing in the opposite direction. What many critics saw as an obsession with blackness —however expressed—also helped many black Americans overcome the brainwashing, the ego castration to which many had been subjected from infancy to young adulthood.

We had been nourished in a society which denied us a cloak of dignity and distorted our aesthetic values. We had been bombarded with stimuli which made us believe our presence in America was unreal or nonexistent, which so thwarted our self-concept that not only did we believe we were inferior but many were forced to act the role. We even became disgusted with the way we looked.

Young black students helped to reverse this behavior and attitude. They helped to turn self-hate into a positive image—a self-concept, self-love, and esteem—of racial pride and dignity. This was a profound revolution, so profound that many have not thoroughly understood its implications.

I strongly believe that the movement toward a positive self-concept is one of the greatest legacies black Americans could have received. Black colleges and their black students helped Americans realize that the first real step to freedom is to break the shackles of psychological bondage—to free oneself from the prisons of self-hate and despair—to recognize, as did the poet, "Stone walls do not a prison make, nor iron bars a cage."

The surge toward black studies must be carefully monitored and interpreted. Black colleges have within their command the expertise to set the standards, the guidelines for the honest and scholarly study of the black experience. Because black studies have more than intellectual and scholarly utility and because they are also psychologically necessary, there is a need for establishing centers of scholarship, study, and inquiry. Black colleges can provide these services. The ramifications are broad and substantial. A proper study of the black experience can assist all of higher education in healing broken egos and restoring dignity, esteem, and confidence in black students whose motivations have been suppressed.

We can succeed in reopening the doors that have been closed to so many students whose potential was judged by defective instruments developed for the majority culture. Black colleges can force the creation of new educational models for the cultural atypical, the underprepared and undermotivated student. I doubt that white colleges are competent or committed enough to meet this critical need. Their response to black student protest in the sixties does little to allay suspicions and doubts. Confronted by black student demands, many educators retreated while others simply fled. Many of these colleges merely pacified black students with phony black studies courses, often taught by instant, overnight experts.

I vividly recall the frantic telephone call from a dean of a predominantly white college. He desperately needed a black faculty member because the black student union was poised outside his office. I inquired about the necessary qualifications; he replied that these were unimportant. The professor simply had to be black. I inquired further about salary. This was not important either. He was willing to pay twenty to twenty-five thousand dollars for a clearly visible afro. This is only one example of the kind of lunacy which prevailed during that period. Fortunately, many of the ideological controversies which colleges created were soon exposed for the sham they were.

Black colleges and black educators are needed more than ever to ensure that the teaching of the black perspective is honest and true. These colleges know better than do any others how to teach students that black is beautiful. But more than that, these institutions can help black students understand that when they enter the real world of competition, they will stand alone; their success or failure will depend on their adaptable intellectual tools and not on what their black heroes have accomplished. If black colleges can provide the models for understanding and teaching the black experience, they will move America a little closer to full freedom and equality.

The second argument in the case for black colleges is that without them the quest for equal opportunity is a fantasy, a dream never to be fulfilled. The current occupational trend shows an increase in the white-collar and a decrease in the blue-collar sector. In the latter category we find the largest number of blacks. If black Americans are to enter the occupational mainstream at levels that will enable them to influence the style of life of this country, we must do more to increase educational opportunity. The number of blacks in higher education must be substantially increased during the decade of the seventies and beyond.

It appears that universal higher education may become more of a public responsibility. If this happens, the lessening of financial barriers will enable larger numbers of blacks to enter higher education. There is little persuasive evidence to suggest that predominantly white colleges will absorb this responsibility. The risk or cost of educating large numbers of black students is very high for the predominantly white college. Entrance examination scores would deny college admission to many of these students. Moreover, the experience of these colleges with high-risk students is recent and limited. Some of them still consider black students as intellectually indigent and uneducable. It is not reasonable to assume that they will shift their priorities and mission to accommodate a large portion of the expected increase in black enrollment.

On the other hand, the education of black students had been and still is the business of black colleges. These colleges have a mission that extends beyond minority access to higher education. They are committed to maximizing the probability of minority success in higher education. As a group, these colleges have been the most open in American society. They have developed special competence in educating a highly diversified clientele which includes the gifted, the average, as well as the cultural atypical and underprepared student.

They have been objects of attack and have been branded by some as second-rate and as academic disaster areas. It is unfortunate that the critics have been unable to grasp the full impact of these colleges. The real meaning of quality education has eluded these critics. They have never understood that quality in higher education is not found in admissions criteria or in test scores. Rather, it lies in the capacity of a college to promote and induce profound changes in its students.

The important question is not whether a black college produces graduates on a par with Harvard or Princeton. This is not its primary task. If it provides the opportunity for a student to acquire the learning tools of life, to raise the level of his intellectual understanding, to develop the skills necessary to compete effectively in the world of work, and to actualize his potential as a human being, then this college has accomplished its mission.

The relevant test of quality is the before and after—the personal change which the college provokes—the creation of the opportunity for a person to go as far as his abilities will permit. When judged by this standard the black college stands tall among its white counterparts. Many of the prestige-type institutions of higher learning admit students who are already like the products they intend to graduate. Many are more interested in predicting their track records than in promoting profound personal growth. They are like the physician who prefers to treat only the healthy.

The education of increasing numbers of black Americans is such an important and critical priority that it cannot be left to institutions to fit into their schedules. This responsibility must be assumed by colleges which have as their essential mission the education of black youth. As we seek to define educational opportunity we must recognize that one of its components is providing black students with multiple options. They must have the freedom to choose a black college. This freedom is real only if these colleges survive.

Why is this freedom of choice so important? Hundreds of years of socioeconomic deprivation have left their mark. Black students with castrated egos, damaged self-images, and poor academic preparation must be given the opportunity to have their personhood restored. For many black students, the black college is the only environment in which this personal objective can be accomplished. They would prefer the comforting climate of a black campus with black adult and peer model figures to one which may be coldly hostile and unfamiliar. They should not be denied this freedom of choice. It may be their only hope for personal success.

This same freedom of choice must also be available for white

Americans. White students are attending black colleges in increasing numbers. They are studying under black teachers and are interacting with black students and black adults. The environment is obviously different from what they would experience in predominantly white colleges. They become minority citizens for the first time. The cultural shock and psychological reorientation could have profound positive impacts on the lives of these students.

I once heard a white student in a black college remark about his experience. All his life he had considered himself free. Prior to entering college he had been in an integrated environment but it was one dominated and controlled by whites. He never once related to a black authority figure. Now he had discovered what it meant to be a minority. But more important, he acquired a deep understanding of the meaning of freedom—an aspiration he had previously taken for granted. This understanding, coupled with a new awareness of the black experience, gave him a new sense of purpose. He deeply believed that he had acquired sensitivities and developed a capacity for leadership in human relations. This experience would not have been available to him in a predominantly white college.

Black colleges can perform this unique service of expanding the educational options available to both black and white Americans. They can become new kinds of laboratories for experimentation in human relations. In this role, black colleges can provide white Americans with educational opportunities that may free them from their own bondage and enable them to assume new leadership positions within our society.

In our pursuit of equal opportunity as a goal for all Americans, we must be certain we understand all of its dimensions. When we consider the historical conditions and inequities imposed on black Americans, we know that justice requires more than equal treatment. Any system which treats black and white colleges alike is inherently discriminatory. The opportunity we seek for black youth must therefore be more than equal. They cannot be asked to begin a race when they are already behind at the starting line. The historical deprivations have created inequalities which can only be remedied by over-equal opportunity for black youth. Only then will we close the gap which now separates white and black Americans.

The third argument is that black colleges are indispensable power bases within their communities. Their potential for influencing change and improving the quality of life has been clearly demonstrated over the years. These colleges can be strengthened to increase their impact on formulating solutions to many of our urban ills. This role of urban extension in the decade of the seventies will become a major priority for many or most of our nation's black colleges. The elimination of poverty and the ghetto are priority goals to be realized within this century.

Black colleges have a responsibility to provide the knowledge base which the appropriate agencies in society can use to make alternative judgments and decisions. These colleges must produce the managers, the professionals, the intelligent and skilled manpower —persons who will assume leadership roles and serve as change agents in the larger society. The record for the black college is more than admirable. America can ill afford to lose such a vital resource.

The lessons of experience are powerful and enduring. Blacks have little reason to believe that the interest of the black community will be adequately promoted by white institutions and white leadership. The credibility of black colleges within the black community is high. To ensure this believability and hope, the leadership of these colleges must remain ostensibly and visibly black. We must understand that simple involvement for black Americans is not sufficient. Shared power and control must also be promoted. The black college as a power base can guarantee these goals.

I have argued that black colleges are necessary for the survival of America. We cannot permit integration or mergers to engulf us, destroy our identities, and thus diminish our service. We live in a multiracial and pluralistic society. Our educational institutions must reflect this reality. As a black American, I will passionately resist the misuse of the slogan or aim of integration to eliminate or reduce our institutions.

I have seen the decline of black high school administrators in the south—black principals more qualified than their white counterparts have been reduced to the demeaning status of assistant principals in charge of buses. I have seen the elimination of black schools and their absorption by white ones with the consequent discarding of the symbols of black pride. I have witnessed resegregation in the midst of desegregation with accompanying humiliation and dehumanization of black children and with the dominant culture more in complete command. I recall the black high school students in a western North Carolina city who one morning suddenly discovered they no longer had a school song and trophy case, symbols of deep emotional meaning for them.

This is the dilemma of integration. Promote it we must, but not at our educational and psychological detriment. When and if HEW insists that many of our colleges must lose their racial identification, we must understand what this really means. We must rise to protest. Under the guise of integration, black colleges may lose their identities as black colleges and simply become predominantly white with minority enrollments. We fail to see that racial identification has ceased to be. It has simply changed its form. What we have then are all predominantly white colleges. The racial identity is still there but now it is white.

We are told that the real concern is not the label or identity of the college but the increase in educational opportunity for black youth. The issue, we are told, is minority access to higher education. This opportunity is more illusory than real. The dominant and genuine concern is not so much minority access to higher education as it is minority success in higher education. This is where the black colleges have made their case and proven their competence.

So long as our society is infected with any vestige of racism and disregard for human dignity, there will always be a need for black colleges to answer the needs of black Americans. We will remain symbols of pride, possession, and power for our people. We still belong to them. They have an emotional investment and stake in our present and in our future. We have a responsibility to them to continue to be the citadels of leadership and influence. More than all other institutions in America, the black colleges can indeed serve as architects of the destiny of black Americans.

There is a clear need for both blacks and whites to see distinguished black achievements and to see black professionals in command of a major societal power base. The mere presence of these colleges is bound to affect society's values. With these colleges, black Americans have a feeling of hope. We are not yet ready to exchange these concrete possessions for fleeting dreams. With this in mind, all of us, black and white, must signal the coming of a new era—one in which token philanthropy is replaced with public responsibility for the education of *all* Americans. We cannot ignore the lessons of history. A people denied is a nation destroyed.

Robert Kennedy once said, "Some men see things as they are and ask why. I dream of things that never were and ask why not." Martin Luther King had a dream that he never saw fulfilled. Both men dreamed and cried out for a better America. They died for their cause. But we still live and can dedicate our lives to the principles they advocated. Our dreams must not become dreams deferred. They must blossom into the realities which will make of America the true land of opportunity.

8

Equity for Women
in Higher Education

Bernice Sandler

For many of us, the words *women's liberation* evoke images of radical, man-hating, bra-burning women. My friends in the women's movement—and many of them are married, to men—tell me that bras were never burned and that the more serious and important activities of the women's movement rarely get the attention of the press.

Women and men, too, are becoming increasingly aware and concerned about discrimination in education. How many readers of these pages know that formal charges of sex discrimination have been filed against more than 360 colleges and universities in the past two years? How many know that none of these charges has yet been refuted by the Department of Health, Education, and Welfare in its subsequent investigations? Some of our finest institutions have been charged: Columbia University, Harvard University, Yale University, the University of Michigan, the University of Wisconsin, the University of Minnesota, the University of Chicago, and the entire state university and college systems of the states of New York, New Jersey, California, and Florida.

I do not want to imply that these institutions or any others that I mention are worse than others, for they are not, or that our campuses are worse than the rest of society. But certainly, of all the areas in our society that have come under criticism for their treatment of women, the most frequent target has been higher education. Perhaps because education holds out the promise of equality and equal opportunity women are most angry. They have discovered that the promise, for them, is broken and that the myth of equality is just that, a myth. They were told that education is a woman's field, and they have now seen study after study, report after report, which clearly indicate that women are second-class citizens on the campus. The anger and the discontent of women are sharpest in academia.

Although women have been allowed to attend institutions of higher learning for more than a century, many institutions are still not used to the idea. To some degree, most colleges can be described as vast men's clubs where women are at best tolerated as foreign visitors but never admitted as equals, for education is designed as though the only people who ever attended school were young, single, and male. Women are not seen as serious students but as pleasant decorations on the campus, to lighten a young man's heart and perhaps to find husbands for themselves.

On campus after campus, women have begun to examine their status as faculty, as staff, and as students. They are examining virtually the entire structure of the university, evaluating institutional policies and practices for their effects on women. They have provided evidence to show that sex discrimination on the campus is real and not a myth. Women are the newest and potentially the largest and certainly the fastest growing advocacy group in the academic community and in society at large. On many campuses they have stunned both faculty and administrators with formal accusations of discrimination and with demands for changes in hiring practices, personnel policies, student admissions, fringe benefits, and curriculum content.

The university community is puzzled and, like Freud, it asks, "What is it women really want?" What women are asking for is equality of opportunity. Now certainly everyone agrees to that. But what does equal opportunity really mean? It is more than asking one's colleague if he knows a good man for the job and then, after the man is hired, saying, "Of course, I'd have been glad to hire a qualified woman if I could have found one." It is more than saying "We want the best students we can find" and then turning away young women who are better qualified than the young men accepted. Equal opportunity is more than saying "We believe in equal pay for equal work" and then paying a woman less because she is married and does not need as much, and paying another woman less because she is *not* married and therefore does not need as much.

Equal opportunity is more than saying "We treat women fairly, the same way we treat men, but we don't want young women in our department because they get married. We don't want a married woman because she'll probably have children. We don't want a woman with young children because she can't possibly be committed. And as for the woman who waited until her children were older, she's much too old for work or study, and isn't it a pity that she's been out for so long and didn't start sooner."

That is not equal opportunity.

What women are asking for is to be free of the myths that are used to deny them the opportunities that are the birthright of their brothers. For example, there is a myth that there is no discrimination on the campus, that things have been getting better for women; yet many studies, including more than a thousand pages of hearings held by Representative Edith Green, have shown that the position of women in academe has actually been deteriorating. The percentage of women graduate students is less now than it was in 1930. The expansion of faculty in the postwar period was largely one of male expansion; the proportion of women faculty has dropped continuously over the past one hundred years, from a third of the positions in 1870 to less than a fourth today. Many institutions have a lower proportion of women faculty now than they had in 1930. Even worse, at least one prestigious Midwestern university has a lower proportion of women on its faculty now than it did in 1899.

Women are far more likely to be hired by the lower-paying, less well-known institutions. When they are hired, they are likely to be promoted far more slowly than men. The higher the rank, the fewer the women. Study after study has documented the fact that women with the same qualifications as men are hired less frequently, at lower ranks, promoted more slowly, and receive less pay than do their male colleagues. Ninety per cent of men with doctorates and twenty years of academic experience will be full professors; for women with the identical qualifications, barely half will be at that rank. There are women who have been temporary employees, without fringe benefits or chance of promotion, for more than ten years. Some women have been assistant professors for more than twenty years while others earn as little as half of what their male colleagues earn; there are even women who have worked for years with no pay at all. Many women students are frankly told that their department is looking for "bright young men." Many women students have entered undergraduate work with hopes of becoming physicians and have settled for being medical technicians; others have wanted to become scientists but are teaching high school science instead because professors tell them these are not suitable fields for women. There are professors who still assert that "women shouldn't be professionals" and who believe that education is wasted on women, despite the fact that the more education a woman has the more likely she is to work, and despite the fact that 91 per cent of the women with doctorates work.[1]

The "shortage of qualified women" is also a myth. Of course if there were no discrimination in admissions, there would be more women on the campus. Still, on too many campuses, women are not hired in any number approaching the actual number of doctorates awarded to women. For example, in psychology, women receive 23 per cent of all doctorates; that is about the same percentage

---

[1] Eighty-one per cent of women doctorates surveyed in one study were working full-time; 79 per cent had not interrupted their careers in the ten years after they got their doctorates. Should the reader think that 81 per cent is not a respectable figure, let me point out that only 81 per cent of all men work, and of men with doctorates only 69 per cent work in their original field of study.

of women listed as psychologists in the National Register of Scientific and Technological Personnel. In 1970–1971 at Rutgers, the percentage of women faculty was 9 per cent; at the University of Maryland, 6 per cent; at the University of Wisconsin, 3 per cent; at Columbia University, 0 per cent, despite the fact that Columbia awarded about 36 per cent of its doctorates in psychology to women. These are fairly typical figures; these institutions are no worse than any others.[2] At one well-known California institution, the two women hired this year were the first females hired for the faculty of the psychology department since 1924. The problem is not limited to psychology or to the institutions named. This pattern is found in institution after institution, in department after department.

Sex discrimination is the last socially acceptable prejudice. It is so ingrained in our society that many who practice it are simply unaware that they are hurting women. Much of it is unconscious and not deliberate, but that does not make it hurt any the less. Many of the most ardent supporters of civil rights of blacks, Indians, Spanish-speaking Americans, and other minorities do not view sex discrimination as "real" discrimination. They fail to notice that half of each minority group are women. I am reminded of a program for disadvantaged students which provided a transitional year at one of our major universities. All thirty of the disadvantaged students turned out to be male. Too often helping minorities has meant helping minority males only, and helping women has meant white women only.

Such discrimination against half of our citizens is wasteful and shameful, but it is all legal. There are no federal laws which forbid such discrimination. Title VII of the Civil Rights Act of 1964, which forbids sex discrimination in employment, exempts faculty in educational institutions. Title VI of the same Act forbids discrimination in federally assisted programs, but it only applies to race, color, and national origin, not sex. The Equal Pay Act excludes professional, executive, and administrative employees. Even the U. S. Commission on Civil Rights has no jurisdiction over sex

---

[2] The more prestigious and better known the institution, the worse the status of women. Women are far more likely to end up at the lesser-known institutions and in community colleges where they constitute about 40 per cent of the faculty where opportunities for research and professional advancement are less, and where salaries are lower.

discrimination; it is limited by law to matters pertaining to race, color, religion, and national origin, but not sex.

The only remedy that women have is the Executive Order which forbids federal contractors from discriminating in employment. It does not cover institutions which have no federal contracts, nor does it cover discrimination against students. It is an administrative remedy at best and does not have the status of law. Moreover, its enforcement by the Department of Health, Education, and Welfare has been the subject of bitter criticism by women's groups and the university world. The Women's Equity Action League (WEAL), the women's civil rights group that spearheaded the campaign to get the Order enforced with regard to sex discrimination in universities, has called for a congressional investigation of HEW's handling of the sex discrimination investigations on the campus.

Women throughout the academic world are asking for a revision of all policies that affect women in a negative way. For example, even though a nepotism policy may apply to both husbands and wives, the differential impact is clearly on wives, whatever the policy itself may state. And so women have been pressing for the end of these policies. At the University of Arizona, five faculty wives sued the university to end its nepotism rules, which were subsequently dropped.

Numerous studies have shown that academic women earn less than men even when identically qualified. In one study that examined a variety of factors, such as number of papers given at professional meetings, honors, publications, and the like, a woman's sex cost her on the average about $845 per year. Women are asking for "equity adjustments" on numerous campuses. These raises are exempt from current wage controls. The University of Maryland and the University of Maine, for example, have set aside small funds to raise the salaries of women, and at the University of Wisconsin 600 women recently received such equity adjustments.

Women are asking for comprehensive plans of affirmative action to "remedy the effects of past discrimination." These plans, which are mandatory for all federal contractors, require the university to do more than merely cease discriminating. He—and the university employer is almost always a "he"—must go out of his way to see that women are treated fairly. This requirement does not mean that unqualified women must be hired but that the university must develop ways to make certain that women are recruited and considered and that whatever criteria are used for men will be applied equally to women. A roster of academic women is vitally needed, and several of the women's caucuses in the professional disciplines have begun to develop talent banks. Institutions need to get the word out that they are recruiting women in earnest. I recently saw one flyer for a junior faculty member at Yale that stated: "Women and minorities are welcome to apply." (It would have been even better if the flyer had stated: "Women and minorities, including minority women, are welcome to apply.")

What women are asking for is essentially the jobs that men now hold. They are tired and angry about being the cheap labor force of the academic community, of being the last hired and the first fired. They want to become associate professors, full professors, department chairmen, deans, and even college presidents. Were it not for the Catholic Sisters, the number of women college presidents would be far less than the number of whooping cranes. Perhaps the first affirmative action we should take is to declare women college presidents an endangered species.

Women are asking for nothing less than the full integration of women on the campus. The very essence of American opportunity is education. We cannot afford to waste fully half of our talented resources. To begin with, we are going to have to consider any overt discrimination by faculty, administrative officers, and anyone else on the campus as a serious breach of conduct, for not only is it a violation of federal policy but it violates our sense of ethics and fairness. Grievance procedures concerning discrimination are going to have to be developed, for on some campuses there is no way for a woman to go through university or college channels if she feels she has been discriminated against on the basis of her sex. Numerous women who have been actively fighting sex discrimination have lost their jobs and literally have no means of redress. Tenure rules can be revised so that women (and men) can obtain tenure even if they work part-time. Already at Harvard, Princeton, and Stanford, part-time faculty can ascend the tenure ladder to full professorship, albeit at a slower rate.

Child care centers are going to become a part of the campus, although the need for them should have been obvious long ago to those who held that women were poor risks because of motherhood. These centers should be available to the children of both male and female faculty, staff, and students. For those who wonder where the money will come from for these centers, women are quick to point out the lovely golf course and the expensive athletic facilities that many institutions are able to finance.

Fringe benefits are coming under a good deal of criticism. TIAA and other retirement plans, based on actuarial tables, pay women less (16 per cent less under TIAA), even though the women contribute the same amount as the men they have worked alongside. The rationale is that women live longer. However, the mortality gap between whites and blacks is far greater than that between men and women, yet we would all be up in arms if insurance companies were to have differential rates based on race rather than sex.

Maternity leave policies are going to have to be revised. On some campuses wives of faculty members can get maternity coverage on their health insurance but women faculty members cannot get the same benefit. In other places women cannot use sick leave for childbirth, nor do they retain their jobs if they leave, even for a short period for childbirth or childrearing. Women who leave their jobs or schoolwork for a year or two of childbearing are viewed very differently from the young men who spend two years away because of military service. The length of time that a woman is out because of pregnancy and childbirth when she is unable to work should be a medical decision between the woman and her doctor. When she is out for medical reasons she should be covered by health insurance and sick leave just as every other temporary disability is covered, be it hernia, heart attack, or prostatism. If the woman wants extended time off for childbearing, the policy should at least be the same as it is for other personal leaves of absence, such as the leave men take for military service.

Nepotism rules need to be revised. Recently Stanford, Oberlin, and the universities of Maine, Michigan, and Minnesota have revised or abolished their nepotism rules so that husbands and wives can work in the same department, provided both meet the standards of employment and that neither is involved in making employment decisions about the other. Moreover, part-time work is going to have to be paid at a rate comparable to that for full-time work, prorated. Fringe benefits for part-timers can be prorated as necessary.

There is every indication that the Congress will extend the Equal Pay Act to cover executives, professionals, and administrators, which means that women faculty will be covered by the Act. Equal pay for equal work is going to have to be a reality on our campuses. It is also clear that we are going to have to hire more than just a few token women here and there. And they are going to end up in positions of power, such as the academic dean, vice-president, and presidents of institutions, too. Women will have to be appointed to all kinds of committees, including search committees, to academic councils and senates, and to boards of trustees, and in more than token numbers. Department heads are going to be held accountable for whether they have really sought out women or have merely checked the usual informal sources of recruitment which typically exclude women.

On some campuses department heads who want to hire white males for the faculty are asked to explain in detail what they did to recruit women and minorities, including minority women, and why none were hired. Highly developed plans to recruit, hire, and promote women will have to be developed on every campus that has federal contracts, with review mechanisms to implement and evaluate the effectiveness of these plans. Equally important, these affirmative action plans which are sometimes kept secret must be made public; indeed, women must have the opportunity not only to evaluate these plans but women must be involved in the development of such plans.

Like it or not, we are going to see numerical goals for hiring women. This is required under the Executive Order for federal contractors, along with timetables and plans for the achievement of these goals. Goals are very different from quotas, for quotas are fixed and exclusionary by definition; in contrast goals are flexible and are an attempt to increase the number of a previously excluded group. Under numerical goals, no employer is ever forced to hire an unqualified person; if the institution honestly seeks to find women and cannot meet its goals, there is no penalty if it has indeed made what is called a "good faith" effort. The goals are merely targets which the employer tries to achieve. They have been upheld by the

Supreme Court, and we will see numerical goals for women and minorities, including minority women, on every campus which has government contracts. Will this make it harder for white males to find jobs? To some degree, yes. For years women have been accused of using their sex to get ahead on the job, but it is men who have used their sex as a way of keeping down the competition of women. As one able woman recently observed, "The time has come when a mediocre woman ought to be able to go as far as a mediocre man."

At the student level, nothing short of open admissions for women in all coeducational institutions can suffice. Many institutions place a ceiling on the number of qualified women students they will admit, while permitting admittance of men with lower qualifications. Although the percentage of women undergraduates has been increasing since the 1950s so that it is now 41 per cent, it is still less now than the percentage of women undergraduates in 1920, when girls were 47 per cent of the undergraduates, or in 1899 when 53 per cent of all undergraduate degrees went to women. About 75 to 90 per cent (depending on the particular study) of the well-qualified students who do not go on to college are women.

Sometimes, lack of dormitory space is given as the excuse: "We'd like to have more girls but we just don't have living space for them." Yet dormitories, like hotels, apartments, and houses, are not built any differently for one sex or the other. When Yale converted some of its all-male dormitories for women students, it only needed to add new locks and full-length mirrors. Some institutions that claim a shortage of dormitory space for women refuse to let their women students live off campus, although men students are allowed that privilege. In any case, lack of dormitory space should cease to be an excuse for keeping women students out of college.

We also need to reconsider our reasons for excluding part-time students at either the undergraduate or graduate levels. These rules work a particular hardship on women students with family responsibilities as well as on less affluent students. There is no indication that these students are any less committed than full-time students. Residence requirements which provide a limited time to earn a degree need to be reexamined in light of the impact that this restriction has in discouraging women from attending and completing school. And is there any reason, other than academic tradition, that prevents schools from giving scholarships on a part-time basis?

Certainly, financial aid policies will need to be reevaluated, particularly in terms of the large number of scholarships that are restricted to men only.

We also need to encourage women to return to school if they desire to do so. Many of our best students were the World War II veterans who had been out of school for several years. Women who decide to return are similarly well motivated and should not be denied the opportunity to learn. Many schools which welcome retired military officers who return to school to prepare for a second career discourage women who wish to return for the identical training. Although some schools have special programs for mature adults who wish to return to college, most of these programs are out of the mainstream of campus life.

Curriculum reform is essential if women are to overcome the handicaps of sex-role stereotypes. About seven hundred women's studies courses are being taught this year. Anyone who has looked at the extensive reading lists of many of these courses knows that they are not frivolous but highly academic, enriching the perspectives of traditional fields. For many young women (and men, too) these courses serve a very real purpose in helping young women to examine themselves as women for the first time in their lives. By confronting themselves as women, they can begin to deal with the contradictions and conflicts in their lives. For this purpose, the women's studies courses serve a unique role, for unlike many academic courses they are directly relevant to the lives of their students. They are consciousness-raising with intelligence and without hysteria. Just as blacks have rightfully said that their history has been stolen from them, so it can be said of women and their history. Young men and women need to learn such things as that the cotton gin was not invented by Eli Whitney but by the widow of the Revolutionary War General Nathaniel Greene. She assigned the patent to Whitney because as a good businesswoman she knew that no one would buy a new machine invented by a "fool woman."

Faculty should also be aware of the role of women within their own academic disciplines. Certainly a history course which deals with civil rights must include the civil rights of women; a psychology course that deals with the socialization of children must discuss how girls are socialized in contrast to boys. Faculty, along with students, have begun to examine textbooks and other academic materials for their handling of women. One study examined twenty-seven leading textbooks used in college level American History courses. No book devoted more than 2 per cent of its pages to women; one had .05 of 1 per cent devoted to women. In many books Harriet Beecher Stowe and Eleanor Roosevelt were not even mentioned. Pressure on publishers from academicians will be enormously helpful in getting changes in textbooks that influence our young people.

At Alverno College in Milwaukee, Wisconsin, faculty met for two days in the fall of 1971 to evaluate how they were making their courses specifically relevant to the education of women and how they could supplement or revise their materials and teaching methods to do so. Other groups have taken surveys at their institutions or within their disciplines to see whether or not women are included in appropriate course content.

Often it has been said that women can be helped to raise their aspirations by providing them with good counseling. Although better counseling would be helpful, it is not likely to help most of our young women change their lives or reevaluate their vocational plans unless something else occurs. Blacks did not need better counseling in order to raise their aspirations; what they needed to have was a keen sense of the discrimination they face and the knowledge that overcoming the barriers was indeed possible. We must sharpen the discontent of women and we are going to have to teach our young women to struggle against the injustice of discrimination. Our women students need to know that the majority of women work for twenty-five years or more, whether or not they marry, whether or not they take time out to raise children. Moreover, a woman who works full-time with a bachelor's degree earns about the same median income as a man who is a high school dropout.

If we are to come to grips with the problems of population control, we must achieve equal opportunity for women. Childbearing and childrearing will consume a smaller proportion of women's lives than previously; at age thirty-five the youngest children of most women will be in school, and what will women do with the rest of their lives? If discrimination in education and in employment continues, then too many women will continue to choose to have too many babies, despite the pill, birth control information, and abortion reform.

The hardest thing about the women's movement is that there is no real enemy that one can hate with self-righteous justification. Men are not the enemy, for surely many of them have been hurt, perhaps in different ways, by the same rigid stereotypes that hurt women. Certainly we need compassion for all those women and men alike, who have been crippled by their experiences in the past. We need compassion for those women who act with an impatience born out of bitterness and despair; and we need compassion for those men who tell us that their wives are "perfectly happy." We will have to have more compassion as male backlash increases. For surely as women make gains, there will indeed be more resistance.

Yet for all of us, what will be hardest to change is our own attitudes and assumptions about what women want, what women are really like, what women need. We—women and men both—are going to have to work with women in ways which we perhaps have never done before, in full partnership. Our society has trained us all to think that women and men can only relate to each other as marriage partners, as lovers, or in an up-down relationship, like that of the male boss and the female assistant. Yet the lives of women and men are joined together, inextricably. We cannot escape each other, nor do we wish to do so. But we are no longer to be limited to such relationships as wife and husband, mother and son, daughter and father, secretary and boss. All of us will need to help each other as we grope together to work out the problems that will arise as women's traditional roles shift toward greater equality of opportunity.

The times are changing. No longer will women weep when discrimination hurts. No longer will women grow bitter when they are denied the opportunities that are the birthright of their brothers. For women have something else to do. They have learned that the hand that rocks the cradle can, indeed, rock the boat.

PART THREE

The Anachronism of the Gentleman Scholar

The San Francisco Chronicle *recently carried about a dozen news items about corruption, fraud, and chicanery among practitioners of the most respected professions. For example, forty-one attorneys were hauled before the California Supreme Court last year for professional misconduct, and the California State Bar Association processed complaints of misconduct against 3800 other California attorneys.**

Corruption is not new to the professions, but, among the status professions, it used to be said that professors, along with men of the cloth, were exceptions. Until well after World War II, the public stereotype of the professor held him to be an idealist who preferred ideas to things. And even in academia the widespread image of the professor established him as a dedicated man who remained dignified at all times and who accepted his genteel poverty without complaint. The old Protestant ethic, with its polarity

---

* R. Bartlett, "Warning to Lawyers on Self-Policing," *San Francisco Chronicle*, August 11, 1972, p. 20.

of work and pleasure, proved an effective tranquilizer: one might reasonably expect to be well rewarded if one accepted the unpleasantness of work, but how could anyone complain about being allowed, however poorly paid, to do nothing but pursue the pleasures of scholarship?

Within a single generation, the image of the professor has been reversed. The professor turns out to be no more ethereal and no more ethical than doctors, lawyers, merchants, chiefs. Professors, too, now have "rights," and they sometimes exercise them with voices too loud for their colleagues' comfort. These voices demand, among other things, changes in the economic conditions which affect professors' lives, in the activities which universities and colleges undertake, in the conditions under which professors work. A generation ago it was still possible to silence such demands with a single gesture, a finger pointed with scorn toward what has been historically associated with racketeering, unrest, and illiteracy— unionism. But a new day has dawned, as Part Three makes clear.

Two chapters in Part Three deal directly with unionism in academia. "Collective Bargaining on Private Campuses," by Sheldon Steinbach, and "Impact of Unionism on Governance," by E. D. Duryea and Robert Fisk, point to an undeniable trend. The tradition of shared authority—"We don't work for the university; we are the university"—is being replaced by a new concept; collective bargaining is gradually coming to be accepted by faculty members everywhere.

The matter of academic tenure is taken up by Florence Moog in her chapter, "Tenure Is Obsolete." The tenure system, Moog says, "has produced a squirearchy unquestionably content to perpetuate its own limitations," and it must go. She assures us, however, that job security is not obsolete—nor is academic freedom.

Academic ethics is a subject of widespread interest at present and extreme views prevail on all sides, fanned, no doubt, by the case of Bruce Franklin at Stanford University. Laura Bornholdt addresses herself to that subject in "Professional Ethics on Campus." The chapter is provocative, and it is likely to arouse hostility in radicals from both the right and the left. It is to be hoped, however, that they will remain cool enough to appreciate the subtleties and follow the intricacies of Bornholdt's argument.

JOSEPH AXELROD

9

Professional Ethics on Campus

Laura Bornholdt

A spate of headlines has recently served to alert the academic community to the fact that "self-discipline" of the university professoriate has serious soft spots or, viewed differently, that academic freedom is the subject for new scrutiny inside academe as well as outside, by the Right as well as by the Left and the Center. The Angela Davis case at UCLA, the Bruce Franklin case at Stanford, the Roth and Sindermann cases at the Wisconsin State University, Oshkosh, and at Odessa Junior College in Texas, respectively, are clouds much bigger than a man's hand. And they are the nationally visible cases: there are many others around the country which have been reported only locally. The very fact that all of these cases save the Davis case are in the civil courts is one of the danger signals, for United States courts historically have tried not to interfere in internal university policy and the university in turn has sought to settle its internal disputes out of court.

Important as it is, the shadow of the courts is only one source of anxiety in and about academe. Viewing the scene in broad perspective, some observers predict a new McCarthy era, while others fear a politicization of the university comparable to that in Germany in the 1930s with an intimidation of academic freedom by and for the Left. Spokesmen from the extreme Left and from the extreme Right charge that the university as it now exists indoctrinates rather than educates; each proposes new criteria of "accountability" and prescribes new judges to whom the enterprise must account. The Center very properly sees polarization as a threat to free pursuit of truth and as a force capable of destroying the trust which permits diversity of viewpoint and academic freedom to exist.

One remembers De Lawd in *Green Pastures:* "Everthin's comin' loose dat ain't tied down!" We yearn for the common values we are sure we must have had—once. But . . . did we? Hofstadter and Metzger, the historians of academic freedom, maintain that academe is "the most bureaucratically controlled of all professions."[1] Advised of this condition, the proverbial visitor from Mars might look for a binding code of professional ethics as a correlate of bureaucracy, but how misled he would be! The conditions which inspired academic bureaucracy in the first place, and which by and large distinguish academics from the practitioners of other professions, have also served to stunt development of a binding ethical code. The key to professional relationships in academe is the basic and inescapable interaction of X, the individual professor, with Y, his institution (occasionally, with Z, his guild, as well), for it is this affiliation which gives a different set of valences to X's relationship with his client—the student—as compared, say, with the doctor and his patient or the lawyer and his client.

In the past, local institutional traditions and codes have re-

---

[1] R. Hofstadter and W. Metzger, *The Development of Academic Freedom in the United States.* New York: Columbia University Press, 1955, p. 406.

flected a wide range of mores, from the code appropriate for a small, residential, rural, fundamentalist college to that which fits a large, urban, streetcar, public university. Despite the diversity, however, most institutions and 99 per cent of American academics have recognized that certain issues transcend the concern of single institutions, namely, issues related to academic freedom and due process. These issues are at the heart of the teaching-learning enterprise, and they are also the source of its basic and significant ethical norms.

The American academic community recognized long since that academic freedom and due process resist codification as eternal verities: we perceive them as standards to be defined and refined through an evolutionary process. One has only to look at the table of contents of AAUP's "Red Book" to note the way the profession has responded to new problems and new perceptions of old problems.

So what, if anything, is new in 1972?

A close reading of the documents on the Angela Davis case makes one conscious of the fact that although Left and Right in this case were far apart in their understanding of academic freedom and the purpose of the university, *all* parties relied heavily on AAUP statements covering standards of professional ethics. They disagreed on what the facts were and how they fitted into the AAUP codes of behavior, and they disagreed in their interpretation of the reasons— ostensible and/or real—for the Regents' action, but not on the standards. This point is stressed not to analyze the Davis case in detail but to move from the general fear of politicization of the university to another factor for disquiet—the fact that the AAUP, having achieved in its brief span of fifty-seven years the remarkable feat of establishing itself as the arbiter of most professional conflicts and having become the guardian of the American academic conscience, now faces new challenges for leadership of the profession and is in the throes of change as it responds to these challenges.

AAUP has long had an influence far beyond its numbers (the fact that its ninety thousand members represent only 15 per cent of the potential membership suggests how many free loaders there are in academe!). Yet the rapid spread of faculty unions has induced a majority of AAUP's Council members to conclude that if AAUP is to survive, it must attempt the double role of keeper of the academic conscience and protector of academic freedom, on the

one hand, and agent for collective bargaining on the other. Whatever the prospects for AAUP's success in collective bargaining, the
decision means a new vulnerability—inside academe—for AAUP in
its old role. Already advocates of faculty unionization claim that
binding arbitration by an agreed upon third party will be cheaper,
faster, more equitable than AAUP's familiar investigatory procedures. AAUP's standard of judgment by peers, they say, is not
essential to academic health but painlessly expendable.

The implications of faculty unionization for professional
ethics deserve a separate program or programs and a different
commentator. The old order is shaken and the nature of the new
one is not yet apparent. What is clear is that union spokesmen are
unsympathetic to the old rhetoric of service and to such axioms as
"Teaching and research are their own reward" and "The professor
is first and foremost a moral and intellectual being." Once-accepted
truths are bluntly challenged: "[There is no truth in the belief]
that professors . . . are entitled to make management decisions.
The tragedy is that so many administrators, governing boards, and
legislatures have been conned into accepting this irresponsible
doctrine."[2] The professor is above all wage earner and employee like
other men; he has a role in a marketplace situation; like other union
men, he may expect to appeal to a third party if arbitration is in
order. Teachers' strikes are not a cause for moral outrage but a
legitimate form of economic pressure. William Boyd recently com-
mented on the strains which collective bargaining places on traditional faculty values, concluding: "The employee-professor in the
new world may turn out to be a better paid individual in a spiritually poorer environment."[3] What's-in-it-for-me? *has* to be the leit-
motif.

In contrast to the open materialism of union proponents, the
revitalized Left offers its idealistic critique of academe. Its spokesmen are not interested in adding to the material blessings of the
university's professors (whom they regard as all too often self-
serving, even toadies for a ruling class) but in redirecting the university to its proper functions of social service and enlightenment
of the People. They do not want separation of labor from manage-

[2] M. Liebermann, "Professors, Unite!" *Harper's*, 1971, *243*, 69.
[3] W. Boyd, "Collective Bargaining in Academe: Causes and Consequences." *Liberal Education*, 1971, *57*, 314.

ment, but they want replacement of management, both administration and boards of trustees, and a new perspective on university priorities. Aiken asks: "Why is it that virtually a whole generation of the choicest students and junior faculty are so revolted by the grubbiness, pretentiousness, and vulgarity of the multiversity . . . by its deadly 'functions,' including . . . its incredible commencement days with their honorary degrees for retired generals, and the ghost written speeches in justification of some manifest destiny or other?"[4]

Although he is not completely sanguine about the future, Aiken believes the university is still viable and essential. Not all the radicals who dream of a new society aborning, however, share his view. Angela Davis and Bruce Franklin would contend that the structure of the university and most of the personnel are so morally rotten that the university itself must go. And what does all or any of this have to do with professional ethics? Simply that an ethical code presupposes an ideal of a well-governed institution: the ethical code and the idealized institution are warp and woof of a fabric-in-weaving.

We are surrounded with evidence that the ferment in academe of the past decade has sometimes subtly, sometimes bluntly, sometimes in detail, sometimes overall, challenged the codes of faculty conduct which once maintained and the assumptions on which they were based. In the "general authority crisis" of the university in the sixties, the faculty failed—usually institution by institution as well as nationally—to identify a set of values held in common. Instead, the value of institutional survival dictated faculty accommodation to pluralism and led to tolerance of diversity on a new scale. In ten years, the accepted life-style for a growing segment of the professoriate has moved from contemplation to active involvement, from bland gentility to broad earthiness, from tacit acceptance of middle-class standards to defiant support of the People, from a posture of socialization to tradition to a near-norm of dissent.

Cultural historians will one day have a gold mine in describing the evolution of new faculty cultures in the 1960s. The establishment of instant universities and the rapid expansion of many old

---

[4] H. Aiken, *Predicament of the University*. Bloomington: University of Indiana Press, 1971, p. 133.

ones, the impact on faculty relationships of the shift from university to multiversity, the seller's market for faculty services, the changes in society generally, all have worked for wider tolerance of personal behavior. What is not clear is whether the profession needs now to resume a search for values held in common if it is to survive the tests of self-discipline which are confronting it.

Against this broad background, I turn to a specific case with major significance for professional ethics in the future—the revocation of tenure by the Board of Trustees of Stanford University in the case of Bruce Franklin, associate professor of English. As one studies the "Decision of the Advisory Board of Stanford University in the Matter of Professor H. Bruce Franklin,"[5] one notes first that the Board found it necessary to preface its investigation of the charges with a survey of "Fundamental Issues and Standards." To quote some key concepts:

(1) The faculty of the university is a small community, characterized by face-to-face contact and personal interaction. Legislation proscribing conduct in a disciplinary context is rare; when it occurs, it merely codifies previously shared understandings.

(2) Faculty members relate to the institution more through practice and informally negotiated consensus rather than through hierarchically codified rule. Rules of conduct thus trace their source to slowly evolving tradition rather than abrupt acts of legislative intervention by persons in positions of formal authority. . . . [There is] no need for the kind of detailed directions that guide the armies of bureaucrats upon which larger organizations often rely for administering centrally-determined policies.[6]

Affirmed in the Franklin Board's decision are the concepts of community, localism, tradition (largely unwritten), and of faculty sharing in institutional policy-making and administration, also referred to as "a web of largely unwritten rules as tough and living as the British Constitution." In accounting for the ways in which the code of academics differs from that of other professions, the Stanford Board suggested: "Faculty members chose their profession in part

[5] The *Text of the Advisory Board Report* together with three Appendices was published by Stanford University, Palo Alto, California, and dated January 5, 1972.
[6] *Report,* p. 3.

because they embrace traditional faculty norms, therefore performing willingly what written rules coerce in other systems." The hypothetical act so described suggests a constantly renewed social
contract, voluntarily adhered to even though "dissent from a rule,
or even from the entire system of rules, obviously exists, and must
exist to furnish the motive power for necessary change." (Here one
must raise the question of how meaningful voluntary subscription to
the "web" can be if it is possible to subscribe to the whole while also
"dissent[ing] . . . from the entire system of rules.")[7]

The university for its part "must accommodate the question-
ing of contemporary goals and structures . . . even . . . the view
that the university, or the professoriate, should not survive. . . .
The code of the institution does, however, demand that the speech
and conduct of a professor stay behind the line of inciting or
physically causing the impairment of the institution's functions,
especially its function as a forum in which *other* points of view can
also be heard."[8]

Having agreed upon a working definition of academic freedom as a reciprocal responsibility of institution and individual
professor, the Board found, unanimously, that the university had a
right to restrain freedom of speech *beyond* the scope of Constitutional protection if either of two "central university interests" were
in jeopardy: "protection of members of the university community
and university facilities against risk of serious injury or damage"
and "protection against coercive intrusion on the intellectual transactions which the university seeks to foster."[9]

In reaching this position, the Franklin committee rejected an
intervention presented by a group of their faculty colleagues which
argued against such a university prerogative and maintained that
the university had no right to restrain speech in any way. By implication, the position taken by the intervening group rejected localism
and tradition (one is reminded of the student complaint of "sandbox
government") in favor of external standards.

This is a line or argument which is revolutionary in American higher education and the more remarkable in that it comes out
of an institution where faculty participation in policy-making is real

[7] *Report*, p. 4.
[8] *Report*, p. 4.
[9] *Report*, p. 4.

and not sandbox, where control over basic institutional decisions is not lost in a pyramid of boards. The intervention inspired the Board to sum up its defense of tradition by saying: "It is not obvious why the university should be dependent on external prosecution policy, which may respond to a number of factors but which is unlikely to reflect any sensitive judgment of university interests as a central concern. It does seem clear that sound decisions . . . require the kind of intimate familiarity with the facts of the case that can be best provided by professional peers."[10] Were such a statement addressed to the California Board of Regents it would be old-hat; the fact that it was addressed primarily to faculty colleagues makes it a bell in the night.

What the Franklin case says—loudly—is that political differences in the 1970s have generated mistrust so intense that a minority of faculty are prepared to contend that academic freedom must be divorced from institutional control if it is to be genuinely free and not politically partial. The idea of the university as an "extended family system" is dead when distinguished professors proclaim their preference for civil supervision of academic freedom. The most poignant note struck in the Stanford *Report* is the statement: "A major element in Professor Franklin's treatment of issues in the university is an attempt to disembody the institution from the human beings who make it up . . . [G]uilt is . . . globalized to the entire institution. . . . The dehumanizing process extends to the treatment of the individuals so labeled: they are . . . 'pigs,' 'fascists,' 'lackeys,' and the like."[11]

The other headline-making cases—Roth, Sindermann, and Davis—resemble the Franklin case as they reflect the heavy political weather of our day, but they differ from it because they concern nontenured faculty and because the position of the faculty member is not that of defendant but of accuser. Each case focuses on the nonrenewal of contract for a junior faculty member who alleges that whatever the appearance, the fact that his contract was not renewed was a violation of his basic rights as a person, a citizen, a professor.

Even in a calm political era, a time of mutual trust, strong

[10] *Report,* p. 4.
[11] *Report,* p. 11.

institutional loyalties, and a sellers' market for faculty, problems of negative decision on tenure can be divisive. The difference in 1972 is that this is not such an era; many cases raise uncomfortably murky political issues and are divisive in a new way. As tenure decisions loom for academics who like Angela Davis and Robert Sindermann have taken unpopular, controversial positions in quarrels which have often torn institutions apart, there is a new element of self-doubt about the system: "How do I know why I don't want A as a colleague?" (or why the Department of Sociology does not want him) which in turn leads to misgivings about the system of peer judgment and of local control.

In the Roth and Sindermann cases one observes a conventional (reassuring?) opposition of faculty and administration which is reflected in the *amicus curiae* briefs presented. The AAUP, the NEA, and the AFT presented *amicus* briefs in support of Roth and Sindermann, while the AAC, ACE, American Association of State Colleges and Universities, and the National Association of State Universities and Land Grant Colleges presented *amicus* briefs for the institutions.

The practical consequences of the Supreme Court's action in these two cases can be far-reaching, their substance is important. Yet the implications of these cases do not shake the foundations of professional ethics as does the Franklin case. All parties want to retain the distinction between tenured and nontenured faculty. All save one of the parties agree that the normal resolution of similar cases should follow institutional standards (guided, perhaps, by AAUP norms and with the improvisation of new safeguards), not fall to civil courts.

The exception is important, for the AFT in its brief suggested that it would be "improper—and of little benefit" for an institution which had already decided to terminate a teacher's contract to hold an impartial hearing by way of review. The remedy they propose is that the appeal be taken outside the institution, not directly to the civil courts, but to a proto-court. The same idea is heard in other contexts, with some faculty suggesting that the quasi-courts consist of panels of lawyers, others that the panels be made up of faculty from another institution to ensure objectivity. The appeal of such devices suggests that we are heading into an era of unusual reliance on machinery, oblivious to the fact that the people who control them will be more important than the machines which are designed and the fact that quasi-courts are unlikely to increase the trust and mutual respect which make the institution viable.

Yet another solution was proposed by Henry Saltzman, the president of Pratt Institute, in a recent issue of the *Chronicle of Higher Education*. Saltzman suggests the whole matter of tenure be removed from the judgment of the individual institution which grants it and given to a National Tenured Professor Accreditation Board. The Board would bestow tenure (following guidelines provided by the institution), review the tenured at five-year intervals, and renew it as justified.[12]

Mort Sahl taught us all that great truth: "The future lies ahead." In the complex area under discussion, it would be easy to be pessimistic about that future. Quite apart from the nightmare of university takeover by the Right or the Left, there is a basis for gloomy forecasts—an *Academic Clocktower Orange*. The old consensus of scholars and gentlemen (for what it was worth) disappeared long since and the new search for external authority to resolve academic disputes suggests a serious collapse of self-confidence. Moreover, we can expect that in the future there will be more monitoring of institutional standards and mores—the "web of tradition"—from outside academe. We are heading into an era in which federal regulatory agencies, such as NLRB and the Civil Rights Division of HEW and the Department of Labor, as well as federal grant-making agencies such as OE, will scrutinize university policies more closely than ever before, policies which reflect faculty/faculty as well as faculty/administrative judgments and standards. We can expect that the number of appeals from institutional judgments to civil courts will increase and that this in turn will have an influence on how decisions are made within the institution. (One has only to contemplate the human cost to the Stanford community of the Franklin trial to wonder how many faculty members could carry the burden of the seven men on the Board and how often any institution could survive it.) On the whole, we must expect a widening gulf between faculty and administration as such trends as these

---

[12] H. Saltzman, "Proposing a National Board To Accredit Tenured Professors." *Chronicle of Higher Education,* November 8, 1971, p. 8.

work themselves out, and though a few administrators and faculty will hail this separation as progress, it will be deplored by many more as an undermining of the structure. Both faculty and administrators will be under new pressures to conform to patterns which are set outside the university.

One must anticipate, too, an increasingly important role for lawyers in the internal governance of the university. With resort to the courts more frequent and with personnel procedures ever more formal and technically prescribed, all parties will opt for expert legal counsel over amateur logicians. If the academic community experiments with quasi-courts or a national tenure board, their effect will be a diminution of institutional autonomy and an endorsement of the point of view that local academic peers don't necessarily make the best professional judgments.

Yet some things can be done to relieve the gloom—by individuals, by institutions, by guilds. If enough academics in enough institutions will give systematic and sustained thought to the issues, the movement to abdicate institutional authority to an outside agency, whether a quasi-court or the civil courts, can be quashed with little difficulty. The academy has fought hard for the right to set its own standards and monitor them, and once that right is lost, Humpty's egg is gone forever.

One way to generate such systematic thought is wide reading of the Stanford Board's decision, for that *Report* comes to grips with the basic issues which make professional ethics possible in 1972 or any other time. The values it affirms are conservative ones, but they are designed to conserve the conditions in which dissent is possible. (Shortly after the *Report* was made public, Daniel Ellsberg made a speech in Palo Alto condemning the decision as unjust and politically biased. He later admitted that he had not read the *Report*. There will be many Ellsbergs, for it is not bedside reading.)

Stanford's example suggests an institutional exercise as well as a personal one. A full year before the Franklin trial took place, the Stanford AAUP chapter began work on "recommendations on standards and procedures for faculty self-discipline"—a kind of faculty bill of rights and responsibilities. Discussion of the AAUP *Bill of Rights* provided the entire community with an opportunity to ventilate many issues—essentially the impact of new life styles and new political strategies on the mores of the "old university"—*before* these issues were personalized in Bruce Franklin.

The Kerr Commission recently urged every institution to organize its faculty, students, trustees, and administrators in a similar task. If institutional preference is to survive, it must be restated in the light of the revolutions of the past decade. Working out institutional bills of rights will be difficult, given the splintered constituencies in most institutions and the gray zones to be assorted. But it will be easier to do before a challenge than after, and there will be a chance of retaining local determination.

Committees of several guilds, notably the American Political Science Association, have shown an interest in rethinking the ethical problems of members of their particular guild, though they have tended to focus on the characteristics of their field which make it desirable to spell out the ethics of grantsmanship and of research involving human beings. They have assumed that AAUP would carry the burden of representing all guilds in matters of ethics in teaching. This reliance leads to a final point. Surely if AAUP did not exist, we would desperately set about organizing it. If participation in collective bargaining serves to reduce AAUP's effectiveness as guardian of academic freedom and keeper of the conscience for higher education, higher education will be naked before its real enemies. One can hope, piously, that the AFT and the NEA will be as convinced of that truth as the AAUP. A realist would insist, however, that only angels could exercise the restraint that would be called for in the competition for the bargaining rights of individual institutions. In any event, there is one other hope, for there is one more full-dress debate scheduled within AAUP. In my judgment, the health of academe will look much better if the membership rejects its Council recommendation to get into collective bargaining in a major way.

❧ 10 ❧

Impact of Unionism on Governance

E. D. Duryea, Robert S. Fisk

"**U**nions!" Ten years ago an ugly word in academic circles, an idea many viewed as repugnant to the essential nature of professional service. Today, though one would hardly say unionism is accepted in academe, collective bargaining certainly has gained a credibility and an acceptance which does open up the possibility of its having a very substantial impact in the 1970s. It poses a basis for faculty-administrative relationships quite different from what is now the case. It presents—for good or bad—an alternative mode to established forms of academic government associated with senates and committees. It can and very likely will strongly challenge the collegial nature of "shared authority" which has been the primary rationale for faculty participation in college and university government.[1]

Data documenting the growth of this phenomenon are still uncertain, partly because it is difficult to be precise in a fluid situation and partly because mechanisms have yet to be established for accurate reporting. In November 1971 the *New York Times* reported a study by Joseph W. Garbarino for the Carnegie Commission on Higher Education identifying 133 institutions which have recognized collective bargaining agents. Garbarino estimated that fifty thousand or possibly more faculty members and professional staff members have joined bargaining units. The trend toward unionism in the two-year colleges is the more pronounced, yet the evidence also reveals a substantial intrusion of collective bargaining into the four-year colleges and universities. The *Times* article listed thirty-two upper institutions including the two major public universities in New York—City University and the State University— both of which have voted in bargaining agents and completed contracts for faculty members and professional staff. State colleges and universities in New Jersey, Pennsylvania, Massachusetts, and Michigan have joined the list.

Concurrently a growing body of professional literature addresses this subject, attesting to the potential impact of bargaining in higher education. Content ranges from specific considerations related to the negotiation process and the substance of contracts to the broader implications bargaining holds for college and university organization.

We propose here to consider the impact of unionism by examining the conditions which have supported faculty endorsement of collective bargaining and the implications which this endorsement presents for the established organizational relationships. The following observations grow out of the literature, a study of the evolution of the corporate nature of college and university government, and

---

[1] The most complete statement of the concept of shared authority currently available is that found in the 1967 report of a Special Task Force of the American Association for Higher Education and National Education Association, *Faculty Participation in Academic Governance*. It contrasts sharply with the adversary relationship believed by many to be implicit in unionism.

our personal observations in the bargaining process of the State University of New York.[2]

Collective bargaining based on union organization has undoubtedly gained support as a consequence of conditions often unique to specific institutions. Ineffectual or repressive administrations have stimulated unionism as a counterforce to authoritarian presidents or governing boards. Other institutions have lacked a tradition of faculty participation in academic governance. Permissive legislation existing in nineteen states has expedited bargaining and undoubtedly stimulated an interest in this form of relationship. Recent decisions by the National Labor Relations Board have encouraged bargaining in private institutions. Threats to employment security and a slowdown in faculty salary improvement growing out of the current economic recession may contribute to the pressures for unionization. Another factor is the concern of many nonteaching professionals who feel themselves effectively disenfranchised by their inability to share in the governing authority accorded academic staff in many institutions.

The specific influences prodding academicians and other professionals to turn to collective bargaining are numerous, and not all bear on every situation. More fundamentally, in our view, the emergence of unions relates significantly to the changing nature of college and university government.

Since the formation of the early colleges in the seventeenth and eighteenth centuries, governing boards have existed as "the institution" on grants of authority from colonial or state governments, either as public or private corporations. In this century, and as a counterforce to the formal authority of boards, faculty members have strived for and gained an increasingly significant role in governance, especially for academic affairs. The essence of this role is the concept of "shared authority" implemented by faculty senates and other governing units which in major universities exercise very

[2] The Senate Professional Association, representing faculty members and nonteaching professional staff members of the various campuses in the State University of New York, signed a contract with the state last August. SPA won the bargaining election in a runoff with an affiliate of the American Federation of Teachers. AAUP had been eliminated in a prior election. At the time of the bargaining election SPA was supported by the National Education Association and the New York State Teachers Association with whom it now has a formal affiliation.

substantial powers. Paralleling this development, academic departments have emerged not nearly so much as administrative subunits as basic units for faculty authority, with great influence stemming from their power to initiate and oversee significant academic policies. Departments at most major institutions, thus, function on a collegial basis more attuned to the senior professoriate than to deans and presidents.

This combination of departmental collegiality and overall faculty self-governance in matters affecting academic policy and personnel has increasingly characterized the stronger colleges and universities. Faculty participation in this tradition receives legitimization from statutes and bylaws approved by governing boards and, at times, simply by tradition itself. The authority has been delegated by boards, in other words, and depends in the last analysis on the formal, corporate authority of the boards.

In our view the rapid expansion of higher education since the end of World War II has supported two new conditions which threaten to affect seriously the continued evolution of this traditional governance pattern. One is derived from the very substantial increase in public funding essential for this expansion. As higher education has become a major investment for state governments, concerned legislators and governors have begun to insist on far greater coordination and accountability. State agencies such as budget offices, legislative committees, and civil service commissions have begun to raise questions and establish policies which in their effect transcend the corporate role of governing boards. For private institutions it appears inevitable that similar actions will follow in the wake of major public support. For public colleges and universities the intrusions exist today in very tangible form, not least of which is the consideration of professional staff members and faculty who are often employees of the state rather than the board. The relative autonomy achieved by higher education through its corporate base has begun to lose out to these intrusions and will probably continue to be eroded. As a consequence, faculty members may find their traditional powers no longer capable of being supported by governing boards and thus will conclude that they must seek alternative modes for the protection of their interests and the maintenance of their roles in the academic enterprise.

The other force is the physical expansion itself, primarily in the public sector. Teacher training institutions in becoming state colleges have increased in size. New state colleges have been formed. In both situations the concept of shared authority seldom has had the opportunity to take firm root. A single governing board often serves a number of such colleges spread geographically throughout a state. In the last two decades a rapid expansion in the number of faculty members has occurred primarily in institutions lacking experience in the traditional patterns of governance. They have faced, in many instances, presidents and other administrators also lacking in any commitment to faculty participation in governance. As a consequence these faculties have and will continue to prove more amenable to alternative models for developing and protecting their interests, the most obvious of which is that associated with collective bargaining.

Clearly the picture is far more complex than the landscape sketched here. Yet these two conditions do pose pressures for change in governance. To compound the situation, the public's negative reaction to campus violence and dissent and the need for serious financial retrenchment by most state governments have reinforced intrusions which threaten the continued viability of governance based on shared authority.

In the context of these forces accompanying the expansion of higher education collective bargaining in just a few years has gained momentum. The press of faculty members to share in the processes of governance is taking the form of "across the table" bargaining. This bargaining affects decision-making in virtually every aspect, from the roles of academic senates and other governing bodies to decisions on the specifics of working conditions and economic benefits. We consider three major directions of change manifested in institutions with negotiated contracts. Each of these establishes in a fundamental way a new basis for faculty-administrative relationships. The first has to do with the substitution of contracts for arrangements which were subject in the last analysis to approval by governing boards. The second concerns the shift in the judicial function from a final review by governing boards, as has been the practice, to a process leading ultimately to compulsory arbitration. The third is a potential shift in responsibility for interpreting the academic function to the public. There will be less reliance on boards and presidents and more involvement by bargaining organizations.

First, we believe that a primary change in policy-making may result from the substitution of contracts for the more traditional, delegated forms of decision-making. Once a bargaining unit gains recognition and then a contract, both parties must adhere to rulings and judgments based on the contract by such agencies as state employee relations boards, the National Labor Relations Board (for private institutions), and the courts. During the period under contract faculty members will find themselves far less vulnerable to deliberate, or innocent, vagaries in administrative and board policies such as those resulting from changes in leadership or from external pressures. Simultaneously, board members and major administrative officers may anticipate a more stable situation in that faculty members and professional staff cannot turn nearly so readily to new issues or to personal appeals and claims of special privilege. The ground rules are, for the time being, set in writing. Specific matters not covered by the agreement must usually await the next round of bargaining.

In addition to providing new stability, the formalization of relationships will delineate the functions of the two major segments of the institution. An individual will find himself classified as "faculty/employee" or as "administration/management." For the many individuals whose roles now place them in both categories, this dichotomy could force difficult choices. It may well lead to what many will believe to be a most unfortunate bifurcation. For others, however, it will represent a welcome opportunity for clarification of role, particularly in decision-making. There will be some shifting about. Present contracts, for example, differ in the inclusion or exclusion of departmental chairmen as members of the bargaining unit. At present writing much depends on the manner of their selection and their role with the administrative hierarchy. Definition of the bargaining unit should clarify responsibility, yet it may place administrative status and responsibiilty on some chairmen who believe strongly in a peer relationship with departmental colleagues.

Less clear and certainly at this time far more uncertain are the ultimate roles and relationships for established faculty governing bodies such as senates. As noted above, these bodies have attained status and power, particularly on major campuses, through tradition and ultimately formal recognition in campus statutes and regulations, with their status resting finally on the corporate role of the governing boards—which have sanctioned their power. A contractual basis for faculty government could make a senate's role more independent and positive. Conversely, a contract may shift the real basis for participation in governance to the bargaining agency, largely or totally supplanting the senate. Whatever the outcome for the respective roles of senates and bargaining agencies, however, a very important circumstance will ensue: these governing arrangements can become contractual and thus beyond the authority of boards to alter except at the time of formal negotiations. All matters spelled out by contract will remain for the period of that contract subject to it and to interpretations of it, beyond the authority of senates or administrative officers or boards to change.

Among the other logical outcomes of contractual relationships will be an increase in the potential for consultation between administrators and professional staff members, an interchange established by explicit requirement rather than by personal disposition, acquaintance, expediency, or tradition. The first clear evidence of this outcome already has appeared in provisions for the handling of grievances. But it is often spelled out in further provision for faculty input on personnel policies, allocation of resources, and academic affairs and may spread to many aspects of management as traditional concerns of academicians blend with the explicating force of unionism. What have been traditional desires could become contractual provisions, depending on how the consultation process develops and the flavor it takes on. Where good communication processes and flexibility characterize the consultations, contracts may prove to be more general than specific. A formal relationship may lead to increased advocacy by professional staff and a pushing onto the bargaining table of many matters heretofore taken for granted.

Conceivably the response to this latter circumstance will reinforce it. "That's what the contract says" might be a general reaction to the concerns of either party by the other. The result may be highly detailed agreements, unless both sides recognize the value of flexibility. A new set of relationships, contractually specified, can spread over academe. Ultimately a greater constancy, a situation less subject to change resulting from such incidents as new presidents and board members, can prevail.

The second fundamental difference likely to characterize higher education under collective bargaining has to do with the nature of the judicial process available to faculty. In institutions with union contracts governing boards no longer will serve as courts of final appeal. Every indication is that, upon signing an agreement, boards will lose this role. Contractual provision and arbitration will become the final recourse. The processes associated with a new word in the academic vocabulary, *grievances,* may prove the most fundamentally significant outcome.

Customarily, the grievance procedure spells out a series of steps instituted to force decisions within time limits far more specific and urgent than those now customary. It will provide for much more formal advocacy of the cause of the complainant and augment his personal resources with those of a collective group. Pushing the case itself and winning it where possible—and hopefully justly—will become important organizationally for the bargaining unit, if it is to be sustained in the next election. Unless prior agreement is reached, both grievant and administration will face an ultimate test of their respective positions in the form of compulsory arbitration.[3]

In well-established institutions with a tradition of collegial evaluation younger faculty members can be formally in conflict with senior departmental colleagues on promotion and tenure decisions. Thus grievances may emerge which lie primarily between members of a bargaining unit rather than solely between a faculty member and the administration. But perhaps more novel concerns will emerge from resorting to arbitration, a process which involves serious risks for both sides of a grievance. For the professional staff member, for example, arbitration places the resolution of important personal considerations in the hands of a third party. For a department it may cause an important tenure question to be resolved by a person external to a discipline, thus affecting the "purity" of that discipline on a given campus. By an administrator and a board of

---

[3] At this time the more typical arrangement, especially for state institutions. But the possibilities of a strike over an issue of extreme importance cannot be totally discounted.

trustees arbitration may be viewed as a surrender of fundamental powers to govern in a manner consistent with their public charge.

Whatever the nature of grievance and other matters subject to reviews of a judicial nature, collective bargaining clearly will alter contemporary suppositions. But it is premature to prognosticate specifically in this dimension until there has evolved both practice over time and a body of court decisions related to contracts and particularly contracts within higher education.

The third direction of change relates to the public image of a college or a university, which frequently reflects the influence of strong personalities such as presidents and faculty leaders or dissidents who obtain the attention of external constituencies. The interpretation of an institution and its service, upon which rests general public support, usually has been a special responsibility of a president or chancellor, often in cooperation with the governing board. Innumerable instances illustrate the impact of presidents with ability and charisma and of strong board members and their capacity to create an effective image for their institution. Often faculty members left out of this public relations process have felt impotent, even when they wished to convey more accurately and effectively the academic aspects of the enterprise; but more frequently they have simply ignored this kind of responsibility.

The nature of collective negotiations and bargaining organizations, frequently of a state and national dimension, engenders new attitudes and proffers a new potential for institutional public interpretation. In public colleges and universities, union pressure for higher compensation and a variety of improvements for members will bring on resistance. This resistance will call for responses which convey to the public the nature of the services which make these increases appropriate. Similarly, organizations at private institutions will feel called on to defend their bargaining positions to alumni, students, and families, as well as to the public in general. Out of this situation academics will gain a new comprehension of the need to interpret their enterprise effectively. This interpretation will have to come from the unions themselves as an integral part of their pressures to achieve propositions made at the bargaining table. It offers the potential for a much more aggressive public posture and, conceivably, for public institutions in particular, a posture calculated to elicit supportive public attention.

This discussion leads us to two residual considerations which underlie the impact of collective bargaining on higher education. The first relates to the traditional concepts held by academicians and professional staff members about their roles. The essence of these concepts is embodied in the idea of shared authority. More than one faculty member has said, "We do not work for the university. We *are* the university."

The professional holds a unique responsibility for what he does in teaching, research, and the other special services, one that transcends normal ideas of work loads, hours, formal evaluation of service, and the entire nature of this service. From this point of view, administrators serve primarily to make the work of the professional more effective in his own terms, and thus decision-making should be an activity in which all participate on equal terms. Thus, one moves between an academic and an administrative position easily and for some individuals quite regularly. Officers of a senate meet with presidents as peers in a common enterprise.

Collective bargaining in its traditional nature assumes an employee-employer relationship, a fundamentally competitive relationship in which the interests of the employee are continually set against those of the institution as interpreted by its administrators or management. What collective bargaining in higher education does is to bring into the open the implicit dualism in the role of a faculty member as both professional and employee. The academic milieu has tended to understate the latter role. A primary task for faculty unions, in our judgment, is to evolve a point of view in collective bargaining which supports rather than mitigates the professional role and enhances the concept of an academic community.

The second impact of bargaining is more a possibility than an actuality as yet, but it may prove to be critically important. Our concern grows out of the erosion of the corporate nature and powers of governing boards. What has been identified as the "quasi-public utility" nature of higher education supports increasing supervision by segments of state governments in the wake of increasing financial support. It seems quite clear, therefore, that the autonomy of colleges and universities is very much at stake. A new force to assist in protecting the autonomy of the academic enterprise becomes important for higher education. We suggest, therefore, that by organizing for collective bargaining faculties and professional staff can achieve a new power base. By doing so they can help maintain that essential balance between institutional autonomy and public accountability which until now has been maintained by the corporate nature of governing boards.

☙ 11 ❧

Collective Bargaining on Private Campuses

Sheldon Elliot Steinbach

In June 1970, the National Labor Relations Board, upon petition by employees at Cornell and Syracuse universities, decided that it would best effectuate the policies of the National Labor Relations Act to assert jurisdiction over private, nonprofit colleges and universities. The decision, which overruled a prior Labor Board case, has eased the way for academic and nonacademic personnel to organize and bargain collectively with private colleges and universities. The few cases decided by the Board and the issues raised in these cases and in others still pending have made institutions take cognizance of and reassess the impact of the assumption of jurisdiction by the NLRB.

116

The National Labor Relations Board, established in 1935, is empowered to mitigate and eliminate obstructions to the free flow of interstate commerce by encouraging collective bargaining and by providing protection for the exercise by workers of the freedom of association, self-organization, and the designation of their own representatives for negotiating with regard to the wages, hours, and conditions of their employment. The National Labor Relations Act provides that "the term 'employer' . . . shall not include . . . any state or political subdivision thereof," thereby excluding from coverage all employees at public colleges and universities.[1]

The basic legislation establishing the NLRB enabled private higher education to be exempt from coverage by providing that "the Board has the discretionary power to decline to assert jurisdiction over any labor dispute . . . where in the opinion of the Board the effect of such labor dispute on commerce is not sufficiently substantial to warrant the exercise of its jurisdiction."[2]

Prior to 1970, the Board relied on its decision in *Trustees of Columbia University.*[3] In that case, the Community and Social Agency Employees Union petitioned for representational rights for a unit consisting of all clerical employees in the libraries of Columbia University. The Board held that jurisdiction would not be asserted "over a nonprofit, educational institution where the activities involved are noncommercial in nature and intimately connected with the charitable purposes and educational activities of the institution."[4] The Board in the *Columbia* case acknowledged that the institution's activities "affected commerce" and that the dollar volume jurisdictional standard set by the Board had been met; however, the Board relied heavily on the Conference Report on the Labor Management Relations Act of 1947, which seemed to endorse prior Board decisions that nonprofit organizations engaged in noncommercial activities should not be considered as affecting commerce so as to bring them within the coverage of the Act.[5]

In 1970, Cornell and Syracuse faced a unique problem when groups of their nonacademic employees began to organize. Both

[1] 61 Stat 137 (1947), 29 U.S.C. Sec. 152(2).
[2] 14(c)(1).
[3] 97 NLRB 424 (1951).
[4] Ibid. at 427.
[5] 7 H.R. 510 80th Long. 1st Sess. 32 (1947).

institutions are located in New York State, which at the time was one of the eight states[6] in the country that had labor legislation written or interpreted so as to expressly cover employees of private educational institutions. Their choice was a simple one: should they subject themselves to the jurisdiction of the State Labor Relations Board, or would they fare better under the Federal regulatory process?

A comparison of the New York State labor relations statute with the National Labor Relations Act reveals noteworthy differences that constitute an unwritten footnote to the arguments propounded by Cornell and adopted by the NLRB in reversing its long-standing decision. Without having to examine every difference between the respective statutes, one quickly notes the benefits accruing to employers under the N.L.R.A. Under New York State law there is no ban on organizational picketing or union unfair labor practices, both of which are unlawful under the Taft-Hartley section of the Labor Management Relations Act. State law permits a closed shop, whereas the N.L.R.A. outlaws the closed shop, permitting only a union or agency shop.

Federal law also provides rules pertaining to bargaining unit determinations that favor the employer. State law enables supervisors to be certified as a distinct unit and provides that they, along with guards and professional employees, may be included in units with rank and file employees. Under NLRB rules, supervisors are excluded from any bargaining unit, guards must be in a separate unit, and professionals must be granted a separate vote before they can be included in a more encompassing bargaining unit. Furthermore, New York State law requires the granting of a request for a craft unit, whereas the NLRB normally looks with disfavor on a proliferation of small craft units or the granting of craft severance.

The N.L.R.A. also guarantees "employer free speech" during union election campaigns, provides a procedure for adjudication of jurisdictional disputes, and contains a six-month statute of limitations on the filing of unfair labor practice charges. State law contained none of these statutory protections for the employer. The more advantageous aspects of federal law, as compared to New

[6] Colorado, Connecticut, Hawaii, Massachusetts, Michigan, Minnesota, New York, Wisconsin.

York State law, motivated Cornell and Syracuse to petition the NLRB to assert jurisdiction over private colleges and universities.

The Cornell and Syracuse petitions caused the NLRB to reexamine the decision rendered in *Trustees of Columbia University* in light of changed circumstances and the presentation of substantial evidence of the impact of these institutions on interstate commerce. After the arguments on both sides had been fully aired (twenty-seven amicus briefs having been filed), the Board decided to assert its jurisdiction over private, nonprofit educational institutions.

The Board, in rendering its decision, accepted three basic arguments of the petitioners. First, the institutions contended that colleges and universities do not merely substantially affect commerce but have a "massive impact on interstate commerce." The Board noted the changes in colleges and universities during the two decades since the decision in the *Columbia* case, commenting particularly on the growth of the student body, increased number of employees, expansion of the physical plant, and the magnitude of the general operating budgets. The Board also recognized that institutions' income is not solely derived from traditional sources such as tuition, fees, and gifts, but is comprised to a substantial extent of monies derived from activities which are commercial in nature. Therefore, it could no longer be said that private institutions of higher education do not exercise a real impact on interstate commerce.

Second, the expanded role played by the federal government in higher education constituted a substantial change from the situation that had prevailed in 1951. Direct federal expenditures for private and public education in 1969 approached five billion dollars, which was only a portion of the funds expended for education through a host of other programs which provided federal support subsidies or which conveyed monies through sponsored research projects. The Board further took cognizance of the evolving pattern of federal legislation that grants to employees in the nonprofit sector the same protection and benefits accorded to employees in the profit-making sphere, such as minimum wage and unemployment compensation.

Lastly, the Board recognized that only fifteen states had enacted labor relations laws, and of that number only eight covered employees of private educational institutions. Looking at the other side of the picture, the Board noted that there were thirty-five states without labor codes to handle labor disputes at private colleges and universitie3 and that the assertion of jurisdiction was necessary in order to have an "effective and uniform application of the national labor policy."

With consideration given to the three foregoing arguments, the Board overruled their decision in *Columbia University,* but simultaneously stated that it was not prepared to establish jurisdictional standards for private colleges and universities as a class.

The Board announced that it would exercise its seldom used rule-making power to set the jurisdictional criteria for all pending and future cases. A Notice of Proposed Rule Making was published in the *Federal Register* for the express purpose of gathering economic data from all private colleges and universities "to the end that the Board's jurisdiction may be asserted over those private colleges and universities whose impact on commerce may be deemed substantial but not over those whose impact may be deemed insubstantial."[7] After considering the thirty responses to the notice, the Board determined that it will assert jurisdiction over private, nonprofit colleges and universities which receive gross annual revenues of at least one million dollars. NLRB jurisdiction is usually exercised over commercial service establishments if the outflow or inflow of goods or services transmitted in interstate commerce exceeds fifty thousand dollars. It is estimated that under the one-million standard "some 80 per cent of all private colleges and universities and approximately 95 per cent of all full- and part-time nonprofessional personnel will be within the reach of the Act."[8]

With the foundation laid for the right to organize and bargain collectively at private institutions, observers of the higher education scene began to experience mixed reactions. Some anticipated the gradual destruction of the academic community due to the establishment of an adversary relationship between faculty and administration, while others looked forward to the collective determination of wages, hours, and conditions of employment.

The first post-*Cornell* decision involved two cases relating to the C. W. Post and Brooklyn centers of Long Island University.

[7] 35 Fed Reg 11270 (1970).
[8] 35 Fed Reg 18370 (1970).

In both instances the United Federation of College Teachers, American Federation of Teachers, AFL-CIO, petitioned for representation rights for a unit consisting of all professional employees engaged directly or indirectly in student instruction, including all adjunct professionals. The institution took the position that jurisdiction should not be asserted over its professional personnel and that if such jurisdiction is applied, a distinct unit should be established for full-time faculty and separate units established for any other categories. In addition, the parties disagreed as to the supervisory status of certain employees.

In deciding the *C. W. Post*[9] case, the Board noted that to some extent it was entering an "uncharted area." It made a clear determination that, even though faculty have quasi–policy-making and supervisory authority, it is "exercised by them only as a group" and therefore they are excluded from being classified as supervisors within the meaning of Section 2(11) of the Act.

The Board next considered the nature of an appropriate bargaining unit. It analyzed in depth the status of the adjunct teaching staff, taking particular note that they: generally teach twelve semester hours or less a year, do not receive the full range of fringe benefits, maintain additional employment elsewhere, exist in high ratio to full-time employees, and are unable to achieve tenure. Both the university and the union cited state labor board decisions supporting their respective positions, but the Board found no "clear-cut pattern or practice of collective bargaining in the academic field" and proceeded to invoke its ordinary unit determination rules which compelled a conclusion that adjunct faculty should be included in the same unit with full-time faculty, since they "are regular part-time professional employees whose qualifications and chief function, teaching, are identical with those of full-time faculty."

The petitioners sought to have deans, division chairmen, and department chairmen excluded from the unit as supervisors, whereas the employer requested their inclusion. The Board found that division chairmen coordinate the work of several departments, and review and pass on all matters affecting the budget of the division, and that department chairmen, usually selected by the dean

[9] 189 NLRB 109 (1971).

in consultation with faculty (although sometimes elected by the department faculty), have some responsibility for hiring new faculty members by conducting interviews with candidates and discussing the prospective appointment and faculty promotions with the dean. The dean was found to be the chief administrative officer who is responsible for the budget and who, like the other officers considered, maintains a reduced teaching load. In view of the facts assembled, the Board found that deans, department chairmen, and division chairmen "exercise the authority to make effective recommendations as to the hiring and status of faculty members and other employees" and as such are supervisors within the meaning of the N.L.R.A. and are therefore excluded from the unit.

The Board also included in the unit librarians and research associates on the grounds that they are "engaged in functions closely related to teaching" and "based upon the intellectual character of his duties and his qualifications" respectively.

Similar problems relating to what constitutes an appropriate unit and the supervisory authority of deans and division chairmen were argued and decided in the same way in the *Brooklyn Center* case.[10] The decision disregarded the pleas of the two unions petitioning for bargaining rights, the UFCT and the AAUP, that department chairmen be included in the unit and not classified as supervisory employees. In addition, the Board found that the Director of Libraries, Director of Placement, Registrars, Associate Registrars, and the Director of Admissions direct the work of other employees and are thus supervisors.

The Board in May 1971 decided the *University of New Haven*[11] case, which dealt with the single question of whether adjunct faculty should be included in a unit with full-time faculty. Unlike the *C. W. Post* case, for reasons of election strategy, the employer here sought the inclusion of part-time faculty in the unit, whereas the unions opposed the addition of these employees. A review of the position of adjunct faculty revealed that aside from the number of hours involved, the lack of fringe benefits, the higher rate of turnover, "their function—teaching, the manner in which they perform it, and the conditions under which they operate—appears

---

[10] 189 NLRB 110 (1971).
[11] 190 NLRB 102 (1971).

to be identical to the corresponding work of full-time faculty."
Finding the facts in this case essentially like those in the *C. W. Post*
case, the Board found appropriate a unit of full-time and regular
part-time professional employees. The Board noted, however, that if
both parties stipulated the exclusion of part-time employees, the
Board would have excluded them from the unit.[12]

On June 22, 1971, the American Association of University
Professors filed a petition asking the National Labor Relations Board
to consider formulating general rules to clarify issues in representation cases involving faculty members at private colleges and universities. The petition listed three areas in which "guiding rules could
make a useful contribution": definition of supervisors; appropriate
organizations to serve as bargaining representatives; and the status
of teaching fellows, research associates, and part-time teachers.

The petition contended that the Board is confronted with
a novel situation involving a unique relationship between faculty
members and the college or university that "has no counterpart in
any industrial setting with which the Board has substantial experience." Approximately one month later the NLRB denied the petition, stating that:

> *The Board considers that the Petition properly points out
> that the Board's unit determinations in this area should take into
> account certain practices and organizational srtuctures which do not
> parallel the traditional practices and organizational structures in
> private industry. The Board's information to date, however, suggests
> that there is also a great variety in this regard within the academic
> community, and also that the practices and structures in universities
> and colleges are undergoing a period of change and experimenta-
> tion. The Board believes that to adopt inflexible rules for units of
> teaching employees at this time might well introduce too great an
> element of rigidity and prevent the Board from adapting its ap-
> proach to a highly pluralistic and fluid set of conditions. Accord-
> ingly, the Board shall deny the petition.*

The Board said, however, that it would welcome the fruits of any
research which had been done in the area.

The decision following the NLRB's refusal to utilize its

[12] *Oxbridge Mill,* 109 NLRB 868 fn. 9 at 870.

rule-making powers was the *Fordham University* case,[13] wherein a three-member panel of the board voted 2 to 1 to include department chairmen in the same unit with other professional employees, but agreed without dissent that the law school faculty was sufficiently unique to constitute a separate bargaining unit.

The Board found, in making its decision regarding department chairmen, that decisions on appointment and promotion were made by the department as a group rather than by the chairman alone and that if the chairman's recommendation is given greater weight, it merely reflects his knowledge and experience rather than any supervisory authority. It was further noted that chairmen: prepare the budget with the aid of the faculty, have salary recommendations subject to review by at least three levels of administrative authority, do not direct the work of faculty members, and, perhaps most significantly, "are considered by faculty members to be representatives of the faculty rather than the administration." Accordingly, the majority found the department chairmen not to be supervisors within the meaning of the National Labor Relations Act.

Board member Ralph E. Kennedy, after noting the duties of department chairmen spelled out in the University Handbook which included "preparing the department budget and supervising expenditures; recommending faculty appointments; reappointments, tenure and promotions . . . assigning schedules to each department member after consultation," found these duties to be substantially similar to those activities performed by department chairmen categorized as supervisors in the *C. W. Post* case and therefore, in his dissent, stated that he would exclude them from the unit.

The majority distinguished the *Fordham* case by noting that expert testimony compelled the conclusion that at some institutions department chairmen were part of the faculty and at others they were considered part of the administration. Unlike those of Fordham, the statutes of Long Island University specifically required the recommendation of the department chairman before the granting of tenure, and deans were directed to act on the recommendation of the department chairmen in making new appointments.

The Board disposed of the question concerning part-time

[13] 193 NLRB 23 (1971).

faculty by relying on the fact that the situation was essentially the same as in the *New Haven* case. They also found no reasons to exclude Jesuit priests from the unit, because "there is no evidence that membership in the Order is in any way inconsistent with collective bargaining."

In what was the first of many decisions that will involve similar issues in the years ahead, the Board agreed to sever the law school from the larger bargaining unit because this faculty "constitutes an identifiable group of employees whose separate community of interests is not irrevocably submerged in the broader interest which they share with other faculty members." The Board decided that, because the law faculty has specialized training, a separate administration and building, little interchange with other faculty members, a separate school calendar, and is inextricably intertwined with regulations issued by the New York Court of Appeals, the American Bar Association, and the Association of American Law Schools, an overall unit which would include the Law School with the entire Fordham University faculty would be inappropriate. It would seem that all law schools would be considered separate entities for collective bargaining purposes. And what about medical, dental, engineering, and a host of other schools which may wish to claim severance from the university-wide bargaining unit?

On October 6, 1971, the Board rendered its decision in the *University of Detroit* case.[14] The Board again followed its decision in the *University of New Haven* case and found that university part-time faculty members are part-time professional employees having a substantial community of interest with full-time faculty members and should therefore be included in the unit. The Board, however, was compelled to establish a test to ensure that only part-time faculty members with a substantial stake in the wages, hours, and conditions of employment had the right to vote. Accordingly, a 4 to 1 full-time to part-time hours taught ratio was extracted from the *New Haven* case, where part-time faculty teaching three or more hours per week were included with full-time faculty members teaching twelve hours per week. Therefore, in the law school where a full-time teacher usually teaches four two-credit-hour courses a term,

[14] 193 NLRB 95 (1971).

anyone teaching two hours per week a semester would be eligible to be in the unit.

In a reverse situation from the *Fordham* case, the University of Detroit contended that department chairmen are faculty members, while the petitioner, the University of Detroit chapter of the American Association of University Professors, argued that they have supervisory authority and should be excluded from the unit. The board found that the chairman makes one of several recommendations to appropriate university officials pertaining to appointment, promotion, tenure, or discharge of faculty members and that the university regards him as a faculty member who represents his colleagues at university senate meetings, carrying out his position without receiving any additional compensation. The Board followed its decision in *Fordham* and held that department chairmen are not supervisors. Member Kennedy, for the reasons stated in his dissent in the *Fordham* case, dissented again.

Thus the few cases decided since the NLRB's assumption of jurisdiction over private colleges and universities have set down some guidelines for unit determination with regard to adjunct faculty, department chairmen, and other professional and nonprofessional employees of the institution. The decisions are but a few of many pending which raise many other questions in this relatively unexplored area of labor law.

Two institutions have felt the impact of the assumption of jurisdiction by the NLRB by being slapped with unfair labor practice charges. The National Labor Relations Act is designed to protect employees' organizational activities for purposes of collective bargaining. Union activities do not afford an employee protection against discharge for cause. However, the reason for discharge, no matter how valid, can be investigated to determine whether the employer's motives might be deemed unlawful. Discharge of an ineffective employee, which is lawful in character, may become discriminatory if circumstances indicate that it was the employer's hostility toward an employee's protected union activities which carried the greatest weight in reaching the decision to terminate the individual.

Both Lawrence Institute of Technology and Monmouth College officials were unable to clearly demonstrate that the reasons for terminating several academic employees were motivated solely by their lack of competence. In each instance, the trial examiners found that the reasons given for dismissal failed to withstand scrutiny and gave rise to the finding that the institution had committed an unfair labor practice by interfering with the employee's right to self-organization. Private colleges and universities must now take note of the fact that probationary employees can be discharged for cause or no cause at any time before achieving tenure except where the termination is motivated by the employer's desire to "encourage or discourage membership in any labor organization."

As a result of being adjudged in violation of the National Labor Relations Act, the institutions were ordered to cease and desist from discouraging membership in the union concerned and to take the following affirmative action: (1) offer immediate and full reinstatement to their former position to the employees discharged or, if the job does not exist, to a substantially equivalent position, without prejudice to their seniority or other rights, and make them whole with regard to any loss of pay suffered; (2) for sixty days, post on campus in conspicuous places, including all places where notices to faculty and employees are customarily posted, a notice signed by the administration stating that the discharged employees will be offered reemployment and that the institution will neither discriminate against any employee for union activity nor interfere with any employee's right to join the union.

The assumption of jurisdiction by the NLRB over private colleges and universities raises many issues in itself without focusing on the general problems relating to the rise of collective bargaining on campus. Aside from the organizational mood on some campuses and the impact of state legislation on the right of public employees to participate in collective negotiations, one finds the NLRB's reversal of position in the *Cornell* case having substantial impact on the higher education community.

The mere fact that employees of private colleges and universities can use the machinery of the NLRB will facilitate the movement on some campuses toward abandonment of the "shared authority principle" and the implementation of collective bargaining as the medium for resolving questions concerning faculty wages, hours, and conditions of employment. Federal labor law is well litigated and will be helpful in most areas to both the administration and the employees. Although guidance may be scanty on some issues, in general, administrators will find greater guidance and protection under the federal law than under any of the state labor relations laws.

Undoubtedly, there will be a spill-over effect from the federal to the state level. At last count, approximately nineteen states have public employee labor relations laws that cover employees of colleges and universities. The example set by the assumption of jurisdiction by a federal agency should hasten the enactment of further state legislation in this area.

The National Labor Relations Act presents some disadvantages and problems to colleges. The problem relating to strikes is still to be realized. Federal law permits strikes at private institutions, whereas public institutions are regulated by state statutes which, except in two states, flatly prohibit the use of the strike weapon. For years commentators have urged that public employees be granted the same right to strike that their counterparts in private enterprise enjoy in those areas where it does not materially affect the health, safety, or welfare of the public. Conceivably, the ability of faculty at private schools to strike will add one more inequitable distinction that will aid in the drive of public employees in education to gain the right to strike.

The jurisdictional standards established by the Board will only cover 80 per cent of the private colleges and universities. Therefore, there are some institutions that will fall in the gap between federal and state coverage. It is maintained that the Board has failed to assert its jurisdiction to its fullest extent because of a lack of sufficient manpower and a determination that an institution that receives less than one million dollars in annual gross revenue has an insubstantial impact on commerce. These arguments seem unpersuasive when compared to the facts that the Board normally exercises jurisdiction over commercial establishments having a flow of goods or services which exceeds fifty thousand dollars and that its failure to assert jurisdiction leaves employees of some private colleges without adequate protection in forty-two states.

Over the past two years, it has become apparent that faculty at both private and public institutions have received substantial organizational and staff support from the national offices of the AFT, AAUP, and NEA. College administrators, and often their attorneys, have found a need for back-up material and advice. Un-

like unions, which coordinate an organizational drive and the negotiation of a contract by pooling accumulated experience gained at
other campuses, college administrators are forced to deal with the
entire process of collective negotiations without sufficient knowledge
of what has transpired at other institutions. In order to meet the
problem, schools throughout the country ought to begin to share
information and informal advice regarding specific organizational,
contractual, and arbitrational problems. Hopefully, once armed
with this collective information, private colleges will be better able to
read and react to the handwriting on the wall.

𝔁 12 𝔁

Tenure Is Obsolete

Florence Moog

𝕴s tenure obsolete?[1] Before tackling that question, let us deal with two antecedent questions: Is job security obsolete? I think not. College and university teachers profit by a reasonable assurance of continued employment because it frees them from anxieties that might militate against harmonious and fruitful relationships with students and colleagues. Is academic freedom obsolete? Again, the answer is definitely "No." The freedom to express, without penalty,

---

[1] This chapter is based on an address given at the 1972 National Conference on Higher Education in which the author took the affirmative side of this question. Tenure was "defended" at that conference by William Van Alstyne, whose point of view is presented in the article cited in footnote 3 and also in an essay, "Tenure and Collective Bargaining," that appeared in the 1971 AAHE yearbook, *New Teaching, New Learning: Current Issues in Higher Education 1971* (San Francisco: Jossey-Bass, 1971).

opinions that may offend influential persons on the campus and off must be recognized as an essential right; without it, scholarship becomes pointless.

Tenure in a sense merely wraps up academic freedom and job security in one neat package, but it does so in a way that provides little chance for redress when the tenured individual fails to live up to his academic responsibilities. Apologists for the system challenge this contention, claiming that abuses of tenure could be readily dealt with if administrators would just put themselves to a little trouble about the matter. So it may be in an ideal world. But as a veteran of forty years in the academic ranks, from freshman to professor, I subscribe to Nat Hentoff's view that tenure protects against everything but "death, retirement, or assassinating a member of the board of trustees." In practice, routine incompetence and neglect are no threat to the security of the tenured. The system lacks accountability, and hence it is left free to damage the interests of students, hamper the careers of scholars beyond the pale, and tarnish the image of the university.

To say that tenure is obsolete implies that it once functioned more effectively than it does now. The idea that those accepted as members of the guild should hold their positions for life goes back to the medieval origins of the universities. American universities adopted the practice of tenure at an early stage, and the principles governing tenure were first codified by the American Association of University Professors in 1915. At that time even the largest universities were small by present-day standards. Teaching was the primary enterprise, and research proceeded at a leisurely pace. The external pressures and external money sources that are so distracting now were unheard of then. The university of 1915 was still a small and relatively homogeneous community in which everyday contacts could provide the feedback that kept the system in balance.

The modern multiversity by contrast lacks the sense of community and unity of purpose that once governed educational institutions. Even within the core of the institution, the faculty of arts and sciences, diversity increases as members develop different perceptions of their roles in a rapidly changing society. Loyalties are divided as the pecuniotropic sense sniffs out what pays off, and the whole enterprise is warped by the increasing rewards of gamesmanship and smart public relations. In this situation interpersonal relations no longer provide the kind of feedback that might keep the institution aimed at such appropriate goals as the teaching of students.

According to present rules, a decision on tenure must be made before an assistant professor reaches the end of his sixth year of teaching. If his colleagues have considered his record conscientiously and fairly, there is a good expectation that the man they recommend will continue to carry on significant scholarly work in his own special area, that he will teach effectively and not evade his responsibilities as a teacher, and that he will assume his share of "community service" jobs. In return, the young professor expects to be immune from arbitrary dismissal, even though he may pursue inquiries and advocate views not generally approved or accepted. The modal age at which tenure is granted being about thirty-two years, this period of immunity is likely to cover about thirty-five years.

At this point we have to confront the discrepancies between the theory and practice of tenure. The theory, as promulgated by the AAUP, says that a person may lose tenure for gross incompetence, gross neglect, moral turpitude, or conviction for treason. (It is interesting that simple unqualified incompetence and neglect are not reasons for interrupting a thirty-five-year guarantee of employment.) Let us take a hypothetical case of a man who manages to clear the tenure hurdle at thirty-three. Fifteen years later his scholarly work has dwindled into trivia or nothingness, his teaching has become dull and stereotyped, his community service has faded away because he fails to take any interest in it. What are the chances that this man will lose his tenure? The records indicate that the chances are all but nonexistent. Merely failing to measure up to any or all of the responsibilities that tenure should carry with it is no cause for losing tenure. Our hypothetical sluggard will continue to be employed; and if he does nothing else, he will continue to teach. The students will have to bear it somehow.

Certainly tenure can be lost for what is recognized as adequate cause. A recent well-publicized case at Stanford University is an instructive example. H. Bruce Franklin is said to be the first tenured professor to be dismissed at Stanford in seventy years. The action against him was in no way related to his teaching or scholarly attainments. Even by going back seventy years, we do not find any case of gross incompetence or gross neglect surfacing at Stanford; the turn-of-the-century action appears to have involved a man who, rather prematurely, advocated public ownership of railroads.

In a period when public confidence in universities sinks as costs rise, when students are dissatisfied and young scholars are frustrated by the shrinking job market, a system lacking effective accountability is indeed obsolete. The frequent attacks on the tenure system in recent years are a danger signal that ought to be heeded. If the values of the past are to be conserved, we will have to get rid of the obsession that the tenured professoriate must be a law unto itself. Some accommodation has to be made. Possible alternatives are to replace tenure with renewable contracts or to acquiesce in a system of collective bargaining. The latter, though it is already serving the interests of the untenured majorities in a number of large universities, is not well suited to an enterprise in which people need to function as individuals. I feel that contracts offer the more feasible, as well as the more desirable, solution.

Although this is neither the time nor the place to propose a new plan of academic employment in detail, it may be useful to consider some guidelines. The distinction between tenured and nontenured faculty should be abolished. The present probationary period might be replaced by a series of short contracts, of perhaps three years, followed by longer contracts, possibly of seven years. Each seven-year contract would include a sabbatical year, which in case of nonrenewal might facilitate the search or preparation for new employment. Since faculty people are not always equally strong in teaching and research, I like Paul Woodring's suggestion that each faculty member should have the option, at the end of each contract period, of having his performance evaluated as a whole or primarily in terms of his teaching or his research.

No one who has had a front seat at the faculty follies for as long as I have would underestimate the difficulty of adopting a sound evaluation system and putting it into action. But if we can make the hard choice, as we are now required to do, between thirty-five years' employment and nothing, we can find the means to deal with periodic review as well. In part the job will be much the same as the tenured decision now. But I think two new considerations should be added, one concerning the professor's relation to his department, the other his impact on his students.

When a young man is granted tenure, it is because, among other reasons, his area of expertise fills a need of his department. Obviously the scholar himself must be the judge of the direction in which his work will go; but tenure can be interpreted as a license to abandon the area of specialty for something more attractive, whether the change is in the general interest or not. Thus we have such extravagances as a department recommending for tenure a third specialist in a minor though important field—because the first two had lost interest in the field. Some people might call this practice academic freedom; but when a similar activity is indulged in by other enterprises we sometimes label it "featherbedding." A contract of limited duration would require each professor to face up honestly to the problem of doing the job he was hired to do or of seeking a new post for which his altered interests fit him.

Another reason for granting tenure is that the candidate is presumably a competent teacher. This is in fact the aspect of his qualifications about which his senior colleagues are likely to be least well informed and sometimes not very deeply concerned. The major weakness of the tenure system is the extent to which it ignores the interests of students. Indeed, discussions about tenure often go on without reference to students at all. For example, in an article on tenure by Fritz Machlup[2] the word *student* is not used even once. To the long-term inhabitants of the campus students may be only "birds of passage," but the brief passage is significant for each student (and expensive for his family). I strongly believe that the decision to renew faculty contracts should be based in part on student evaluations. The entering freshman ought to know that throughout his college career he will be expected to pass on the work of his teachers. If students are persuaded that their evaluations will be taken into serious account, rather than merely serving as a means for blowing off steam, I am confident that they will do their job conscientiously and well.

Replacing tenure by renewable contracts would admittedly lessen the security of many faculty appointments. If such a system were put into effective operation, some people would be cut off before retirement age. Providing suitable compensation in these cases

[2] F. Machlup, "Tenure." *Encyclopedia of Education.* New York: Macmillan, 1971.

is a problem that would have to be solved if a contract system were to become acceptable; a means of financing early retirement would also facilitate acceptance of a new system. But I feel that the magnitude of this problem is often exaggerated by people who seem to assume that under a system of contracts dismissals would be commonplace. On the contrary, it is likely that the knowledge that one's performance would be reviewed at intervals would in itself take care of much of the slackness that must now be tolerated.

The contention that abolition of tenure would adversely affect faculty morale is another argument that is often overemphasized. For those in the probationary period the change might be beneficial, for these people would no longer have to look forward to the traumatic decision between everything and nothing—a decision that, in difficult cases, is sometimes made with unintentional caprice. Those beyond the present probationary period would of course lose the support of the structure which, in the words of Harvard's University Committee on Governance, "by freeing its members from other pressures and anxieties often allows the spirit and imagination of even the seemingly desiccated to soar." This notion seems to contradict the evidence that throughout human history the greatest creative achievements have been the work of untenured minds, but I will not press this point. Instead, I simply offer my own testimony, as a member of the sex that rarely gets an even break at Harvard or elsewhere, that a stiff dose of insecurity may be remarkably stimulating.

But what of academic freedom? Though tenure may be challenged on other grounds, it is widely regarded as indispensable because it guards the freedom of each scholar to think independently and to express his opinions without fear of reprisal. In today's climate the end of a contract period would no doubt be seized on in some cases as a means of ridding the campus of an able teacher and scholar who advocated views unpopular with higher authorities on and off the campus. The renewal procedures would have to be hedged about with guarantees of academic due process similar to those that now exist. It would be important to establish that the renewal of a seven-year contract would be *earned* by satisfactory service, not merely given, as is true of the granting of tenure today, for reasons that are neither defined nor definable. Van Alstyne expresses the indeterminacy of the criteria for tenure rather nicely, pointing out that the probationer has a period of six years in which to prove his excellence, "assuming . . . that the institution does not in the meantime find others who it thinks may show greater promise or otherwise better meet its needs than he."[3]

Amid the clamor that we must retain tenure to protect academic freedom, a rude question goes almost unasked: academic freedom for whom? Not for blacks, certainly. Not for women. I assert that tenure has been a significant item among the procedures that have kept the faculties of colleges and universities in this country overwhelmingly white and male—and altogether complacent about the situation. Is it not curious that the protection of tenure frees a man to see what is wrong everywhere except in the place where he might do something about it? More than thirty-five years have passed since Eleanor Roosevelt forcibly directed public attention to the magnitude of discrimination against Negroes. What white faculty was moved to effective action to begin to prepare blacks for scholarly careers? With the feminist agitation that led to the Nineteenth Amendment more than a half century behind us, our universities have been willing to grant Ph.D.s to women in considerable numbers; but how many male professors have challenged the practices that close the privileged ranks of the tenured professoriate to their own female students? The changes that have recently begun to occur we owe to the militancy of blacks and to the vocal dissatisfaction of women, plus a strong assist from the federal government.

In saying these things I am not contradicting my earlier assertion that academic freedom is not obsolete. What is worn out is the view that the protection of tenure assures society that the faculties of its educational institutions will be made up of free minds, independent in thought and courageous in advocacy. On the contrary, the system has produced a squirearchy unquestioningly content to perpetuate its own limitations. Abolishing tenure is not going to cure everything that is wrong on our campuses, much less elsewhere. But I think it is a step toward a more open and a more altruistic society.

[3] W. Van Alstyne, "Tenure: A Summary, Explanation, and 'Defense.'" *AAUP Bulletin,* 1971, *57,* 331.

PART FOUR

Breaking Time-Space
Patterns

If, for a moment, we stand away and look objectively at our standard pattern for awarding degrees, we discover that it is rather peculiar. We have developed ingenious schemes for accrediting schooling but no adequate means for judging a person's education. The standard certification pattern in present use is completely bound up with class meetings and course enrollments, with credits and points and grades. Yet, more often than not, these mechanisms prevent, rather than facilitate, learning.

One of the worst aspects of the system, unfortunately, is that these certification patterns discourage young people from attempting to master a field of knowledge or a set of skills on their own. But even when a student manages to achieve such a goal in spite of the system—when he has filed petitions and obtained special signatures—the achievement, except under unusual circumstances, goes unrecognized and unrewarded.

No wonder, then, that during the past decade there has been much agitation for the development of new patterns for certification and for educational programs that exist outside the regular higher education establishment. A number of new and exciting programs have appeared, both for college-age students and for mature adults. Jane Lichtman, in her chapter, "Free Universities," describes some of these programs—how and when they were organized, how they differ from standard degree programs, and what impact they have had on curricular innovation in the standard programs.

The necessity for breaking the time and space barriers that have hindered educational progress is discussed by Morris Keeton in "Dilemmas in Accrediting Off-Campus Learning" and by Stephen Bailey in "Flexible Time-Space Programs: A Plea for Caution." But these authors insist that certain problems must be solved before we can adopt these new learning modes, and they pinpoint some of the problems.

The subject is complex, with many facets. Arland Christ-Janer, in "Credit by Examination," and Samuel Gould, in "Less Talk, More Action," examine the educational potential of the external degree. Christ-Janer suggests alternate routes to what he calls the traditional academic model and demonstrates how the external degree concept might free educators from many unnecessary fetters. Gould, exploring in a wide context, spells out the advantages of the development and institutionalization of the external degree for colleges and universities.

The five essays of Part Four, then, propose, each from within its own perspective, how educators can liberate themselves and their students from the conventional time-space patterns that now govern campus lives.

JOSEPH AXELROD

13

Dilemmas in Accrediting Off-Campus Learning

Morris Keeton

The effort to give due recognition to learning achieved away from campus is important in its own right. It can make possible some services in higher education that cannot be accomplished on campus and other services that are less well done on campus than off. But this effort is also important in the effects it can have on the ways we accredit learning on campus.

On-campus crediting has been done in seriously defective ways. In responsible crediting, the award of credit will signal learning gains of defined types, and the methods used to determine what credit is awarded will be valid and reliable. In this sense present practices in academic accountability leave much to be desired. Most "grading" and reporting of credit awards rest on poorly defined or unstated objectives and on measures that have poor reliability and validity. We have managed, on campus, to avoid directly confronting the causes of these unsound practices, but we are not so easily satisfied when off-campus learning is in question. The consequent press for valid and reliable methods in making those awards may help us with the larger problem of on-campus crediting.

The problems of facilitating greater academic accountability are not all internal to the evaluating and reporting processes, however. External obstacles abound. The worst of them turn around two things: the attempt of local faculty or of state and regional accreditors to restrict the list of valid educational aims to those which have previously been in use and in the best odor; and the habit of insisting on old tests of what is good even while employing the rhetoric of accepting new objectives.

To make sure that my meaning is understood, let me say briefly in what sense I use the terms *validity* and *reliability*. By a valid measure or method, I mean one that does in fact measure the thing it is intended to measure. By a reliable one I mean a measure or method that yields the same finding when applied on different occasions to the same or equivalent things to be measured. Let me illustrate.

A quarter of a century ago I took part in a twenty-college study to create better ways of assessing learning. I was on a team which developed some new tests of performance in critical thinking. But what is critical thinking? We made a list of dozens of component skills that form elements of critical thinking on different occasions. We could not create adequate tests for all of them, so we selected a limited list of skills that both seemed important and seemed within our means to measure. We then took these objectives one by one, invented items to use in testing a subject's skill, and tried the items out on particular subjects. In testing, for example, whether a student could correctly infer whether a given conclusion followed deductively from given premises, we found that some test items were often answered correctly by students who got the answer for the wrong reason. The item was thus not a valid one, for what it tested as often as not was skill in getting the answer rather than in getting it by a correct method of reasoning.

Subsequently I was involved in an experiment with some fifteen faculty members in which we all shared the objective of improving the student's performance in critical thinking skills. In all cases this objective had one of the highest priorities. In only two of the fifteen cases did the instructors succeed in generating a measurably significant degree of gain in critical thinking skills; yet the course grades awarded reflected the usual distribution of As, Bs, and so on. No one was really disturbed about the grade awards. If, however, it should emerge that someone were giving off-campus credit in so demonstrably fraudulent a way, I would expect an uproar.

A reliable measure, I am saying, gives close to the same reading on the same thing measured when the measurement is repeated. This does not mean that the measurement must be mechanical or simple. For example, I once had classes which were trying to improve their writing of critical essays. We identified some thirteen characteristics that would typify the best essays. The weighting of scores on the thirteen different factors could not be given a mechanistic formulation. Yet after training a group of reader-graders, we were able to get reliabilities of over .80 on the correlations of overall scores on the whole essay by two or more readers of the same essay.

How, then, can improved academic accountability be achieved in accrediting off-campus learning? Let me address this question by talking about how to tackle different obstacles to getting more valid and more reliable measuring of learning in off-campus situations and getting these methods accepted and recognized by those who determine publicly acceptable credentialing.

First, we must broaden the list of objectives acceptable for credit as higher education. We have hailed the CLEP tests as a breakthrough toward enabling students to gain recognition for learning without doing it in regular college courses. The CLEP tests, however, are essentially abstractions from very traditional liberal arts and disciplinary objectives. If anything, their availability widens the service gap between those for whom those objectives are appropriate and those who need different kinds of postsecondary education. Let me resort to illustration to make my point.

Edward Miller, at thirty-seven, is weight-lifting champion

of Minnesota. He has been champion of several state and federal penitentiaries in the West and the Midwest, having introduced the sport in some of these places while in residence. Most of his life from age nine to age twenty-seven was spent inside prisons. Today he works as a counselor at a prison near Minneapolis. He is seeking insight into both his own life and the revolutions that are convulsing our world. The kinds of things measured on most of the CLEP tests give no measure of the learning he has already achieved or of that he most needs. (It is not, by the way, his weight-lifting skills for which he seeks or needs credit.) It is also not, for the most part, vocational or technical training that he needs, though he is on the way toward becoming some kind of professional in the prison counseling and rehabilitation field. A set of standardized tests of any kind is probably inappropriate, first because such tests begin from objectives that either just miss or do not remotely connect with the aims appropriate to his further education, or because the form of such test fails to enable him to show what he knows and can do. Such tests are neither valid nor reliable for his purpose. What is more likely to work is a panel of people of different competences who by observing his work and interviewing him about his ideas and his questions can discern what he has learned and how rapidly he is gaining in understanding.

If we were to take seriously the concept that higher education should liberate men from the limitations of their earlier ignorance, prejudices, cultural and family backgrounds, and preoccupations, Miller's program of study is much more appropriate for a baccalaureate than that of the great majority of undergraduate students resident on college campuses today. Yet our accrediting practices are such that the burden of proof is on him, not them.

The way to broaden the list of objectives acceptable for credit in higher education, I think, is not to wait for consensus in educational meetings but to start using our own colleges' authority to accredit as a vehicle for legitimating the work of people like Edward Miller. In defending our credentials, in turn, we will force accrediting associations and state and professional bodies to broaden their own objectives. In many cases they want to do so anyway and are hanging back because of the attacks they anticipate from our professional associations.

Second, we must be able to cope with unusual student backgrounds and competences. In deciding what to give credit for, we are used to giving paper-and-pencil tests and assigning essays, reports, or theses. If a student enters who lacks writing skills, not to speak of oral communication skills, we direct him first to brush up those skills, and only then do we think of him as competent to think on the deeper and more complex issues of thought and life. This attitude of ours, however, is manifestly wrong. Again I illustrate.

Many years ago I had an opportunity to take an administrative post in Germany for the American Friends Service Committee. I had qualified in German for the language requirement for the bachelor's degree, and I had passed the Harvard University test for a Ph.D.-level reading knowledge of German. I had even used the language in research on my dissertation. But I could not pass the time of day in German nor grasp another person's meaning in the normal flow of the simplest conversation. Fortunately Harry Steinhauer, a scholar's scholar in comparative languages and literature, was willing to coach me. His recipe was to discuss in German with three of us faculty members the most puzzling philosophical and political questions in the simplest of linguistic forms. If he had prescribed that I first master German listening and speaking skills and then take up questions worthy of challenging my wit, I would have found the prescription impractical and stultifying.

In New York City today The Teachers Inc. has developed a program for paraprofessionals in teaching, with students drawn from the communities they are to serve. Many of these students are in their late twenties or thirties but still at entrance could not pass a strong college test of English writing and reading skills. Yet almost without exception, they are more astute in political and human relations, in child behavior and in family life, both in their talk about these things and in their behavior, than most of our college seniors. They are, by present standards, at early high school level in the traditional academic tool subjects and at college senior level in certain disciplines and especially in complex interdisciplinary areas. Since some of them lack English skills, they also lack the professional jargon on which we normally build advanced discussion and writing of complex interdisciplinary studies. How then can they be taught or credentialed? Essentially in the same way in which Harry Steinhauer taught me, for he used not my large English vocabulary and facility but my halting and limited German as the vehicle that had to be raised to the level of functioning which would serve the level of apprehension and reflection I brought to my studies.

To cope with unusual student backgrounds and competences in off-campus studies, then, we must adjust our attitudes as teachers and administrators to the actual student needs with which we deal. Again, this is best done, I think, not by resolutions but by setting up situations in which the task has to be done.

Third, we must learn to cope with atypical learning resources and with the absence of conventional feedback on learning achieved. Goshen College recently asked a panel of expert accreditors to examine its studies abroad. They found the program one of the best available. But they noted the dearth of access in an under-developed country to the usual kinds of library services. Yet students were trying to write conventional research papers. In fact, they were in the midst of ideal conditions for original data-taking and for applying the best that is known in research method to original questions and problems. The examiners recommended that they cease trying to do the usual undergraduate research papers, which could only be done in a second-best way, and start using their firsthand experience as the resource for an intellectually more challenging task—the field phase of original research.

Typically, students studying abroad or using other forms of experience abroad cannot bring back to the home college the usual array of grades on the usual array of subjects listed in their home catalogs as appropriate for the bachelor's degree. The university abroad is attuned to an entirely different set of objectives and priorities, and its ways of accrediting are not aimed to fit American college patterns. It is true that accommodating professors or universities or examining boards can be induced to send back something resembling our transcripts. But the whole game of doing so is an invalid and unreliable enterprise. It would be much more appropriate to reconsider what objectives are appropriate for students in those settings and to enlarge what we recognize as higher education to include these aims. Then we should ask further what valid and reliable means can be devised for assessing the learning on those objectives and for verifying the results.

This observation applies far more broadly than just to experience abroad. As interest in work-study and in so-called experiential learning grows, we ought to recognize the need and the opportunity to choose afresh where we will direct our efforts and how to monitor the quality of the endeavors. We have graduated far too many seniors who are facile with words but insensitive to meanings and to people. The opportunity to use jobs and other environments as learning laboratories is an unprecedented boon, but only if we do not go on trying to use CLEP tests and AGREs to find out how good the boon is. Again let me illustrate.

In response to a citizen association, which students helped to organize, the developer of Columbia, Maryland, a new town, allocated funds to inventory the natural resources of a five hundred-acre stream valley running through the town site. To do the inventory the students had to have professional supervisors, to learn how to inventory birds, land mammals, water quality, and vegetation, and to learn how to assemble, integrate, and interpret these diverse forms of data. Since they hoped that the natural resources would be saved but knew that some human uses would be a necessary trade-off for this preservation, they also had to study the potential impact of increasing population and of different alternative uses of the natural area for recreation, education, and real estate development. And finally they had to cope with the problem of persuading the public and public officials to heed the recommendations. All the basic work for this project took place within some six months and in the context of a field center without any substantial library of its own, most particularly without the kind of technical library required for this project.

For purposes of accrediting, two types of problem arise with such a project. How can we measure what was learned? And how can we get the external accrediting authorities to continue legitimation for work done without permanent library, faculty, or classrooms? In power to motivate students to learn, in the level of energy evoked, in the intensity of intellectual application during the work, I have rarely seen the equal of this project. But only if "the accreditors," both within the campuses and within the external accrediting bodies, ditch their old rules and use their own good sense and judgment will any kind of reasonable response be made to these new opportunities in off-campus learning.

Fourth, we must acknowledge alien philosophical outlooks on learning. The toughest problem I have encountered in accrediting off-campus studies has to do with accepting into the faculty people who seem consciously or unconsciously to indoctrinate students in a perspective which the present faculty thinks erroneous. A sequel is the problem of accepting the curricula which these new faculty devise and which set the issues for study and the methods of study in ways the usual faculty believe will produce wrong or short-sighted outcomes. Since the whole environment of learning, and not just what goes on in classes, has a profound effect on what is learned, this concern extends to a situation in which an authoritarian style of administration is used or in which a life style is practiced which discourages individuals who would practice a different life style. I suspect this concern enters into the reluctance of many faculty to let doctors, attorneys, government employees, and other varieties of practitioner act as bona fide faculty, even on campus, but particularly in settings where the regular faculty cannot keep tabs on what is occurring and control the result by their own counterinfluence.

Many faculty members deny that they teach values or elicit a value-defined outlook on life. Yet all campuses are cultures in miniature, and their design is also a design for indoctrination. The thing that disturbs us about these "alien" philosophies and outlooks, whether they be what we have known as "ideologies" or as "professional orientation" (as in social work professions, for example) is that we disapprove of them or disagree with them. We are willing to be open-minded about all the details but not about these most comprehensive and most critical values.

The greatest obstacle to the progress we need in accrediting off-campus learning is our own ideas and habits about what is good practice. I include in *us* student expectations, faculty standards, administrative priorities, and external accrediting standards. If any of you get into the position, as I have recently had to be, of defending your institution's credentials while it goes about trying to extend the frontiers of opportunity in off-campus learning, you will constantly encounter these forces. For example, the students of the established home campus will worry about the reputation being created away from campus by students who use the honored name of the mother institution to gain sanction for their crazy ventures. The faculty may fear, and possibly correctly, that the institution does not know how to manage these ventures well, that it is draining off leadership and other resources in trying to do them and thereby weakening the mother campus, and that the things being recorded for credit out there are not what the faculty intended when they granted permission for independent study and for student-initiated courses. The administrators will try to go on doing business as usual in their financial aid practices, in their admissions procedures, in their handling of financial transactions, and in their practices surrounding the granting of credits and transcripts. The state and regional accreditors will have a hard time figuring out how they can even consider accrediting these experiments, much less how the off-campus activities can possibly meet the standards for facilities, faculty, library, time in class, capital in the bank, and syllabi and course descriptions telling in advance just how learning is going to occur and what will be learned. This last perhaps is most revealing of the dilemmas of accrediting off-campus learning. The very heart of learning is not mere memorization but a process in which unexpected things emerge. To define excellence in learning as having the most detailed syllabi describing how learning will occur and what will be learned is the very antithesis of what higher education should be. Yet this is where we are today.

Where we ought to be is far different: we ought to be considering new definitions of liberal education and hence of our degrees. We should be looking for settings and mixes of students and faculty and tasks for learning which are better related than are present options to both present students and new ones. We ought to be inventing methods of evaluation and crediting that are valid and reliable in relation to these people and these rethought objectives of higher education.

If the movement toward off-campus learning can force us out into the unknown where something genuinely novel can be discovered and where the study of a problem requires the invention of a new approach to its solution, we will at the same time be forced to invent improved ways of identifying and appraising learning, wherever it occurs. With any gain we make in those tasks, we ought also to attack the obstacles to improving the service of higher education to those for whom the ideal arena for learning is not on campus but outside its current walls.

One of the key opportunities that off-campus learning opens up is the opportunity to give students genuine exposure to conflicting outlooks, opposing philosophies, different styles of life, and different priorities for human effort. In theory the very definition of higher education includes the commitment to critical inquiry about anything and everything, but especially about the most important things. Therefore, in theory, we should welcome with open arms the possibility of exposing students to other cultures than that of our own campus. In fact, however, we are hurt and threatened by having our very life priorities and perspective doubted and by the possibility that we might have to face a world which has been fundamentally changed with the assistance of our own teaching institutions. Until the holders of the power to give and withhold accreditation can be brought to permit a polycultural definition of the accreditable, the colleges that venture upon truly polycultural education, at home or away, will be risking their own credentials. This very risk is one I think should be taken by those who see the point and have the position to influence their colleges to see and heed it.

❧ 14 ❧

Free Universities

Jane Lichtman

In 1964 at Berkeley, California, students embroiled in the Free Speech Movement created the first free university on the steps of Sproul Hall. They called their creation FUB—the Free University of Berkeley. One year later, January 1966, and fifty miles away, graduate students at Stanford University announced the birth of a new type of university to provide the impetus for change[1] in the American educational establishment, the Free University of Palo Alto (later changed to Midpeninsula Free University). After these West Coast beginnings, free universities began to leapfrog across the nation. Six months later there were two more free universities: FUNY—the Free University of New York—started in a Fourteenth Street warehouse, and the Experimental College at

[1] "Free University of Palo Alto." Brochure of courses. Palo Alto, California, January 1966.

149

San Francisco State College initiated its first courses to create a "counter environment for freedom" *within* the gates of its huge parent. It was the first of the free universities to be established by a student body organization and to receive the support of the administration.

Since 1965, in every state of the nation, free universities have spread like local brush fires. In March 1972 there were about 150 free universities operating. Most of these were started in the late sixties. (Their average was 2.6 years in January 1972.)[2] The youngest of them—the Free University Knoxville, Southwest Illinois Learning Cooperative, and Epimetheus in Michigan—first offered courses and discussion groups in January 1972. The oldest, the Free University of Berkeley, started in December 1964. Thousands of students had gathered on the Sproul Hall steps during the Free Speech Movement. They were angry, frustrated, and feeling impotent. Sit-ins and surrounding police cars might gain publicity, but in the long run, many of them were convinced, their lives in the university would be changed little by these actions. One afternoon, as they were sitting on the steps, someone suggested that they secede from the university and create another university, a "free university." The new university could be a lot like the plaza, a place for dialogue and open forums, a place of intense emotions as well as dispassionate inquiry, a place of greetings, meetings, movement, gathering, love, fights, life. That circus-like atmosphere could be the curriculum of the new university. The whimsical and the serious would have equal hearings. This new university would be the marketplace for ideas of everyone in Berkeley. Almost immediately, the Free University of Berkeley moved off campus to continue and to grow outside the University of California.

Since then, other free universities have developed during equally volatile times. In the aftermath of the Kent State killings and the announcement of the movement of U. S. forces into Cambodia in spring 1970, several free universities were produced.

May 1970, Albuquerque, New Mexico: At the University of New Mexico, national guardsmen with bayonets raised confronted angry and confused mobs of students. Danger to lives and property

---

[2] J. Lichtman, *FUD* (*Free University Directory*). Washington, D.C.: American Association for Higher Education, 1972.

was conceivable and imminent. It could go either way: "In the world behind my eyes I see a hazy picture of a volcano with two vents: one is creativeness and one is destructiveness," says Sylvia Ashton-Warner describing an angry child.[3] In order to save the child, Ashton-Warner hands him a ball of clay. In order to save the University of New Mexico, tensions had to be released, and, if remotely possible, in creative and productive ways. Suddenly the idea of a new university, Amistad (Friendship) University, circulated. Its purpose would be to "discuss, study and act upon those problems and concerns of our society that normally are not covered in the university curriculum." The catalog explained that "our guiding principle is that education, learning, cannot be strait-jacketed into fifty-minute lectures or bulky textbooks, and it cannot be measured by competitive grades, quizzes, and diplomas."[4] After two days, 1500 people enrolled in 80 discussion groups. At the end of the first week, the new university was one-fifth the size of the old university.[5] This creative fashioning of an acceptable alternative to destruction eased the University of New Mexico out of a very difficult situation.

May 1970, Bowling Green, Ohio: At the same time, the State University in Bowling Green was similarly polarized. "Business as usual" was unacceptable, but the only alternative seemed to be no business—the student strike. During this time, all segments of the university worked together to form a New University, designed to "allow a respite from routine so that significant action can be taken by those students who feel committed to working immediately and intensely for a better understanding of the problems and a chance to help diminish them by whatever means seem feasible, legal, and sensible. In the end, the goal of the New University is action in the contemporary world."[6] All told, 3600 people enrolled in 133 new courses during the month of May.[7]

[3] S. Ashton-Warner, *Spinster: The Story of a Teacher of Maori Children.* New York: Simon and Schuster, 1958.

[4] "Amistad: The Free University." First brochure of courses. Albuquerque, New Mexico: May–June 1970.

[5] "Position Report No. 1." Albuquerque, New Mexico, Summer 1970.

[6] "Goals and Purposes of the New University." Bowling Green, Ohio, May 1970.

[7] Interview with Carol Sloman at Bowling Green State University, March 1971.

These free universities serve to channel aggression away from the universities into some avenues which are seen by the students and faculty as responsive to the deficiencies of normal university learning. They are steam valves, protections from explosions. But as products, they are different from the culture out of which they arise. The new environment is characterized by confrontation, joint inquiry, active participation, and open community involvement.

They also have a longer-term impact on the university. Some courses started in these free universities—Humanizing the University, History and Goals of Women's Liberation, History of Peace, Ecology and the University—continue as university credit courses after the free university passes. New curricular interdisciplinary programs start off-campus and end up as part of the regular curriculum. Honors programs stressing independent study only for the most capable students are broadened to include a greater cross section of the university. New courses are no longer so remote from the students' interests and daily lives. Modified grading patterns—pass/fail, satisfactory/unsatisfactory, pass/no pass—are partial outcomes of some explosive free universities. More important, the sense of urgency, the involvement in structuring an intimate learning experience is new for many students. The rhetoric of the academic scholar and the educational reformer merge at times like these. Personal involvement in intellectual inquiry and research has never before been so meaningful to many of the participants. A teacher-student relationship of responsiveness and interaction, as well as joint inquiry, emerges. Once this intensity has been experienced, it is hard to forget. Both faculty and students say that this involvement does not remain only within the free university; it is sought elsewhere too.

Most free universities do not start during crises, however. They evolve slowly. Many develop as student educational activities out of the Dean of Students' Office. They are characterized by drug seminars, ecology-action programs and projects, birth control counseling, education seminars, election-year political forums, encounter and sensitivity groups, workshops in crafts (macrame, upholstering, tie dyeing), groups in the arts (life drawing, theatre troupes, creative writing), training in daily needs (auto repair, law for the common man, electricity), and sports, such as football, rocketry, frisbee—which has been a credit course in at least one regular university—akido, judo, yoga, and penny-pitching. The free university in these instances is a supplement to the classroom, not too different from a university's other student-initiated extracurricular activities.

Other free universities which are university-centered focus on changing the curriculum of the college, rather than supplementing it. The Experimental College at San Francisco State College is perhaps the best example. It started in the spring of 1965 with two noncredit freshman seminars which were student-run and intended to get students to think critically about their education. (Today, these are called Dis-Orientation sessions at other universities, to distinguish them from the more common Freshman Orientations.) Throughout its first years, the Experimental College was intended to be rigorously academic, yet to activate students with a knowledge of social and political problems. What was experimental, however, was not the new courses, but that the impetus came from the students rather than from the faculty.

The idea is that students ought to take responsibility for their own education. The assertion is that you can start learning anywhere, as long as you really care about the problem you tackle and how well you tackle it. The method is one which asks you to learn how you learn, so you can set the highest conceptual standards of accomplishment for yourself. The assumption is that you are capable of making an open-ended contract with yourself to do some learning, and capable of playing a major role in evaluating your own performance. The claim is that if people, students, faculty, and administrators work with each other in these ways, the finest quality education will occur.[8]

By the spring of 1966, twenty-two courses for 350 students were arranged. Seventeen faculty members sponsored Experimental College credit courses; 66 students got credit for these courses.[9] One year after its inception, seventy-five experimental courses were included in the curriculum.[10] Robert Smith, who later became presi-

[8] "Experimental College, Fall 1966." Catalog of courses. San Francisco.

[9] "Experimental College, Fall 1967." Catalog of courses. San Francisco.

[10] Terry Lunsford, "Educational Innovations in Response to Student Activism: Developments at Berkeley and San Francisco State College." In *Innovation in Higher Education, Proceedings of a Conference Sponsored by the University of the State of New York, June 18–20, 1967.* Washington, D.C.: ERIC Clearinghouse.

dent at San Francisco State, wrote that "the successes of the student college would contrast with the failings of the faculty college."[11] John Summerskill, president of San Francisco State during the first year of the Experimental College, said that "it would have been better if the faculty had created an experimental unit at the college as a place to try out new ideas, new ways of presenting material, new concepts for integrating rational, emotional, and sensory experience. But the faculty did not take the leadership, so the students did."[12] Faculty members in 1971 recalled that the Experimental College encouraged them to try new things in their regular college classes.

Introducing the universities to new ideas is, perhaps, the most important function of free universities. They acclimatize universities and colleges to unpracticed, disregarded areas and ideas. For a while, these are considered "nonacademic," "radical," "irresponsible," "not of scholarly worthiness," and so on. But their presence in the vicinity of the university builds tolerance, allowing the community to embody them later. Black studies, astrology, and encounter groups are some examples of topics that started first in the free university and were later adapted to the university. On many campuses, there is a causal connection between the free university and the establishment, in the regular program, of independent study options, learning contracts, schools without walls, experimenting units (such as New College at the University of Alabama), January terms and 4–1–4 programs, campuses in the community and campuses in the dormitories, and programs connecting scholarship with active service.

A look at the free university curricula foretells future regular college and university adaptations. Some 1971 free university courses which will, in the next few years, be offered increasingly in the university curricula are: yoga (which is already offered for credit in ROTC quads, dormitory lounges, and philosophy classrooms), science fiction, comic books (perhaps the art in superhero comix, or how to make comedy, or why the comics hold such fascination). Everyone will be liberated. There will be studies and

[11] R. Smith, R. Axen, and D. Pentony, *By Any Means Necessary.* San Francisco: Jossey-Bass, 1970.
[12] J. Summerskill, *President Seven.* New York: World Publishing, 1971.

groups in women's, men's, kids', gay, black, Chicano, Puerto Rican, and "average" liberation. There will be liberation through drugs (alcohol and aspirin included) and liberation through the mind (yoga, Krishna consciousness, and Jesus freaks). Interdisciplinary courses such as Music as Poetry and the Novel and the Film will be common. Practical law, consumer research, and how to get a divorce will be offered to undergraduates. Larger facilities will be built for the larger enrollments in the arts and crafts: life drawing, theatre troupes and productions, painting classes. Business courses will include popular classes for the small businessman—on mini-businesses, cooperatives, different economic systems such as barter-ing, and maybe even on how to panhandle (creatively) or how to get a foundation grant. Departments of education will concentrate more on changing standard teacher-student relationships, on open classrooms and no classrooms, rather than training their students to teach as their own teachers did. More students will learn how to farm the land and grow vegetables with more understanding. The family—nuclear and extended—will be increasingly highlighted. Contemporary music—underground, rock, electric, bluegrass—will be taken by more and more students. Soon, users of Ma Bell will be able to take courses in telephone tunes. Traditional physical education will not be as popular as rock climbing, mountain climb-ing, judo, yoga, akido, and backpacking. Students will be increas-ingly concerned with structures and architecture—how the square, monochromatic classroom with separate places for separate individ-uals influences learning. Domes will be built, classrooms and halls will change color and contrast, and classrooms as such may go out of existence altogether. Encounter and sensitivity will reach every department's graduate and undergraduate curriculum as well as the professions. A curriculum study committee of the Association of American Law Schools recently proposed major changes in law training, one of which was the alteration of teaching methods, in-cluding the introduction of "human relations training" instead of the traditional "torts, contracts, and property titles."[13] Instead of black-white encounters, there will continue to be student-faculty encounters, psychodrama, sociodrama, and even sexadrama. Lead-ership training may give way to training for cooperation (Con-sciousness III generation upcoming). Mysticism, witchcraft, as-

[13] *Chronicle of Higher Education,* January 3, 1972.

trology, ESP, the occult, and eastern religions will become common university courses. ("In 1971 there are ten times as many students taking astrology as astrophysics," laments Yale physicist, D. Allan Bromley.)[14] There will also be increasing enrollments in courses on Western religions. Even now, students are getting credit for winemaking, witchcraft, barn dismantling, puppetry, nuts and bolts repairing, and jug, jook, washboard and skiffle band music. There will be a theology of the counter-culture and an ecology of the culture. Courses in the environment will persist and will concentrate on the local—the Greening of Indianapolis, Marine Preservation: San Francisco Bay, and perhaps a new one—Chicago Street Cleaning, Chinese Style. Some faculty members will find it hard to understand students who are interested in Jimi Hendrix, Khalil Gibran, Restroom Graffiti, Hobbitlore, the media, and comic books, rather than the traditional "scholarly, learned disciplines." The *Chicago Sun Times, True Confessions, Reader's Digest, Life,* and *Better Homes and Gardens* will take their places beside the more frequently mentioned periodicals such as *Time, Newsweek, Psychology Today,* and *The Public Interest.* The most used journals will be those with the most pictures and the shortest articles. In December 1971, for example, the six most popular books at Utah State University were *The Last Whole Earth Catalog,* Colin Fletcher's *The Complete Walker, The Greening of America, Future Shock,* and *I've Got to Talk to Somebody, God.* A little spicy, "relevant" philosophy was also up there in the form of the *Khalil Gibran Diary.*[15] Rather than studying the manners and morals of remote people, sociology courses will investigate the manners and morals of their own participants: swingers and wife-swappers, pleasure-seekers, and contemporary American nonthinkers. In addition to Thomas Jefferson and Thoreau, other notables such as Al Capp, Walt Disney, John Wayne, Tarzan, and maybe Annette Funicello will be given equal time.

At this point, I would like to comment briefly on my personal feelings about this rapid movement toward instant gratification and impulse stimulation. Somehow I strangely feel apart from this comic-book, pleasure-dome–seeking, surface-perceptual culture.

[14] *Time Magazine,* January 3, 1972.
[15] *Chronicle of Higher Education,* December 6, 1971.

It sometimes seems so plastic—colorful, pretty, changeable, disposable. Personal attitudes of some youth toward one another are often so very simple, warm, and accepting; but too often anguish, self-despair, loneliness, impotence, and an existential maze confront this TV-raised generation. It is a generation used to things that work instantaneously; if they do not, they are thrown out for equally remote new ones, or they are fixed by someone else: the TV repairman for the mechanical box and the psychiatrist or artificial stimulant for the head. But those do not work either. Youth sage Paul Goodman says about these critical youth: "I see them with the Christmas astronauts, flying toward the moon and looking back at an old house, and therefore it makes no difference if they litter it with beer cans."[16] With similar analogies, the free universities are the cosmic wildernesses, the symbolic statues of liberty, calling for the tired, the poor, the humbled, those wanting to escape in order to be free. America, the vast place for individual and societal growth, is no longer fertile. Physical emigration becomes less feasible daily. Mental emigration sometimes works for a short time, but the furious retreat to spiritual truth and worship is a personal faith that is not an alternative for an entire civilization. Too often, the free universities experience an inability to make decisions, to develop long-range plans, to maintain values, and to create something which will be meaningful. This lack of depth, of historical consciousness, of commitment, of deeply believed values, of internal strength is most frightening not to those actually participating but to their peer group. Some members of the peer group become frightened and grope with blind faith for the "old culture." *The New York Times* reports a revival of songs and dances from the fifties among college students. The *Times* writer speculates that its cause is a turn away from the turbulence of today's society to the nostalgia of childhood.[17] But the alternative, the "other culture," is equally devoid of meaning. Where do they go from here?

Not only will courses and the nature of learning change, the institutions and clientele will become more diverse. First, there will be more people participating: an increase from 8.5 million stu-

[16] P. Goodman, *New Reformation, Notes of a Neolithic Conservative.* New York: Random House, 1969.
[17] *The New York Times,* May 15, 1972.

dents in 1970 to 17.4 million by the year 2000.[18] Second, there will be more local learning centers, perhaps called Guerrilla Universities. They will be part of neighborhoods where people live rather than academic enclaves. Courses will be taught by volunteers: the retired, the professional, and the professor. Classes will take place in factories, offices, homes, community centers. All will enter and leave at will, as they now do for sports events and the actual learning will be self-evaluated. The resources for learning will be free to all who cannot pay. They will be not only institutions of traditional education but individual and community advocates; needs for legal and paralegal services and training, consumer protection, economic development, medical services (preventive medicine, nutrition, "barefoot doctors," community medicine) will be met. Courses will be deemphasized in this new university in favor of increased use of existing community resources—the schools, local museums, adult and YMCA education, community agencies, churches, and, most of all, resources of individual neighbors. These advocates will contract with local universities for credit or attach themselves to a regional or national accreditation service.

Currently, for example, the Office of Economic Opportunity is helping to fund the Vermont Regional Community College Commission. An outgrowth of a state educational needs study, its purposes are to take education to those individuals who are "consistently priced out of education" and to use existing facilities and resources.[19] The Commission has arranged with the governing board of the state colleges for college credit through the existing state college system. Facilities currently used are a local library, an area high school, a gas station, a Congregational church, and a trailer park. The joint program is also developing high school diploma programs for school dropouts. Offices for information are in churches, high schools, chambers of commerce, and "over Dunhams of Main Street."

Neighborhood resource networks are starting, with the purpose of connecting all who want to learn with access to available

---

[18] Carnegie Commission on Higher Education, *New Students and New Places.* New York: McGraw-Hill, 1971.

[19] Letter from John Turner, December 8, 1971, Brattleboro, Vermont.

resources. Primarily, they were suggested by Ivan Illich,[20] and people around the nation are starting these "free learning exchanges" where people meet others to exchange something "worth knowing." The Free Learning Exchange in New York City explains: "As we turn our lives more and more over to the care of specialists, it becomes harder to share our insights even with our own families. Our society has an abundance of communications and information systems. Unfortunately, a basic need is still not being met. We have many periodicals to give us the same information, such as what movie is playing at what theater, but there has yet been no service which could tell us which of our neighbors might be interested in discussing that movie."[21] Tutoring in reading could be exchanged for an auto tune-up. Lessons on how to repair plumbing might be exchanged for a good meal or use of the laundry machines. The possibilities are vast.

These networks and guerrilla universities will not be limited to areas of dense population. There will be more traveling buses designed to bring the resources for learning to rural areas. The National Student Association's ELF bus, a traveling resource van, was intended to help design local learning programs, to stimulate people, and then leave for other areas. That bus is now broken down, but there are many other individuals designing similar edumobiles.

These new resources broaden the traditionally narrow ideas of an exclusively academic education designed for an elite clientele to a new conception that includes learning as a practical, necessary instrument for urban societies. What we are seeing, therefore, is not only a technological and population explosion in higher education but also a conceptual explosion.

[20] I. Illich, *Deschooling Society*. New York: Harper and Row, 1971. See also Chapter 25 in the present book.

[21] P. Knatz. From a duplicated sheet explaining and advertising the Free Learning Exchange, 1972.

15

Credit by Examination

Arland F. Christ-Janer

Twenty-five years ago President Truman's Commission on Higher Education declared that the time had come to make higher education equally available to all. The pressures within American society which created universal secondary education—individual, family, corporate, societal—are today moving us inevitably in the direction of universal higher postsecondary education. Current enrollment reports, reflecting the demand for universal higher education, indicate that more than half of the eligible population is enrolled in colleges and universities, and that by the year 2000, 75 to 90 per cent of the eligible population will be enrolled in higher education. Today the public generally believes that higher education is essential and desirable and that some form of postsecondary education is a right, not merely a privilege.

At the crux of the issue of making postsecondary education

available to all is the distinction between universal higher education and full opportunity for access to higher education: the goal is not that everyone should necessarily attend college, but rather that an opportunity to engage in postsecondary educational opportunities be provided for all who wish to attend, are capable of attending, and can benefit from attendance. If we are truly concerned with higher education's social responsibilities, we must see to it that educational opportunities are related to the needs of society and of individual students and are available in a form and under conditions that are likely to attract students. Further, inequities in educational opportunity by ethnic group, geographic location, age, economic status, and other factors must not be allowed to inhibit educational aspirations.

Today the educational establishment is being challenged simultaneously by the need for financial retrenchment and the need to educate an ever increasing number and diversity of students. Many educators now believe that in the next decade, at least, enrollment will increase and these increases can be expected to come from students who are not now attending higher education in great numbers. It has become more evidenced, therefore, that many of the newer students now seeking higher education are a diverse group who have not been attracted to or do not fit the mold of programs presently offered. What then are the implications of the huge numbers, the vastly different mix of students seeking postsecondary education, greater public expectations, and a recognition of the inequities in the pattern of access?

One of the mistakes that higher education has made has been to try to be all things to all people with basically one model of education, essentially the traditional academic model. With respect to the seemingly rigid homogeneity of our educational offerings, it can be said that such an educational system services neither individuals nor society well if society's and individuals' needs are changing.

It seems to me, therefore, that the need is for a coordinated, efficient, and diversified system of postsecondary education which includes all levels and types of institutions and programs and which is flexible enough to make educational opportunity relevant to the educational aspirations of a variety of individuals who differ greatly in competence, interests, motivation, and aptitude. Programs and living conditions which meet the needs and life styles of new student populations—older adult students, servicemen and returning veterans, mature women, those who must work while pursuing their education, students requiring remedial instruction, and others— are being investigated as possible answers to equalizing educational opportunity.

Already, as you know, there has been a good deal of institutional response in this area. The trend is toward a development of attractive alternatives to the traditional four-year college in order to respond to the needs of "nontraditional" students. This trend is being influenced not only by those factors mentioned earlier— the recent growth of higher education, the dichotomy between the ideal and reality of equal educational opportunity, the financial strains on education, the need to match human resources and manpower needs—but also by a society which is demanding new institutional forms in education and in all fields, by a tremendous increase in learning and in the rate of learning that takes place outside the classroom, and by a style of life that requires continuous learning if one is to survive in a world which is constantly changing.

One of the alternative routes to providing opportunity and flexibility in higher education has been the establishment of the credit-by-examination concept. The oldest example of this concept is the University of London, which, since its founding in the nineteenth century, has performed only an examining function. Students not enrolled in constituent colleges or schools of the University may still earn degrees by performing successfully on examinations.

In this country many institutions have instructional programs which allow students to work independently under the supervision and guidance of faculty. In such cases most institutions will grant credit to their own students, but traditionally they have been less prone to recognize independent study which occurs outside the institution's own program. The system of American higher education, based on class attendance and the accumulation of course credits, has always emphasized and rewarded learning acquired in a formal setting more than learning acquired in nontraditional ways. With the pressures on American higher education to do more with less money, many institutions, recognizing that learning can take place in a variety of ways, are beginning to award academic credit by examination as one means of providing educational opportunity while saving money.

Though statistics on current practices among institutions nationally are not available, there is certainly a growing trend among colleges and universities to award credit by examination. In 1960 a survey of the 170 member institutions of the Association of University Evening Colleges and the National University Extension Association found that most of the 131 institutions responding to the survey had programs of advanced placement or credit by examination; 88 per cent of these granted either advanced placement or credit or both.

The role of the College Board in this area goes back to 1956 with the establishment of the Advanced Placement Program (APP). This program grew out of the feeling expressed during that time that there was a tremendous waste of academic talent resulting from students having to repeat courses in college which they essentially had completed in secondary school. APP began under the assumptions that high school teachers could teach college-level courses and that able students, taught such courses in high school, could successfully do sophomore-level work on entrance to college. In 1972 there are 4000 secondary schools participating in APP, as compared to 3,300 in 1971, and there is a long line of thousands of students who have been given advanced placement and/or credit at institutions of higher education.

The APP was and always has been designed for the traditional high school eleventh- or twelfth-grader seeking to secure recognition for college-level work and has always required the explicit commitment of schools, teachers, and students. In the AP program, the curriculum is spelled out rather precisely, the conditions under which instruction takes place are relatively well known, and there are external examinations prepared by those men and women who prepared the course. The examinations, which are only one part of the whole program, are designed to measure a more-or-less prescribed educational experience, which is a totality in that it involves the dynamics of teaching and interaction between student and teacher over a long and definitive period of time.

More recently the Board has established the College-Level Examination Program, which, by contrast, is aimed principally at the nontraditional student regardless of age, educational experience, or social or economic status. Concerned with helping individuals get credit for what they know no matter how or where or when they learned it, CLEP is designed to be of value to the unaffiliated student—usually an adult who may have acquired college-level learning and skills but in uncommon ways. CLEP has no basic syllabus and the examinations measure no prescribed body of knowledge but rather a general level of expectation in the collegiate community pitched at the level of work in subjects given in the first years of college. While someone with a variety of educational experiences might do well on the CLEP examinations, he would not be well advised to take the APP examinations without having had the total experience of APP courses in high school.

In Spring 1972 the College Board received notification from the Carnegie Corporation of a grant of $800,000 to continue the CLEP program over the next four years. This means that over a ten-year period Carnegie has supported the College-Level Examination Program in the amount of $3,100,000. The momentum the CLEP program has acquired, particularly in the last year and a half, is evident in some of the statistics related to it.

The first national monthly test administration took place in October 1967 and four candidates appeared—two in Atlanta and two in Chicago. In October 1971, 1,175 candidates came through the national test centers. A monthly comparison of the last two years shows a striking increase in usage of CLEP tests—in November 1970, for example, 425 candidates took the tests on the national basis; last year during the same month 2,605 candidates took the tests.

The increase in candidates has resulted in a change of policy by the Board which will make the test centers increasingly available to interested individuals. At the end of 1971 we had 60 established test centers; in March 1972 there were 175. By July about 225 test centers were in operation throughout the country.

Institutional participation and support has also grown considerably so that now close to one thousand institutions of higher education are participating in the program. There are striking and imaginative institutional uses practiced at such places as the University of Texas, the University of Maine, the California State Colleges, the University of Iowa, the Johns Hopkins University, the

University of Nebraska, Miami-Dade Junior College, the City University of New York, and the entire Utah system of higher education—all of them different and all of them substantial.

For example, the University of Texas has estimated that it has saved close to 1.6 million dollars in instructional costs through the use of CLEP tests. Last year the University offered all entering freshmen the opportunity to take the American Government Test, a subject examination of the College-Level Examination Program. Approximately 70 per cent of the students were awarded credit. Since many of the CLEP tests award 6 hours of credit, this meant an instructional saving of between $220 and $240 per student per six-semester-hour course.

The University of Utah reports it has saved students (and their parents) nearly a million dollars in tuition this year through CLEP. So far 1,278 students have trimmed a full year off the time required to earn a degree.

Meanwhile, the University of Maine decided to build onto and extend advanced placement opportunities offered to entering freshmen by giving the CLEP General Exams all over the state to the top half of the freshman class. The University estimates that it granted 10,500 teaching hours of credit and 87.9 degrees in credit for this class, saving a quarter of a million dollars. The project as reported received a tremendous amount of publicity and no less than sixty-six institutions of higher education have written and inquired about the project.

At the Evening College of Johns Hopkins University an independent study program based on CLEP has been initiated. Upon successful completion of the examinations, full credit in nine basic courses will be granted to students by the University, which traditionally has provided good educational opportunities for part-time students. The program was designed to encourage people engaged in the difficult process of earning a degree through part-time evening study by permitting them to earn up to thirty credits for independent work.

One of the most interesting and innovative uses of CLEP has been in the Faculty Scholars Program of Florida Atlantic University. At the undergraduate level Florida Atlantic admits only upper-division students. The faculty and administration, however, recognizing that there were also some extremely well-qualified high school graduates who would benefit by beginning their upper-division studies immediately after graduation from secondary school, developed the Faculty Scholars Program for students who have achieved competence in general education comparable to that of a junior college graduate or of a student who has completed his sophomore year in a conventional four-year college. This level of competence is determined by the CLEP General Examinations. Those students accepted are credited with the equivalent of the freshman year of college and are given the opportunity to devote their three remaining years of college study for the bachelor's degree to upper-division courses. The academic performance of the first group of Faculty Scholars gives clear evidence that this exciting and challenging program is working.

At Roosevelt University in Chicago the Bachelor of General Studies program (BGS) was started in 1966 as a special activity for adults over the age of twenty-five. Each of the 1,000 students currently registered had to show competence for college work by receiving suitable scores on all five parts of the CLEP General Examinations. An adult may graduate with as few as 72 credits as opposed to the 120 required of younger students. Recent research completed at Roosevelt revealed that grade-point averages of graduates of the BGS program were significantly higher than those of comparable students in arts and sciences.

Roosevelt's Discovery program is the University's newest and most innovative venture. Smaller than the BGS program, it is designed for those "autonomous self-learners" in the Chicago area who have rare intelligence, ability, and achievement but who do not possess an undergraduate degree. These carefully selected adults, who must score at least 600 on each of the five parts of the CLEP General Examinations, proceed to studies at the graduate level after spending essentially only one semester in the undergraduate division at Roosevelt University.

Likewise, the Advanced Management program of Michigan State University uses the General Examinations in evaluating high-level business executives in the Detroit area. Although some of the applicants have been to college, few actually have bachelor's degrees. Often their previous academic records are so outdated that they are meaningless in evaluating the academic background of the applicant. Further, such records fail to take into account the individual's personal growth through independent study, job experience, travel, and so forth.

Arrangements between the College Board and the United States Armed Forces Institute (USAFI) have long provided for the use of the CLEP General Examinations with military personnel. Under this arrangement several forms of the tests have been provided to USAFI, and a new edition is made available annually. USAFI administers these examinations to servicemen on request, under conditions that safeguard the security of the examinations. Early in 1972 a new contract was signed with USAFI which will also make CLEP Subject Examinations available to servicemen and women.

The Bootstrap Program of the University of Nebraska at Omaha is one of several examples of the use of the CLEP General Examinations with military personnel. Servicemen who want to enroll in "Operation Bootstrap" are required to take the CLEP General Examinations. An individual may earn six credits for scores at or above the twenty-fifth percentile on each of the five parts of the General Examinations, a policy in keeping with the CASE recommendation of the ACE. Approximately 800 Bootstrap students, who average about twenty credits on the General Examinations, graduate each year. They take the same courses in the Bachelor of Arts and the Bachelor of Science programs as regularly admitted younger students. In April 1969 a faculty evaluation of the university's credit-by-examination policy revealed that Bootstrap graduates completed their studies with just under a B average.

One of the most socially useful ways in which the College-Level Examinations are being used is at the Fort Leavenworth Branch of Highland Community Junior College. All the men at this military confinement facility are encouraged to continue their education. For several years the CLEP General Examinations have been given to those entering the junior college program. Credit toward the A.A. degree is awarded to those who score at or above the twenty-fifth percentile. Among the last twenty-five candidates to receive the A.A. degree, twenty-two obtained some credit in this manner; the remaining three had already had prior college work.

While some institutions are cutting back instructional costs through the use of credit by examination, other institutions are looking to CLEP and credit by examination as a source of scholarship funds. The University of Miami, for example, has a policy of granting as much as twenty-four semester hours of credit for the CLEP General Examinations plus additional credit for the Subject Examinations. These are equivalent to one-quarter of the total hours required toward most degrees at the University or a saving of $2000 in tuition plus other expenses incurred during a normal academic year. In notifying prospective students and applicants of its CLEP policy, the University cited it as equivalent to a scholarship. Letters were sent to all applicants admitted to the university, as well as notices to 52,000 National Merit Semi-Finalists and Letter of Commendation winners who responded to the initial correspondence. A CLEP brochure prepared by the University was also sent to more than 6,500 high school guidance counselors.

Credit by examination produces the same result as scholarship money to students and their parents and to colleges themselves. Not only does credit by examination have the same financial result as scholarship money for students it is also a means of recognizing a student's academic talents and advancing him more quickly toward his scholastic objectives. Credit by examination policies, it seems to me, is one way of attracting capable students, rewarding academic accomplishment, and at the same time conserving resources. Institutions struggling to find ways to achieve more results without more resources should explore the relationship of thoughtfully developed and articulated policies and practices of credit and placement by examination to practices and policies of student financial aid.

The popularity of credit by examination is best illustrated by the interest expressed by agencies and organizations of a public nature on a nationwide basis. As many of you who watch television probably know, the Board began a national public service advertising campaign in 1971 with the endorsement of the Advertising Council to bring the opportunities and benefits of credit by examination to the attention of adults. The campaign resulted in an estimated one and a half million dollars of free time and space received from the media, a response from over one hundred thousand citizens interested in the program, and the winning of the CLIO award for the best public service television announcement of the year. In February 1972 we launched a second campaign, again with the support of the Advertising Council, to inform the general public of the possibilities of CLEP.

One of the newest and most exciting developments is the movement among public libraries across the country to cooperate in the CLEP program. Since May 1970, the Serra Regional Library System of the San Diego area has been providing information to the general public on what CLEP is all about, what the examinations are like, who and where the institutions are that grant credit, and where one can register and take the examinations. The libraries have also cooperated in providing advice and guidance in the selection of books and materials for persons wishing to study for the examinations. Similar library projects are under way in the greater Miami area, in St. Louis, and in Dallas. The four CLEP library projects have demonstrated their effectiveness in reaching large numbers of adults and informing them about CLEP. Most recently the Kansas City area and Denver-Boulder area libraries have asked to participate in CLEP.

These experiments have led to an expansion of the Dallas library as a center for independent study toward achieving college-level education. Supported by funding from the National Endowment for the Humanities and the Council on Library Resources, the Independent Study Project has enlisted the cooperation and participation of Southern Methodist University in furnishing faculty guidance, study grades, reading lists, and seminar workshops for the adults in the Program. The project will last two years, beginning August 1, 1971, and concluding September 30, 1973.

The efforts to involve the public libraries in cooperative programs with CLEP stem from some early probes by the Board to determine the needs of adults who were engaged in independent learning activities and to identify the best means for meeting those needs. One of the most important conclusions reached was that in order for unaffiliated adult students to benefit fully from their studies, guidance or advisory services would have to be made available to them. Furthermore, such services were not readily available, with the exception of the reader's advisory services of the public libraries. It was decided, therefore, to encourage library systems to experiment with pilot demonstration projects which would test the feasibility of expanding present activities in continuing education for adults to include guidance services for the individual who may want help in planning a course of independent study that would result in the attainment of college credit.

The importance of CLEP, however, is its centrality to the myriad efforts now under way in higher education to increase the options for more and different students. A great many of the new and flexible approaches to delivering learning depend on the concept of credit by examination as part of their approach. The logical extension, of course, of the concept of credit by examination is the external degree program, which would rely entirely on the examination of students who cannot attend regular college classes and on the awarding of a degree externally—outside an academic institution.

In early 1971 in a speech to the membership of the College Board in New York City, Alan Pifer, president of the Carnegie Corporation, called attention to the need and prospects for degrees in this country that could be earned outside of normal institutional frameworks. Since then, enormous interest and considerable activity has occurred in the whole area of nontraditional study and external degrees. In anticipation of this growing interest, the Board and ETS, with financial support from the Carnegie Corporation, jointly established in March 1971 a Commission on Non-Traditional Study to look into all aspects of nontraditional postsecondary education including the external degree, now in operation or being planned.

In its first report, entitled "New Dimensions for the Learner —A First Look at the Prospects for Nontraditional Study," the Commission concluded that the philosophy of full opportunity in education is appropriate and should be diligently fostered and that the route of nontraditional study will be a major answer to the demand of the American people for more and for equal education beyond secondary school.

In July 1971, the Board and ETS also jointly established an Office of External Degree Plans, now directed by John Summerskill, to provide consulting and advisory services to colleges and universities and other degree-granting agencies which are broadening educational opportunity and recognizing a variety of learning experiences through external degree programs. There has been a good deal of interest and activity in the new office. People have been calling upon it regularly for help in developing their own variant models of external degree systems, including the examining and other validating techniques needed to make those systems possible. With continuing experience, we hope the Office of External Degree Plans can be a major resource in identifying institutions and agencies with common purposes, establishing communication links among them, and helping them find cooperative and supportive approaches to shared problems.

What is required for the external degree is an organized sequence of the measures of accomplishment appropriate for the evaluation of student achievement in studies that may be pursued off campus. While CLEP has the potential of becoming the backbone of any substantial external degree program in the offing, it is worth mentioning that this program is complemented in a significant way by the Undergraduate Program of ETS. Formerly known as the Institutional Testing Program of the Graduate Record Examinations, this program provides major field tests in twenty-five subjects. Added to CLEP's five General Examinations and twenty-nine Subject Examinations, plus four medical technology and Afro-American history examinations in development, this presents a large array of examinations. One of the foreseeable functions of the joint College Board-ETS Office of External Degree Plans may be to coordinate the offerings for CLEP and UP in order to help provide an examination basis for the external degree.

While other indications of accomplishment, such as papers, theses, field and laboratory work, seminars, and special individual residence requirements, might be required in external degree programs, it is my belief that external examinations are of central and prime importance and that CLEP has proved their utility, convenience, and indeed their real and potential value. CLEP now provides a working concept, a tested set of tools, and has helped to create a new educational climate in which the full execution of credit by examination can be made a reality.

❧ 16 ❧

Flexible Time-Space Programs: A Plea for Caution

Stephen K. Bailey

From one who has greeted the idea of external degrees (or, more accurately, flexible space-time higher education) with enthusiasm, and who presently is engaged in designing one model of the general concept, a somber plea for caution and restraint may seem perverse. But the real enemy of successful innovation in any field is untempered enthusiasm leading to the transience and disillusionments of faddism.

Flexible space-time higher education experiments are burgeoning across the nation like toadstools after a summer's rain.

Stimulated in 1970 particularly by Alan Pifer, president of the Carnegie Corporation, and by Ewald B. Nyquist, New York State's Commissioner of Education, buttressed by the beginnings of Britain's Open University, by the Antioch-led consortium known as the University Without Walls, and by the precursor experiments at Oklahoma, Syracuse, and Wisconsin, new flexible space-time programs have since been announced or explored by scores of institutions of higher education—including entire state higher-education systems.

It is, says Alan Pifer, an idea whose time has come. Alas, if we are not careful, it may be an idea whose time will soon have passed.

The case for adopting flexible space-time programs is impressive. If students of any age, with the help of new educational technologies and support systems, can prepare themselves academically at their own pace in a variety of off-campus as well as on-campus educative settings; if, further, they can demonstrate their academic competence through an assessment of the academic worth of life experiences and by college-normed examinations rather than by fulfilling traditional residency and class-attendance requirements, a lot of lives can obviously be freed up. A lot of academic lock steps can be broken. Furthermore, there is at least the hope that great academic economies might be achieved at the very time when, in *real politik* terms, great academic economies *must* be achieved. Other dividends may ensue: invidious and false distinctions between "classroom" and "on-the-job" learning might be eradicated —enabling bridges to be built between hard-hats and long-hairs in our society. Real equality of educational opportunity might be realized whether or not someone has had the good fortune or good breeding (or just plain money) to secure admission to a college campus. The whole community could become the college campus. Sam Gould, some years ago, projected the "communiversity."

That prudently developed flexible space-time programs might move in all of these directions I do not question. The promise is enormous. But, alas, at the bottom of this basket of shiny apples lurk some serpents. And the serpents are dangerous. Unless recognized and carefully removed or contained, the serpents can poison all such programs and can even crawl through the grass of college-campus quadrangles.

Because serpents wiggle, they are hard to count. But I think that I see four of them. The first is the serpent of academic shoddiness. There is, of course, a lot of academic shoddiness *on* campus. But unless very special precautions are taken, credit and degrees for off-campus students by examinations alone can lead to a parade of academic horribles: cram courses organized by fast-buck proprietary schools, a deadly standardization of subject matter, tutoring to the test, meretriciousness in academic performance—in general, in Wallace Sayre's words, "the triumph of technique over purpose."

Americans did not invent degrees by examination. The University of London, presaged by Napoleon, developed the idea of an examining university in 1836. In 1913, the Haldane Commission, reviewing the University of London's seventy-five years of experience with external examinations, came to the devastating conclusion that "both a detailed syllabus and an external examination are inconsistent with the true interests of university education, injurious to the students, degrading to the teachers, and ineffective for the attainment of the ends they are supposed to promote." The Commission goes on to note that to students with the ordeal of examinations hanging over them, "the degree comes first and education is a bad second. . . . They lose theoretic interest in the subjects of study and with it the freedom, the thought, the reflection, the spirit of inquiry which are the atmosphere of university work."[1]

Although one can discount some of this rhetoric as "Oxbridge" hubris, the serpent of academic shoddiness in credit programs largely based upon standard examinations is real. There are ways of protecting against some of these dangers, and, in any case, few large undergraduate colleges in this country with their giant classes and machine-graded examinations have the right to point any finger of scorn at credit by examination alone. The issue is real, however. Test-passing and education are not totally synonymous.

But, alas, this is only one horn of the dilemma. For if flexible space-time programs are allowed to cut away from traditional college-normed examinations and embark on highly experimental credit-giving for subjectively evaluated "experience" and "creative expression," academic standards may be severed from any and all recognizable moorings. In this case, again unless special pains are

---

[1] The London University Commission, 1913, Sec. 85, p. 36.

taken in designing the program, the credit or degrees earned by the external student may have no acceptability for purposes of academic transfer, graduate studies, or employment. So educational shoddiness in flexible space-time programs can take the forms of undue rigidity or undue limpness. In both cases, trouble can ensue.

The second serpent in the basket is the serpent of the garden path. Off-campus degrees will be advertised. They will seem to many an easy way—a royal road—to status. Without adequate counseling, and without adequate educational and psychological support systems, students will pay matriculation fees and then discover that learning by nontraditional methods is hard and often baffling work. Enormous expectations will be initially established followed by the thud of mass attrition. For years, many correspondence schools have come close to fraud by making exorbitant profits from the actuarially determined number of students who drop out of their sullen systems of lonely learning. Without very special devices to overcome these psychological propensities, flexible space-time programs can founder on the quicksand of unstable human motivation.

Third is the serpent of fiscal naivete—the belief that flexible space-time programs are inevitably cheaper to mount and to sustain than on-campus programs. Experience with Syracuse University's external degree in liberal studies over six years suggests that students get a better education than they do on campus but that the off-campus program is more expensive. We have not had enough experience as yet in this country to cost-account the real costs of various types of nontraditional studies. All I am saying here is that there is no obvious reason for believing that quality education can come cheaply when purveyed off campus.

Finally, there is the serpent of projected technological miracles. Of course, cassettes and videotapes and cable TV and auto-tutorial library carrels can help in the instructional process. But in education, hardware is no better than software. If millions of dollars' worth of instructional devices are already dustcovered in campus closets, what makes us believe that similar or even more sophisticated devices will save the world off campus? We are in our infancy in developing academic software suitable to the miracles of instructional hardware. This pattern will not change overnight. A lot of the existing software available for, and advertised as aids to, self-study is unbelievably shoddy. For years ahead, the most valuable learning aid will still be a little pedagogic device called a book.

In sum, serpents lurk. If the serpents are recognized and are carefully removed or contained, flexible space-time programs can be an enormous boon to all Americans seeking higher education. But the serpents are real. They must be watched with exquisite care.

❧ 17 ❧

Less Talk, More Action

Samuel B. Gould

A democratic principle that has been mouthed often enough to become a cliche has suddenly moved into the forefront of lay and academic concern. The concept of full educational opportunity is now a serious goal rather than a convenient platitude. A confluence of forces—political, social, cultural, economic, ethical—is forming relentless pressures that academic institutions cannot ignore if they intend to survive. The notion that everyone should have as much education as he can benefit from is now being examined pragmatically for the first time, and many rather neglected portions of our population are being looked at with new eyes.

Out of this practical scrutiny wells up a realization that the learning process itself, as well as what constitutes pertinent content, is still relatively unexplored. Clearly, we must rethink how we learn and what we learn, how we teach and what we teach. It is equally clear that as a society we must rethink how we live and according to what principles and priorities we shape that living.

As chairman of the Commission on Non-Traditional Study,[1] I have a special vantage point from which to view all these happenings. Even with admittedly incomplete knowledge, an amazing amount of information has poured in about how people and institutions are reacting to the new pressures, what they are doing, or what they are thinking about doing. If not too much movement and progress are evident, there is at least a host of intentions— most of them well motivated, some vaguely conceived, and a few springing out of a desire for publicity or a hope for economy or occasionally a tendency toward cupidity. Altogether they form an intriguing set of techniques that I should like to outline before discussing the dangers and possibilities these manifestations represent.

Different institutions and individuals have reacted to the great outcry for educational change in differing ways. Some are defensive, some noncommittal, some aggressive to the point of fierceness. The only characteristic they have in common is the need to react to *some* way; nobody dares to ignore what is happening whether or not he agrees with it.

One reaction in the defensive category, for example, might be labeled the "Get thee behind me, Satan," technique. This is used by institutions or individuals convinced that we already live in the best of all possible educational worlds. They cordially but firmly maintain that external degrees or any other relatively flexible opportunities for study are inevitably bound to destroy today's standards. Sometimes there are elitist overtones to their arguments and often they reveal a straightforward unwillingness to change much of what they have been doing for the past few decades. In their eyes the external degree is not only inherently different but inherently infectious and debilitating in its academic effects. A certain cogency in this argument will continue unless and until more documentation emerges to prove that their fears are unfounded.

In the noncommittal camp, there are gradations such as the "grasping at straws" or "new wine in old bottles" or, in a slightly

[1] See S. B. Gould and K. P. Cross, *Explorations in Non-Traditional Study*. San Francisco: Jossey-Bass, 1972.

more dramatic form, the "Look, Ma—I'm dancing" technique. These are all designed to show that nontraditional forms have always been used and that all we require is a strengthening of adult continuing education as presently practiced. This will solve everyone's need while keeping educational approaches safely traditional. Once again, there is some validity in this argument, since the statistics of continuing education look impressive and the achievements seem significant. The trouble is that the public wants much more than is currently offered, wants it in a different and more flexible style, and contains large segments which have thus far been served very little, if at all, by continuing education.

On the aggressive side, we have the "You name it, we have it" reaction, the "Get to the head of the line" technique, the "How do I get a piece of the action?" response, and the "On a Clear Day You Can See Forever" approach. The first of these shows an eagerness to supply whatever is requested coupled with an assertion that practically all the new forms are already in being and are regularly employed. Whether this is actually so is open to question, but the intention is clearly apparent. A much more aggressive approach is the second, which reflects the desire to be first with new and well-publicized opportunities even though most of them are comparatively untested. The danger lies in the expectations raised in the mind of the student which may not be capable of realization. New programs and structures have sometimes been announced long before detailed plans have been worked out. The third response comes from the alternative systems, proprietary or plainly commercial, who now identify a large, new market for what they have to offer. And the final reaction is that of the starry-eyed idealists who see a virtually total turning away from present educational practice and an almost limitlessly flexible set of opportunities in a nontraditional approach. In this view, we are moving toward a wonderful new world of marvelously effective educational outcomes growing out of the sheer happiness of learning and requiring no special order or rigor.

I am merely identifying these several approaches, not commenting on them critically. All together, they represent a recognition of the need for change and have drawn a great deal of public attention. Indeed, they form the material for the greatest educational debate of our time. Every conference seems to center on the actual or impending shift to the nontraditional concept. Over and over, we hear the same discussions of these new forms of education, discussions that run the gamut from enthusiasm to distaste to outright horror. And meanwhile, there is still insufficient evidence to prove the merits or limitations of any program that has actually been tried.

If we are not careful, we will *talk* the nontraditional concept to death before we have worked with it sufficiently to prove its effectiveness. We should also beware of transplanting the programs of other institutions to our own rather than creating the particular approach that suits each individual institution. If diversity has been one of the great strengths of American education in the past (and I believe it has been), then we need a fully developed diversity as we create nontraditional opportunity. This does not mean working in academic isolation; rather, institutions should share strengths and relate according to their own objectives and needs, not according to any preconceived pattern used elsewhere.

The educational debate is most productive when it starts with the aims and objectives of the institution itself and when a great part of it takes place on the single campus or on the campuses of a group of institutions close to each other physically and philosophically. And in its early stages at least, the debate should center on an understanding of what is making nontraditionalism inevitable and what attitudes toward change in general are reflected in the thinking of *all* the constituencies of a campus. Unless there is an atmosphere of receptivity leading to acceptance and willingness to move in a new direction, any nontraditional efforts will ultimately prove abortive.

Having described some general aspects of nontraditional study, I would like to present a kind of balance sheet on the external degree, which is one of the most discussed outcomes of unconventional study. Even though such a summary may be incomplete, it can recapitulate many aspects of the debate now going on. And it may draw together in one place the pros and cons, the hopes and pitfalls that such a different educational arrangement has to offer.

The danger of deterioration of standards is undoubtedly mentioned more than any other. And indeed, it should be, since it involves most people's greatest fears about the external degree. There is no doubt that adhering to quality education is difficult when the circumstances surrounding it may be so radically changed. The difficulty is not insoluble, but solutions may be complicated, slow in coming, and probably achievable only after considerable trial and error. And part of this problem concerns a definition of academic standards: are they to be the traditional ones we have always accepted without question, or do these, too, now need re-examination?

A parallel danger is the proliferation of degrees far beyond the great number already troubling many people in academic life. More than sixteen hundred different degrees are now being offered. With the move toward more unconventional approaches, this number will tend to increase. How to be assured that the degree is not debased thereby becomes a very real problem.

Another danger is that of using the external degree as a political instrument. Much has been said about the financial savings derived from this form of education. Expectations have been raised that major capital outlays will no longer be necessary and that additional economies will evolve from new types of curricula and methodology. All this is very tempting to state legislatures so hard pressed to provide funds in large amounts for so many social services in addition to education. The assumption that savings can accrue is perhaps valid also, even though it is yet unproved, provided that proper safeguards for the nature and quality of education are established. A trend is already developing in this country toward more involvement in academic decision-making by legislative committees; the new opportunities offered by the use of the external degree as a substitute for current educational practice may well serve to hasten that trend.

A very real danger rests in the expectations that are being raised in many quarters *without solidly developed program plans* to support them. Two kinds of expectations could turn out to be serious disappointments to the prospective student: first, that the external degree possibilities offered are indeed different enough from the conventional in material or in flexible arrangements to create a truly achievable academic goal; second, that what is being offered the student is more than a motley collection of largely unrelated parts not yet fashioned into a flexible but intellectually rewarding whole. The enthusiasm already generated in thousands of prospective students, particularly those beyond traditional college age, could soon evaporate and change to apathy when their expectations are not met. A relatively small number of good or excellent external degree programs might emerge, but not enough to take adequate care of the needs of hitherto unserved population segments.

The very nature of the modern external degree with its reliance on highly individualized study made possible by television, cassettes, correspondence courses, and the like causes many educators to fear the danger of academic isolation for the student. The cross-stimulation of faculty and students, the classroom or seminar inter-changes of thought among the members, the possibilities that campuses afford—these can easily be lost if the external approach is carried to an extreme. What is the appropriate mixture of personal interplay and solitude necessary to create the appropriate climate for learning? This question is still to be answered completely. And there are so many changes to be rung, so many combinations of organization and method and material that the question may never be answered to everyone's satisfaction. Still, the same danger might be cited for traditional forms of education as they are presently used in some places.

Yet another danger centers on the curricular vagueness with which the external degree can easily be surrounded. Much more has been said and written about style and forms, methods and measurements than about content. An external degree can be highly traditional in intellectual content or actually radical in its material. It can be merely a regrouping of old elements or it can be comprised of totally new ones. Thus far, there have been few attempts to define the subject matter in other than conventional terms. Yet the outcry that has echoed on our campuses has not been only about dullness and ineptitude and rigidity of forms and regulations; it has seriously questioned our intellectual assumptions and the material we use as a result of these assumptions. Is the subject matter we offer always relevant to the needs of these new groups of students? Is there an appropriate linking of the timeless and the contemporary? Is the material for one age group always suitable for another? These are still largely unexplored questions although they are constantly on everyone's lips. The external degree offered by traditional educational institutions in traditional ways may soon be rejected unless such questions are dealt with.

One of the most obvious dangers the external degree presents is its threat to the future of private colleges. If a considerable proportion of students of college age were to discover that alternative systems or patterns of higher education were more closely related to their needs than is the conventional system, and especially if they were to discover that there were financial economies as well, the private colleges would soon find themselves in even worse straits than they are today. Ironically, if the private colleges want to adapt themselves to new forms and approaches, they have the least resources with which to do so. In Great Britain, students below a certain age are ruled out of candidacy for the external degree; I doubt, however, that such a rule could be made generally effective in this country. The effect of nontraditional forms upon these institutions, therefore, may cause some major dislocations in their future development.

A final danger is that the external degree may complicate still further the important debate over what constitutes an educated person. Perhaps this is not a problem at all but a helpful development. We are all so much involved in the impedimenta of learning —the access, the measuring, the grading, the institutional structures, the financing, the governance, the bricks and mortar, the degree-granting process—that we forget the basic issue about internal or external degrees, or, indeed, any portion of what we call education. What is it all intended to achieve? What are the characteristics of an educated person, and what can a college or university or any agency or any experience contribute toward creating such a person? Are the characteristics of an educated person different now because of the changes in our society, and, if so, how do they differ from any earlier concepts? Are the objectives of the external degree different from those of other degrees, or does this degree merely represent another way of reaching the same goal? What are the desirable outcomes of *any* degree to be acquired by the student? These questions are actually more fundamental than those that preoccupy the proponents of change. The answers to them are still vague in contrast to the detailed mechanics of new programs being fashioned. Every institution and every educator will have to wrestle with such questions and answers if more than superficial solutions are to be reached.

The other side of the balance sheet—the possibilities the external degree may hold for higher education—should be set against the dangers I have been suggesting. These advantages are not inconsiderable. And as we think about them we should remember that we do so in the context of strong pressures toward educational reform.

The possibility spoken of most frequently is flexibility of form, a breaking away from earlier and more rigid requirements such as residence on campus, prescribed courses, credit hours, and the like. It allows the occasional interruption of study, the inclusion of work experience or travel or independent projects. It raises the question of judging by competence and performance as well as by the more formal or conventional tools of measurement. Flexibility encompasses the regrouping of knowledge, new interrelationships of disciplines, the use of modules or units of work rather than traditional courses, the use of presently developed electronic teaching devices such as television, radio, cassettes, computers—a great array that can be shaped and reshaped in various combinations as need or change dictates. The path to an external degree can have all or few or none of the characteristics of flexibility, but chances are it will have at least some.

Another possibility closely linked to flexibility is the added diversification of programs and structures and styles of learning that the external degree may encourage. As I said earlier, diversity has always been hailed as a great strength of higher education, and rightly so. The development of multiple approaches through the external degree and nontraditional study in general is a significant addition to that diversity. The student's options are increased in proportion to the number of program variations he can find within reach geographically or in some other way. At a time when educational opportunities are expanding for new populations and more mature age groups, added diversity of programs, structures, and methods is a necessary and desirable component.

A dramatic possibility closely linked to the external degree is the widespread adoption of the concept of individualized learning. The student-mentor relationship has always been championed as coming closer to an ideal learning pattern than does any other. But most traditional institutions, either by choice or by necessity, have moved steadily toward relatively large groupings of students, not only for instruction but for admissions selection, program choices, calendars, and other campus elements. Properly devised and practiced, the guidance of the student through the process that wins him the external degree can be a highly individualized matter. This process can deal more readily and more intelligently with the two most controlling factors in a student's success: his capability for additional learning and the strength and direction of his motivation.

The external degree, together with accompanying nontraditional forms and methods of learning, gives new strength and meaning to the philosophy of lifetime learning. This philosophy has been expounded ever since formal systems of education came into being, but it has never been fully understood or accepted. With new and broader opportunities made available to adult populations, there is at least the likelihood that education may come closer to being understood and welcomed and used as a continuing attribute of life. Whether or not the goal is to acquire a degree, more flexible approaches and more diverse offerings should encourage people to turn more often to education as part of life's enrichment.

I think it is logical to expect that the development of different patterns for the external degree will increase the possibility of more community involvement in the educational process. There is a role for other cultural and social agencies to play as an addition to the patterns of learning and hence a drawing together of the formal and informal. There are additional laboratories in which to work and new kinds of educational talent to use. One can only conjure with the thought of what new understandings, what new sympathetic attitudes and support for education, community involvement could bring about. Such involvement is very likely to happen and, with proper monitoring, can lead to beneficial results on both sides. Few institutions of learning will continue to exist much longer with high walls of aloofness and separatism surrounding them.

Coupled with the burgeoning of community involvement is the possibility of joining academic institutions and alternative systems of learning to create a shared and total process. Business, industry, the military, proprietary institutions of many types—these have unique contributions to make. Their activities are more widespread, more appealing, and stronger already than many of us realize. These systems are, indeed, competitors for the attention of the student in many real ways, and they must be reckoned with as one looks at the whole spectrum of student choice. To ignore them would be folly; to find ways to cooperate with them and to fit their particular and peculiar strengths into the student's individual need as an adjunct to what colleges and universities offer would be a much wiser course of action.

It goes almost without saying that the external degree has great possibilities for affecting the character and style and structure of the internal degree. The traditional pattern in the traditional institution is bound to feel pressures from traditional, college-age students for changes in current practices. This need not mean a weakening of the college or a loss of the sense of rigor and self-discipline in the student. It can mean instead an adaptation to a changing world within a relatively traditional framework for those who prefer a more sheltered and more highly structural educational pattern. This internal degree is a sound part of the diversity I mentioned earlier; the external degree should exert a benign and mild influence rather than create radical change.

The rising interest in the external degree and the thousands of new students of all ages and walks of life that it may attract offer a new and perhaps more positive reason for reassessing the sources, the extent, and allocation of financial support of higher education in the immediate years ahead. We have long been accustomed to certain educational support formulas and programs. It is hard for many of us to imagine others or to look kindly upon the changes that may now be necessary. Even without the impact of educational change and the rising number of clientele, higher education already is in a period of austerity that could, in some specific instances, quickly become a period of disaster. The only things certain about our financial problems are, first, that they will grow more rather than less acute during the next five years and, second, that we shall have to find ways to help ourselves much more than we are presently doing if we expect large amounts of external help as well. Patchwork efforts to stem the tide will soon prove insufficient and even abortive. What is now required is a *total* re-examination of the financial picture as it is and the exploration of many future options, no matter how unconventional, ingenious, or complicated they may seem. The external degree may be one of such options, one that could ease or somehow transfer some of the burden each institution is now carrying.

A final possibility offered by the external degree and the non-traditional approach is more fundamental to the educational process itself rather than to methods or structures or financing. An attitude may be fostered that accepts the swiftness and inevitability of change and the correspondingly changing aspirations of students, whoever and wherever they are. Basic educational objectives may well remain the same for an institution. But within those objectives and guided by them, all sorts of shiftings and adaptations will be necessary, continuously necessary, if society is to be adequately and productively served. A commitment to this kind of realization and a willingness to act on that commitment are, therefore, major factors in how successfully higher education will weather the increasing demands made on it. Life in the educational world has never been easy; it will be even more difficult from now on. But there is no occasion to feel a sense of despair or defeat when we know that the American people want more rather than less education.

The external degree is only one of the phenomena affecting the future of higher education. It can be fashioned wisely or foolishly, boldly or timidly, tentatively or with a sense of commitment. It has both dangers and possibilities, but we should remember that academic traditionalism is equally plagued and blessed. I urge, therefore, that we add more action to the current spate of talk. If we are to have an educational revolution, let us be a controlling influence within it, not controlling in the deadening or defeatist sense of the word, but in providing guarantees that intellectual quality of many sorts is still the touchstone by which we measure our educational goal. Let us use such a revolution to make education stronger —different, no doubt, but stronger—in its contribution to the growth of each individual.

PART FIVE

Curriculum and Instruction

The chapters of Part Five continue to explore the concerns expressed in Part Four, all of them having to do with the settings needed to foster education rather than mere schooling. Three additional avenues are followed in Part Five: one author describes an interdisciplinary program that provides a new way for students to synthesize what they learn; a second author describes a whole new college built on principles of organization vastly different from those of the conventional model; and two authors focus on the college professor's growth as a teacher.

George Francis, in "A Degree Program in Environmental Education," tells about an interdisciplinary degree program in environmental studies. Opponents of interdisciplinary programs usually argue that, desirable though such programs may be, they cannot flourish because they are not department based, departments normally corresponding to single disciplines. But the program Francis describes is based on its own department; hence it has prestige, budget, and support.

In "A Model for an Upper-Division Urban College," David Sweet presents a picture of the newest Minnesota postsecondary institution, Minnesota Metropolitan State College. The operational plan may appear unbelievable to many readers; the standard notions of student body, faculty, physical facilities, courses, student assessment, and degree certification have all been rejected. The plan thus illustrates many of the principles set forth in the chapters of Part Four, breaking as it does all the standard time-space barriers.

The opening and closing chapters of Part Five deal with the improvement of instruction. The central thesis of John Noonan is stated in his title: "Curricular Change: A Strategy for Improving Teaching"—a thesis imaginatively demonstrated by argument and example. John Centra, working from a theoretical framework about the evaluation of teaching, describes in "Evaluating College Teaching: The Rhetoric and the Research" a five-college study he undertook in order to test whether faculty members improve their teaching after receiving certain kinds of student feedback about their effectiveness in the classroom. The results, thus far in the analysis of the data, are negative.

On perhaps nine out of ten campuses, professors plan curricula and carry out teaching tasks in contexts that do not help them grow as educators or encourage improvement in their teaching. The chapters of Part Five suggest that creative and substantial changes in curriculum and instruction are not likely to occur without serious reassessment and rebuilding of the entire degree system. Educational change requires more from the faculty than a periodic pious document or an annual act of will.

JOSEPH AXELROD

❧ 18 ❧

Curricular Change: A Strategy for Improving Teaching

John F. Noonan

One of the forgotten truths in education is that changes in student behavior can be quickened by changes in teacher behavior. Recent attempts to reform colleges and universities by doing something to the curriculum but not to the faculty have not met the high hopes of the planners. William Arrowsmith identified the problem several years ago: "Nothing can be expected of a system in which men who have not themselves been educated presume to educate others."[1] Aristotle and Aquinas were right after all: "A

[1] W. Arrowsmith, "The Future of Teaching." In C. B. T. Lee (Ed.),

thing cannot give what it does not have," even if it does have a Ph.D. The problem, then, is discovering ways to change faculty.

One option is to hire a new faculty and fire the old. As tempting as this might be, it is both inelegant and impractical. The most fireable faculty—the untenured junior staff—are sometimes the best teachers. Besides, even if you could move people in and out of the institution, the product you are buying comes with no written guarantee. Academic credentials, as everyone by now is tired of hearing, certify professors as researchers but only rarely as educators. There are not enough Harbison Award winners to go around, and even if there were, how many colleges can afford their salaries?

Another option is to upgrade the present stock by faculty development programs like the ones described in the excellent monograph done by the Southern Regional Education Board about eight years ago. Included in that inventory were new faculty orientations, workshops, reduced teaching loads, special library collections, classroom visitations, faculty committees, and visiting lecturers. But the authors' conclusion is not consoling. "Despite the frequently expressed feeling that improvement of teaching effectiveness and professional growth are key objectives of faculty development, there is little evidence of vigorous, imaginative, and sustained efforts to facilitate such improvements or growth."[2]

Consultants, workshops, subscriptions to the *Chronicle* and to *Change Magazine* are worthy activities, but not sufficient by themselves. As a total strategy for improving the teaching talents of the faculty, this one rests on the questionable premise that the way to learn how to teach better is to read about it or listen to someone else tell how it is done. This chapter presents another option for improving teaching. It might be nicknamed the immersion method, since I advocate the somewhat unsettling position that the best thing you can do for many faculty is to plunge them into new learning-teaching environments where they must sink or swim. In other words, use the curriculum itself to alter faculty teaching behavior.

Improving College Teaching. Washington, D.C.: American Council on Education, 1967, p. 58.

[2] W. S. Miller and K. M. Wilson, *Faculty Development Procedures In Small Colleges: A Southern Survey.* Atlanta: Southern Regional Education Board Research, 1963, p. 55.

Comparatively little has been written on the effects of curricular change on faculty members. In the fall of 1971, *Liberal Education*[3] published a sketch I made of the impact of several new courses on faculty who taught them. Not a scientifically pure study by any means, the piece was based on observation, written reports, and extensive interviews with the participants. The message was clear: regardless of what was happening to students in those courses, something was happening to their professors. Reaction to the article encouraged me to test the assumption in other settings. Hence part of what I present here is based on a study in process of a cluster-college program at a medium-sized state university in Ohio. The methodology is the same, relying mainly on observation and tape-recorded, in-depth interviews with faculty.

Several course models widely adopted in recent years ought to be viewed in terms of their impact on the faculty. Without intending it, educators who have established interdisciplinary, problem-centered courses, values-oriented courses, and living-learning programs such as cluster colleges have created important catalysts for faculty development. Institutions contemplating major curricular revisions would do well to begin with a two-year transitional phase where the emphasis is on altering faculty behavior. During this period, as many faculty as possible should be encouraged to participate in courses and programs that will help them develop their teaching talents and expand their view of learning. At the end of that time, faculty and students will be in a much better position to discuss major curricular changes. The sketch I will present is not meant to be a finished blueprint. It is conjectural because it is untried. When it is tried, corrections will no doubt be required.

The idea of using the curriculum to the advantage of the faculty is hardly radical. After all, thanks to the work of Joseph Katz, Arthur Chickering, Lewis Mayhew, and many others, it is quite clear that we have taken the curriculum far more seriously than our students have. Why keep up the pretense? If students learn in spite of the courses they enroll in and not often enough because of them, why not make sure someone profits from the exercise?

Nor is the idea new. Seven years ago Wilbert McKeachie proposed it at the annual meeting of the American Council on Edu-

---

[3] J. F. Noonan, "The Impact of Curricular Change on Faculty Behavior," *Liberal Education,* 1971, *57,* 344–58.

cation. He said: "Curricula should be designed, like golf courses or bars, for pleasure—faculty pleasure. I am quite serious in asserting that a primary determinant of the effectiveness of a curriculum is its effect upon the attitudes of the teachers who are to put it into operation."[4]

The problem-centered interdisciplinary course, one of the most widely adopted course patterns recently, can stimulate faculty growth. Take, for example, a freshman course at Findlay College called Self-Understanding Through the Humanities and Fine Arts. The core problem is "man's search for identity." It involves two hundred students and five faculty each term, a student:faculty ratio of 40:1. The faculty are drawn from literature, religion, art, and music. The course has used several teaching models. The first year, for instance, the staff began by dividing the week into a combination of large general classes attended by all faculty and students, and smaller discussion sections conducted by a single instructor. The second time through, however, this approach was abandoned in favor of the high-anxiety version where each member of the staff taught all the disciplines to a fixed group of students without the benefit of general classes run by the specialist.

The first approach, assuming the teaching staff is headed by someone who is both a good teacher and a good manager of people, has the greatest potential as a strategy for faculty teaching development. In the first place, four members of the team get to watch the fifth person handle the general sessions. This may seem insignificant to some people, but how often does it happen outside this setting? If it is true that most of us model our teaching after people who taught us, this method at least enlarges the options. Secondly, it generates shop-talk sessions which are rare among college faculties. Nevitt Sanford reports on a project involving extensive interviews with more than three hundred college faculty about teaching. He found "that undergraduate teaching is not, for professors at four-year colleges and universities, a true profession. Perhaps the most vivid sign of this is the fact that such professors, when they assemble informally or formally, almost never discuss teaching; that is not

---

[4] W. J. McKeachie, "Effective Teaching: The Relevance of the Curriculum." In L. E. Dennis and J. F. Kauffman (Eds.), *The College and the Student*. Washington, D. C.: American Council on Education, 1966, p. 189.

the "shop" they talk. Nor, for that matter, do they discuss the philosophy of education."[5]

Exploiting the potential for shop-talk requires no wizardry. One way is to solicit staff responses to the teaching of the person who ran the last general session. Another is to invite the faculty to share with each other the frustrations and satisfactions of conducting the discussion sections. Such sharing provides a good opportunity to explode some of the mythology that surrounds the discussion method: that it is the students' fault when no one says anything; that the professor should be on one end of every dialogue; that discussions require no advance preparation by either the staff or the students. A course chairman who is savvy about teaching and wise in the ways of human nature can improve the odds that this course structure will make the faculty better teachers.

The second course model, where each instructor assumes full responsibility for all the disciplines as they bear on the basic problem, is the most effective way to end disciplinary nearsightedness. The first time a literature professor has to teach music or art or philosophy, that goes out the window. So, of course, does his tranquility, but no one says learning ought to be a serene process. Arthur Chickering wrote the following about students, but it applies to faculty in a setting like this: "Expressions of discomfort, signs of upset, are not necessarily negative signs. On the contrary, these signs may be evidence that developmentally fruitful encounters are occurring, that stimuli for progress are being felt."[6] Despite the cries of educational irresponsibility raised in certain quarters when anyone encourages people trained in one discipline to teach what they have not earned a Ph.D. in, any good humanities professor should be able to do this on the freshman level. As a matter of fact, there is room in the model for natural scientists, social scientists, coaches, and deans. The market on culture should not be controlled by the division of humanities.

A second type of course highly effective as a strategy for improving teaching is the values-oriented course. At Findlay it is called A Critical Analysis of Values, and in the past three years

---

[5] N. Sanford, "Academic Culture and the Teacher's Development," *Soundings,* 1971, *54,* 359.

[6] A. Chickering, *Education and Identity.* San Francisco: Jossey-Bass, 1969, p. 283.

faculty from a great many disciplines have taught one or more sections of it. Its primary function is to give seniors the opportunity and guidance to examine critically their own values. Hence, a good deal of time is spent by faculty and students asking and answering such questions as: What are values? What are my values? Where have they come from? How do mine compare with yours? What are the values of the profession I am about to enter?

Although the questions are not always immediately clear, it is evident right away that the course demands reflection from faculty and students. This is hardly a surplus commodity in our society, particularly in colleges and universities. One of the distressing discoveries Charles Silberman made in researching *Crisis in the Classroom* was how rarely educators had an intelligible answer to the question, why do you do the things that you do? A course like A Critical Analysis of Values, taught by a professor with an open and honest mind, can stimulate him to become a more reflective person. You can hardly help other people answer questions about their values if you don't do it to yourself at the same time.

During the interviews, faculty who have worked in this course regularly report becoming more aware of their own values as a result. After all, when an attractive blonde coed, responding to some demonic impulse, asks a nervous young professor if he can imagine a set of circumstances which would justify a sexual relationship with a woman not his wife, it is virtually impossible for him not to learn something about himself. A course like this is a natural setting for students to ask professors a host of important questions like: Why do you teach? Why do you teach literature? What is your philosophy of education? What is your philosophy of life? Issues of this sort are seldom going to be raised in the History of British Poetry.

In setting up courses like this and in encouraging non-philosophers to teach them, one ought to be prepared to respond to the purists who will insist that the study of values belongs to the philosophy department. Perhaps one of the reasons higher education seems sterile is our tendency to insist that a person have a Ph.D. in philosophy before we take him seriously as a philosopher. To quote Arrowsmith again, the irony of education in our times is that "we have students concerned to ask the crucial questions—identity, meaning, right and wrong, the good life—and they get in response not bread but a stone. . . . Almost without exception the response of the universities to this profound hunger for education, for compelling examples of human courage and compassionate intelligence, has been mean, parochial, uncomprehending, or cold."[7]

Since this course is really about the people who enroll in it, the professor cannot play the comfortable role of the expert. He may be an axiologist, but that is not what the course is really about. Hence, as the interviews revealed, he has little choice but to set up learning situations within which his students will feel comfortable reflecting on their own values. For someone who has done nothing but lecture, the experience will be trying but beneficial in the long run. The values-centered course is a promising way to help faculty acquire experience in student-centered learning situations.

Finally, faculty who have participated report having learned more about students as a result. With students at the center of the process, reporting on and critically analyzing their beliefs about God, education, drugs, the war, and so on, the instructor is given the opportunity to see students in a new light, where they are something more than candidates for graduate school.

In the winter of 1972 I spent many hours on the campus of one of the state universities in Ohio, interviewing faculty who are participating for the first time in a residential, interdisciplinary humanities program, or cluster college. Although this is a more expensive curricular change than the two preceding, the price is cheap when faculty benefits are calculated.

The program involves 100 students and seven faculty who study together for ten weeks. The faculty, who are from art, literature, history, music, philosophy, and drama, are working on campus with the participants from nine in the morning to late afternoon, often returning at night and on weekends to attend concerts or watch films with them. Unlike the students, who are housed together on two floors in a dormitory, the faculty do not actually live on the campus. Students receive fifteen quarter hours of credit for the program which they apply to the core requirements of their particular college. Enrollment in the cluster college was optional, and a wide range of tastes, abilities, and majors is represented among the participants.

[7] Arrowsmith, p. 61.

The most striking characteristic of the faculty interviewed was their conviction that they were themselves learning a great deal from the program. The brochure states what the cluster college program hopes to do to students, and it is clear that those same phrases apply to faculty: "To provide ways of helping students see the interrelationships among the arts, history, and philosophy; to feel themselves involved with their studies and with other people on a personal basis and especially to become aware of the basic issues of human values and human dignity."

Here are some of the things faculty report learning from the cluster college program: (1) a shedding of the exclusive discipline-oriented view of learning; (2) a willingness to try a variety of methods for assessing learning—portfolios of creative projects, autobiographies, plays, journals; (3) a conviction that they are seeing students from a new and important perspective and that students are viewing them differently. One instructor told me: "A girl wrote a poem about me yesterday. Can you imagine! She said I was her friend. This never happened to me before." (4) a growing uneasiness about the utility or validity of the conventional grading system; (5) a more complete picture of the learning process. As one professor said, "When you throw a question at a student in this program, you do it with a deeper understanding of the forces that are going to be at work in him in answering it." (6) a clearer awareness of the comfortable rut the ordinary curriculum lets you slide into; (7) reinforcement of the idea that learning takes place outside the classroom.

The cluster college is having an impact on its faculty, not because it is giving them a head full of new ideas—although there are some of those—but because it gives them an opportunity to try out ideas they already had acquired, from reading, from hearing other people talk, from students. This program gives them a chance to find out what works and what does not. It is, to put it simply, an educational laboratory, and it is altering the way these educators view learning and teaching, the way they view students, and the way they view themselves.

In the words of one member of the team: "Working closely with students has forced me to see them from a different and, I believe, more meaningful perspective. The usual professorial perspective is functional: we tend to see students in their function as students. As a consequence we endeavor to have them function as better students—to write papers, to participate in class. The emphasis is on doing. Now, however, when the perspective becomes one of seeing students as persons, we see them as they are rather than in terms of what they do."

As difficult as this concept is to verbalize, it ought to be central in an educational institution. In the words of the Hazen report: "Whether it realizes it or not, the college has a major effect upon the development of the whole human personality for the student between the ages of seventeen and twenty-five. . . . The college cannot escape the fact that it does have such an impact, that the quality of life on the campus . . . does shape the personality of its youthful charges. By the very fact that it presumes to inform the minds of the young, the college becomes involved in the development of the whole person."[8] The cluster college faculty are learning what this means. It is, incidentally, an exhausting discovery.

No experiment should be planned without an accompanying system for its evaluation. Educators who use the adjective *experimental* to describe whatever program is new at their institution do violence to the language if they neglect this step. This step is often omitted, however. During the fat fifties and sixties, when enrollments and funds were swelling, other things seemed more important to us. Now, of course, administrators everywhere are caught up in the alchemy of cost-benefit analysis. I say administrators deliberately because most faculty remain suspicious of evaluation.

I would like to suggest, however, that the suspicion decreases as the distance between the area being evaluated and the professor's area of specialization increases. Moreover, the theory concludes, once something is learned about the nature of evaluation, suspicion is decreased even further. The plain truth is that most college faculty do not know very much about evaluation, so naturally they fear the unknown.

To suggest that rigorous evaluative procedures be established from the beginning of an experimental program is not as likely to

---

[8] *The Student in Higher Education.* New Haven, Conn.: The Hazen Foundation, 1968, pp. 5–6.

quicken tensions as to suggest that the same procedures be applied to the chemistry or English departments. In fact, faculty who might ordinarily object to an interdisciplinary experimental program might soften their opposition if they suspected some way could be devised to prove the whole thing a failure a year or two hence.

A variety of benefits can be derived from evaluation. First, faculty who are not used to asking those two rare but important questions—"Is it working?" and "How can we tell?"—will learn what those questions mean. Second, someone besides the faculty in the education department will learn how to write behavioral objectives. Third, if the overall goals of the institution have a high fog index, evaluating this two-year experiment will make that painfully clear; program evaluation cannot take place in a vacuum. In Ralph Tyler's words: "The very fact that it is not possible to make an evaluation until objectives are clearly enough defined so that one can recognize the behavior to be sought means that evaluation is a powerful device for clarifying educational objectives if they have not already been clarified in the curriculum planning process."[9] Like the other steps recommended in this statement, examining institutional goals ought to have a favorable impact on the quality of teaching in the institution. Once people learn how to evaluate experimental learning programs, they just might apply what they learned to their major programs.

Nevitt Sanford has written recently of the need to liberate professors from the "academic culture" which inhibits their growth as educators. Continued growth, he claims, requires "greater awareness on the part of professors of themselves and what they do—of their philosophies, objectives, and styles of teaching; familiarity with alternative ways of attaining their objectives; and recognition of the legitimacy of being interested in students and taking satisfaction from working with them."[10] The scenario presented here should be instrumental in this campaign of liberation. In recommending it, I am not suggesting that faculty and administrators cancel their subscriptions to the *Educational Record* or try to have their names removed from the Jossey-Bass mailing list. I do not think it would be a good idea to ban consultants from the campus either. I wish

[9] R. W. Tyler, *Basic Principles of Curriculum and Instruction.* Chicago: University of Chicago, 1950, p. 80.
[10] Sanford, p. 367.

simply to suggest that we must follow our reading and study and reflection about higher education with action—if we want to improve the quality of teaching and learning on our campuses.

We ought to look closely at the curriculum and see what it is doing to the people who teach in it. We must stop viewing courses and programs as a means for changing student behavior only. Whether it is widely recognized or not, a curriculum ought to do something to faculty behavior. It ought to quicken their development, excite their curiosity, ignite their imagination. This will not happen by accident, of course. Careful planning is required. People who are interested in teaching should be placed in charge of each step of the experiment. Reduced teaching loads are needed. Too many experiments fail because the people who run them are overworked to begin with. If these key individuals are also secure persons, so much the better, because there will be times when the experiment will appear a failure.

Joseph Axelrod and his colleagues observed that "curriculum design and instructional strategy are the two sides of the same coin. . . . It is not likely, therefore, that sound or lasting curriculum change can take place on a campus where the teaching process remains static or where attitudes toward it relegate it to a private sphere—an aspect of a man's *personal* style—which is not subject to discussion."[11] Faculty who view teaching as a static process can hardly be expected to make long-range curricular plans that will make a real difference in the lives of their students. But if those same faculty can be encouraged to break the old molds, if they can be encouraged to adopt a more dynamic view of learning, is it not likely that their plans will be better? My recommendation, then, is that we design a two-year curriculum for faculty before making long-range plans for students.

[11] J. Axelrod, M. B. Freedman, W. Hatch, J. Katz, N. Sanford, *Search for Relevance: The Campus in Crisis.* San Francisco: Jossey-Bass, 1969, p. 73.

💠 19 💠

A Degree Program in Environmental Education

George Francis

💠💠💠💠💠💠💠💠💠💠

The wide range, diversity, and seriousness of situations now recognized to be environmentally significant have given considerable urgency to directing more attention to man-environment relationships as a focus of study, policy, and action.[1] This necessity is derived from the realization that the very question of survival in a habitable world has become top priority as mankind drifts rapidly

[1] See, for example, L. K. Caldwell, *Environment: A Challenge to Modern Society.* New York: Natural History Press, 1970.

into a future of great uncertainty and foreboding. The catalog of particular problems and issues leading to this conclusion is distressingly long. Essentially it comes down to a soaring world population which is increasingly urbanized, relying more and more on sophisticated technologies having awesome potentials and untoward human and environmental consequences. The much discussed "environmental crisis" is really an awareness of the accumulating consequences. They are many and insidious, not always desirable, and can be found at all levels from the global biosphere to local communities.[2]

Confronted with realizations of such magnitude and importance, postsecondary educational institutions are certainly expected to respond. At the very least some awareness is called for as part of a general education for those whose time will span the remaining decades of the twentieth century and overlap into the next. There is also a need to consider the desirability of modifying existing degree programs, establishing new ones, and in some cases orienting the resources of an entire institution toward environmental studies. Only in this way can sufficient numbers of people with the right blend of awareness, determination, and skills be made available to cope with the "environmental challenges."

The difficulties of making innovative changes in conventional universities are well recognized.[3] In the context of environmental studies these difficulties were discussed in a much-quoted article by Hare,[4] and it has even been suggested that the very organization of universities is antithetical to environmental education.[5] The all-embracing feature of "environment" is what creates the problem.

---

[2] There has been an enormous amount of writing on environmental concerns over the past few years. For global perspectives see, for example, the Report of the Study of Critical Environmental Problems (SCEP), *Man's Impact on Global Environment*. Cambridge: Massachusetts Institute of Technology Press, 1970; and G. R. Taylor, *The Doomsday Book; Can the World Survive?* Greenwich, Conn.: Fawcett, 1971.

[3] For a recent discussion see B. J. James, "Niche Defense among Learned Gentlemen: Notes on Organizational Inertia in Universities." *Human Organization* 1971, *30*(3), 223–228.

[4] F. K. Hare, "How Should We Treat Environment?" *Science,* 1970, *167,* 352–355.

[5] R. H. Hall, "University Education and the Natural Environment: Are They Compatible?" *International Journal of Environmental Studies,* 1971, *1*(2), 47–52.

Like other theme-oriented or area studies programs, environmental studies have to cut across the vertical jurisdictions of many established disciplines, but their swath is wider than most as they draw on natural sciences and various professions as well as social sciences and the creative arts.

Nevertheless, quite significant initiatives have been made by colleges and universities in North America and Europe. Many are very recent; those directly involved are just beginning to discover one another, and mutual awareness of these initiatives is still quite limited. Communications among innovators are developing rapidly, however, through conferences,[6] the establishment of organizations such as the National Association for Environmental Education, and the appearance of new journals such as *Environmental Education.*

Environmental programs may arise anywhere within an existing academic structure. The initiative may come from such disciplines as anthropology, biology, geography, or geology which routinely deal with many of the problems from their particular perspectives; from professional schools such as engineering, architecture, public health, forestry and natural resources, or urban and regional planning, all of whose graduates clearly make or influence environmental decisions; or from already broad-based programs of studies such as marine sciences, conservation, or liberal arts which can with little difficulty expand or reorient to major environmental themes.[7] Perhaps this only helps confirm one view that universities have been studying man and his environment all along and what is at issue now is how to do it more effectively.

[6] For example: Organization for Economic Cooperation and Development (OECD), Center for Education Research and Innovation, *Workshop on Environmental Education (at University Level),* University of Tours, France, April 1971; University of Toronto Institute of Environmental Sciences and Engineering, *Environmental Studies—The Role of the University,* Toronto, May 1971; S. McB. Carson, *"Environmental Studies:* The Construction of an 'A' Level Syllabus," National Foundation for Educational Research in England and Wales, 1971; International Union for the Conservation of Nature and Natural Resources (IUCN), *European Working Conference on Environmental Conservation Education,* Ruschlikon near Zurich, Switzerland, December 1971, and the (U.S.) National Association for Environmental Education, *Environmental Education: Progress and Profile,* First Annual Conference, Hot Springs, Arkansas, April 1972.

[7] For examples see "Careers 'Doing Something for the Environment.'" *Changing Times* Kiplinger Magazine, Washington, July 1970.

The aims of new environmental programs may be almost as varied as their origins. Some programs may only look to neighboring disciplines or develop "overview" courses in order to obtain a degree of environmental awareness at either undergraduate or graduate levels within otherwise traditional disciplines and professions.[8] Other programs see their role as training a variety of technical personnel needed to support government and industry commitments to "environmental quality." The more innovative may see possibilities for developing a new type of environmental profession at the graduate level while others see the use of environmental themes along with teaching and learning innovations as one way to revitalize undergraduate education, giving it a particular relevance to the contemporary world and its future.[9]

Clearly this diversity of origins and aims allows for a variety of "models" for environmental education. There are many combinations which might be developed into viable on-going programs, so that environmental education becomes as hard to define as environment itself.

Yet a consensus appears to be emerging about desirable characteristics which environmental education programs should have. Although not fully definitive or unchallengeable, they provide a starting point for distinguishing rather conventional single discipline or professional training programs, which may be labeled "environmental" but otherwise are properly identified with their own discipline or profession, from the more innovative programs which are trying to develop distinctive new approaches. Some may even go unnoticed because they prefer to be known in terms of social ecology, urban affairs, or by some designation other than "environmental." Without denying the contributions of programs retaining a disciplinary affiliation, I suggest that the more interesting models are the newer and more innovative multidisciplinary programs.[10]

[8] This seems to be the more usual situation, particularly in Europe. See, for example, U. Fornstedt, *A Short Report on Environmental Education at the Swedish Universities and Institutes of Higher Learning.* Office of the Chancellor of the Swedish Universities, March 1971; and IUCN, *Conclusions of the European Working Conference on Environmental Conservation Education,* Special Supplement to IUCN Bulletin, February 1972.

[9] See, for example, J. Fischer, "Survival U: Prospectus for a Really Relevant University." *Harper's Magazine,* September 1969.

[10] Examples of both types can be noted in the compilation made by

Prospective models might therefore be examined in terms of how they incorporate certain features thought to be desirable. For example, regardless of their orientation or particular aims, environmental education programs should stress synthesizing and integrating concepts engendering attitudes and values which strive for broad perspectives and the sense of wholeness. The frequent reference to *ecology* as the paradigm indicates this focus. It reflects a considerable hope and expectation that the new "environmental consciousness" will lead to an effective overcoming of the narrowness of viewpoints and the divisiveness resulting from excessive fragmentation of knowledge and skills into innumerable specialties.

An environmental education curriculum must be multidisciplinary in the widest sense. This emphasis is required to give scope to studies which must range over man's complex interrelations with the biophysical, socioeconomic, and man-made physical environments. A systems mode of reasoning about situations is called for and may be built into the program through the application of systems theory, the study of ecology, or by striving for new interdisciplinary concepts.[11] The curriculum must somehow relate individual disciplines with interdisciplinary ideas in some distinctive concurrent or sequential pattern within one degree program or between undergraduate and graduate degree levels.[12]

In the approach to teaching and learning most appropriate to environmental studies there is considerable agreement about the desirability of using problems and issues drawn extensively from "real world" situations and thereby unconstrained by conventional academic boundaries.[13] Closely allied is the value placed on com-

---

L. S. Jayson, *Environmental Science Centers at Institutions of Higher Education*, a survey prepared for the Subcommittee on Science, Research, and Development of the Committee on Science, and Astronautics, U.S. House of Representatives, 91st Congress, First session. Washington, D.C., December 1969.

[11] Suggested, for example, by E. M. Hafner, "Ecography: A New Scientific Discipline." *Environmental Education,* 1970, 2(2), 26–28.

[12] Some possibilities were outlined by J. Michaud and M. Paoletti, "Example of a Theoretical Model of an Interdisciplinary University Oriented Toward Environmental Problems." In OECD: *Seminar on Plurisdisciplinarity and Interdisciplinarity in Universities.* Nice, France, September 1970.

[13] J. S. Steinhart, and S. Cherniack, *The Universities and Environmental Quality—Commitment to Problem Focused Education.* A report to the

munity or other off-campus involvement as an integral part of a total program of studies; experiential learning is reaffirmed again.[14] In order to give the range of experience necessary for both a multidisciplinary approach and a problems focus, more reliance should be placed on approaches other than conventional lectures and seminars, such as team teaching, student-selected projects, and the involvement of nonacademics in the program. Unquestionably, some notion of an expanded campus is a prerequisite for an effective program of environmental education.

Organizational arrangements to assure the viability and growth of environmental programs should include a separate administrative unit within the larger institution to manage the core of the program. This unit needs to have a team of faculty of its own, be able to decide on curriculum and courses, and be able to administer the academic reward system. [15] At the same time the core team must be able to evolve useful communications and cooperation across faculty or departmental boundaries to draw on expertise throughout the university.

It would be virtually impossible for any one person to know at this stage how many environmental education programs now under way in North American and European colleges and universities exhibit these features and could be presented as instructive models. Most programs are too new, they seem to be feeling their way, and they probably are not well known outside their own institutions. Therefore I will confine myself to describing the model with which I have been involved. This program functions at the undergraduate level within an otherwise quite conventionally structured university.

In 1969, the Department of Man-Environment Studies at the University of Waterloo in Ontario began a four-year honors program leading to a Bachelor of Environmental Studies (B.E.S.) degree. The department has its own multidisciplinary faculty equivalent to eleven full-time members, some fifteen persons altogether. Their educational qualifications range over the natural sciences,

President's Environmental Quality Council. Washington, D.C.: Office of Science and Technology, September 1969.

[14] E. M. Hafner, J. M. Fowler, and C. A. Williams, *Environmental Education 1970*. New York: Scientist's Institute for Public Information, 1970.

[15] Steinhart and Cherniack.

social sciences, and fine arts. They also bring to the program a diverse array of nonuniversity but relevant experience as well as enthusiasm for working closely with others interested in problems and issues said to be environmental. By having the traditional autonomy of a university department the program is able to operate its core, experiment with methods and approach, and cooperate with faculty elsewhere in the university on the basis of equality. Current enrollment is about 140 and the steady-state projections predict 200 students for the honors program. Faculty also present courses of general interest to students from elsewhere in the university and participate in the preprofessional training of students heading into fields such as urban and regional planning and architecture.

The aims of the honors program can be formulated in terms of a process notion of education, one which lays the foundation for following a number of different roles or careers through both concurrent and subsequent study. The process encourages students to learn how to learn, find out how to find out, and generally develop these capabilities methodically with increasing sophistication and creative self-direction. These basic general skills can be carried forward, adapted, applied, and refined in many kinds of situations over a lifetime. Environmental education at the undergraduate level provides ample opportunity for developing these skills since it is not artificially constrained by conventional academic boundaries. This program does not preclude more specialized study beginning at the undergraduate level, but it has the advantage of beginning with a wide-ranging approach, thereby providing a basis for students to decide in a much more knowing way how they may wish to proceed.

Key ideas which are guiding development of the curriculum include the following. Studies are oriented around the theme of man-environment interrelationships and range over biophysical, socioeconomic, and man-made physical environments in a search for understanding the main features of these systems. A systems mode of reasoning is encouraged through teaching systems theory, decision theory, and ecology. Regular reference to a future time perspective stresses the idea that the more significant challenge is to conceive alternative possibilities for the future and so to act now to steer toward some preferred situations rather than the most likely ones. This perspective requires understanding the dynamics of social and technological change and suggests providing opportunities for students to acquire understanding and skills which would enable them to participate meaningfully in the change process. Finally, the use of real-world problems and issues helps to bound the enormous array of potential subjects under the environmental education umbrella and enables situations recognized by students to be relevant to be used as effective learning opportunities.

In terms of the actual curriculum, about half of the twenty-two full (two-semester-equivalent) courses required for a degree are stipulated, and most are in the first and second years. The intent of the required courses is to introduce in an integrated manner the wide array of problems, subjects, and perspectives and to develop some elementary skills in searching out relevant information and using it methodically. The wide range of electives can be selected from anywhere in the university and permits each student to explore and then choose a mix of subject and skill courses best suited to his own development needs and career aspirations. This program also enables students to combine environmental studies with some one discipline stream if they so wish.

The core of the curriculum is a sequence of seminar-workshop sessions which run throughout the four-year program. These provide ample opportunity for individual and small-group work on problems students select after consultation with faculty. More than any other courses these are intended to help develop the general problem-identification and problem-solving skills, provide opportunities for working with a variety of media and communication techniques, and encourage the synthesis and integration of subject matter.

A variety of means are used besides the usual lecture and seminar format. Team teaching is used extensively and frequent use is made of visitors from government, industry, and community organizations. Students have considerable latitude to select projects for investigation, including some tied closely to an activist commitment within the larger community.

A number of questions still arise from the day-to-day experience with the program. Discussions recur about the appropriate contents, desired learning processes, and the degree of faculty-imposed structure for various courses being developed. While this situation is hardly unique, the wide scope of environmental studies, drawing as it does from the physical and life sciences, the social sciences, and fine arts, requires that continued attention be paid to what may be essential rather than conventional, and how this may best be incorporated to form a coherent environmental education program. These questions raise a number of different assumptions about acceptable or effective approaches to teaching and learning, providing considerable opportunity for innovation and experimentation.

Man-environment studies, like environmental education generally, find themselves very much in the mainstream of educational concerns today. Given the rates of change now being experienced, the rapid obsolescence of specific knowledge and skills, and the serious doubts about the ability of established institutions to meet the challenges being forcefully put to them, what, in fact, should be the response when the very question of the survival of man is being raised?

A Model for an Upper-Division Urban College

David E. Sweet

Minnesota Metropolitan State College (MMSC) is a new institution. In May–June 1971 the college was authorized by the Minnesota legislature, approved by the governor, and established by the Minnesota State College Board, which appointed the president in late June. Between July 1971 and February 1972 a small group of college officers and faculty developed the plans and procedures for what Clark Kerr has termed "perhaps the most innovative institution of higher education in the United States." Since

February 1 the college has been admitting approximately fifty new students per month.

MMSC has no central campus. We use existing under- or un-utilized facilities throughout the seven-county Twin Cities metropolitan area. The college will not build or buy or steal any structures to put on four acres or forty acres or four hundred acres. Using the entire metropolitan area, we have the best facilities available in America for higher education. The college has the same kind of problems that campus-based institutions have in trying to inventory and mobilize these facilities and resources.

MMSC serves a student body that is beyond the traditional age group of seventeen to twenty-one or eighteen to twenty-two— the immediate post-high school graduate. Seventy-five per cent of MMSC's students are over twenty-five. In addition, the college is committed to provide educational opportunities for the poor, minority groups, and women. Specifically, the students whom MMSC serves are adults who have dropped out of college but who have the potential and desire to complete college degrees; adults who have acquired the equivalent of the first two years of college through work or other experiences including military service; adults who require collegiate-level retraining to meet their personal or professional goals and to cope with the technological demands of the changing economy; adults who transfer from one of the six metropolitan area junior colleges; adults who have completed post-secondary courses in area vocational-technical schools; and adults whose unique higher education needs have not been met by other institutions.

Given the foregoing target population, the college is basically an upper-level institution. This condition is in part a product of our political and educational situation. The metropolitan area includes six state-supported junior colleges and another six, largely state- and federally-supported area vocational-technical schools (in addition to several private colleges and the main branch of the University of Minnesota). In the Twin Cities metropolitan area students have many opportunities to complete the first two years of college work. We do, however, admit students who have completed the equivalent of the first two years of college. Many of our most interesting students have entered the college on this basis. By admitting students who have "the equivalent" of the first two years of college we are able to extend our program to many who might otherwise not be able to complete a degree or other educational objective in a reasonable time period. Potential students can offer anything which makes sense to them to achieve this equivalency admission: formal or informal educational experiences, work, hobbies, reading, innate genius. In establishing criteria and processes for evaluating these students we have been grateful for cooperation from the state junior colleges, which have also entered into discussions with us looking toward the establishment of a cooperative lower-division program modeled on our upper-division program and aimed especially at meeting the needs of equivalency applicants who do not qualify for admission to MMSC.

It seems to us that many of our older students have the same characteristics, problems, and hang-ups that students who are eighteen or nineteen or twenty-one have. The reason for this is not clear. Perhaps it is because these hang-ups are all too human and characteristic of all of us. Or perhaps it's a case of arrested development: if you did not go to college when you were eighteen, you did not get over these hang-ups. Finally, I should note that we are convinced that the educational format outlined below will work with students of all types and ages. The populations of immediate concern to us emerged in large part because they are not well-served by existing institutions, but we are confident that our basic procedures and policies have much broader applicability.

From the very beginning we postulated that the college would have a small core of full-time professional educators—for the most part conventionally trained, degreed, experienced academicians —at the heart of the enterprise. We have surrounded this core with a large number—in a ratio of approximately ten to one—of what we call "community faculty members." These are persons drawn from the Twin Cities metropolitan area who have a demonstrated capacity not only to learn but also to apply what they know. We seek such persons in order that they may share their insights, experiences, and backgrounds with our students.

Without any systematic effort on our part, nearly five hundred individuals applied for membership on the community faculty. Approximately three hundred have now completed our orientation program. When community faculty members complete this orientation program, they are placed in a "bank" of talent, time, and resources from which students may draw. Community faculty members are reimbursed as they complete their work with students. Pay is at the standard rate of full-time faculty members. This is not a way, in other words, to cut instructional costs but a way of expanding the faculty resources available to students.

MMSC is explicitly "pro-city." We believe that much of American higher education and, indeed, much of higher education around the world is anti-city. Institutions have often been deliberately located outside the city in small towns because of the corrupting influence of large urban areas on those involved in higher education. Even where educational institutions have been located physically in the city, they often have chosen to isolate themselves from the life of the people in the city. MMSC is committed to the proposition that our students should come out of their experience with us as individuals who can live, work, and play effectively in the city as masters of their lives and not servants of impersonal (or personal) forces over which they have no control.

In addition to being pro-city and having a different kind of campus, faculty, and student, MMSC is also characterized by two commitments which we believe make its education significantly different. Students are admitted to the college and awarded degrees on the basis of demonstrated competence and not on the basis of credit hours accumulated or courses taken. By *competence* the college means the combination of skill or knowledge (including both mental and motor skills), understanding, and attitudes (or values).

It may help to conceptualize this term *competence* by means of the game of golf. An individual may have the motor skill to raise a thin stick with a bulge on the end of it and swing it down accurately to hit a white pellet, driving the pellet far and straight down a grassy field. He has that motor skill. We do not call him a golfer, however, unless he understands what he is doing and why he is doing it. But even when he has the skill and understanding, one does not say that he is a competent golfer unless he has what is called, for lack of a better term, a "golfer's attitude." If he thinks using a thin stick to hit a small white pellet straight and far down that grassy field is a great waste of time, he is not likely to be a golfer.

We apply the analogy to education. An individual is only

educated when he has the right skill or knowledge, the right understanding, and the right values or attitudes. At MMSC we contend students need competence in five broad areas. The first of these is competence in basic learning and communication. Individuals need competence in reading, speaking, writing, listening, computation, and so on. Each one needs the skills, understanding, and attitudes that relate to communication, to both the projection and the reception of communications.

The second area of competence we call "civic involvement." By this we do not mean simply political competence, although that is included. This area also encompasses the economic, the social, the religious, the cultural. We recognize the fact that most men live in communities. Decisions which are made by these communities affect individuals, shape them. If we are to assist individuals in becoming self-governing, we must teach them to participate effectively in the community, in making community decisions of all kinds. This involvement requires skill. It requires understanding. Above all, it requires an attitude that says that participation in decision-making is worthwhile. One of the failures of contemporary education is that we have often taught the skills and the understanding while convincing students (often implicitly) that it was okay to cop-out by not using what they had been taught.

MMSC is essentially a liberal arts institution. But we believe that nobody should be granted a baccalaureate degree who does not have competence in a vocation, a profession, or career. We believe this because no major social system in the twentieth century—and probably no future society—will grant individuals a share of the goods and services produced unless in some way they contribute to the production or distribution of those goods and services. In other words, individuals must be able to function in the economic marketplace—whether it is a capitalistic, a socialistic, or some other marketplace. And that is what we expect of our graduates. They may be auto mechanics, plumbers, doctors, lawyers, or teachers.

Some students come to us not yet committed to any vocation. Others have a commitment to learning "for its own sake." We try to help this latter group understand that while it is possible for some people to function in contemporary America by pursuing learning for its own sake, most are not able to do so. We try to help them appreciate the realities of the world as they will find it and to equip them to function in that world. To us this means that they must be able to obtain and hold a job.

One of the values of our community faculty is that its members often illustrate in their lives a commitment to "pure" learning coupled with a capacity for fitting into the contemporary economy. For this reason we do not seek community faculty members exclusively for what they can contribute to the vocational competence of our students. We also seek community faculty members who have other kinds of learning to share.

The two broad fields in which we are prepared to assist students in obtaining professional training are administration (both public- and private-sector administration) and in the various fields which fall under the heading of "human services"—social work, rehabilitation services, educational services, and (eventually) health services. Many of our students, of course, come to us having already met the requirement for a demonstrated vocational competence. Some of these seek to use the college to upgrade their status on the job, but others are more interested in the other competence areas.

Our fourth competence area embraces leisure and recreation. We recognize that in addition to being learners and communicators, citizens, and workers, men and women must in some sense "recreate" themselves. Individuals must learn to use wisely what is becoming—at least in America—an increased amount of leisure time. One of the great tragedies of education is that it has tended to turn out people who are fundamentally spectators and not participants. We help our students acquire what we refer to as lifetime leisure competencies. More than this, we try to provide them with an attitude and an understanding which will enable them to develop a continually evolving set of such skills.

The fifth area is called personal growth and assessment or maturation. This area of competence is usually acquired outside the formal curriculum. At MMSC we aim for a capacity to look at yourself, set goals for yourself, modify the goals in the light of changed circumstances, and relate to other people as human beings. Competence includes the capacity to confront with a minimum of trauma the fact that people die, lose jobs, have children— all unexpectedly. It includes, if you will, knowledge of what it means to be human and a capacity to act on that knowledge.

Competence-based education is one of two basic commitments of the college. The second is a conviction that each student must be the principal architect of his own education. The five areas outlined above are not, in our view, the equivalent of traditional college requirements. The college does ask each student to confront these competence areas in a dialogue with his faculty adviser. If in the course of such confrontation the student concludes that this concept of education is not pertinent to his goals and aspirations, then with the active support of his adviser he works out an educational plan which *is* pertinent and meaningful. The college faculty and staff believe passionately that it is indeed the *student's* education; it is his or her life, and he or she must bear responsibility for it. (My intent in the following is to include both sexes, although I will revert to the traditional masculine pronouns for simplicity.) In the final analysis, therefore, the student's educational program must conform to his life goals and situation as he determines them with the help of an adviser, other faculty members, and even other students. If a student looks at this structure of education and says that it is not for him, we can respond to him. We can let him redesign education, but we insist he confront this structure. He must say why it is not for him and why it is not going to work.

We see this structure as a model. We feel it is important for people to have models to knock apart, reassemble, or ignore. Just to present individuals with a great vacuum, telling them they can do anything they want to, confronts them with a situation with which most are incapable of coping. But when confronted with something to out-argue, to out-fight, then most can begin to set objectives for themselves. At MMSC we expect that education will be a cooperative process between the students and the faculty. That process exists at most institutions of higher education most of the time. Students and faculty work together making mutual adjustments that accommodate the needs of both. But everyone knows that in a crunch in most educational institutions the institution (the faculty) wins and not the student.

While we do not want an individual's education to become a confrontation between him and the faculty (individually or collectively), occasionally it does. But mechanisms exist at MMSC for the individual student to win. We want him to encounter a system, to encounter a structure. But when he does, when he makes his case, finally, if he says that what he wants to do is study comic books and get a degree, he will be able to study comic books and he will be able to get a degree for it. The difference—the reason this is not a cop-out or a sell-out as far as we are concerned—is that we would not try to dress up such a program with a fancy academic title. We would just call it "a study of comic books." We would not record the study of comic books as a program in contemporary literature or folklore or sociology, or the counterculture, or in any other way try to confuse anyone who looks at the student's record. I make this point not because I expect anyone to take advantage of this offer, but because I want to illustrate and emphasize the fact that there is no reason for anybody to try to manipulate the MMSC educational system. In this system, no student needs to sign up for courses in which he already knows almost everything that is going to be taught and therefore does not have to make an effort to learn very much. Many take that path through institutions of higher education, threading their way through, learning as little as possible, studying in fields where they already are masters so that they are free to do things that interest them more. What we are saying is: You decide what interests you the most; then we will build your education around it. You do not need to play games with us, therefore, and we do not need to play games with you. In this sense the MMSC student is principal architect of his own education.

Before outlining the educational format—the process with which we attempt to implement the educational structure outlined above—let me mention two other characteristics of the college. First, our governance structure. I think we have created an educational anarchy. For that reason, I am not sure we need a governance structure, but we are constructing one. The basic institution is the College Assembly, made up of all faculty members and other employees, all students, and all members of a group which we call the College Association. This latter group includes anyone who wants to assist the college through various kinds of contributions. The Assembly meets regularly once each three months. All matters of concern to the college come before it, including the making of college regulations and policies. Gradually the college is developing a committee system to supplement the work of the Assembly. This structure is elaborated in an interim constitution, on the grounds that we need to play with our governance system for three or four years before settling into permanent forms.

We actively recruit women and minority group members for positions of major responsibility even when—on the basis of conventional credentialing—they may not be the "most qualified." I justify this policy in part by noting the oft-reported proposition that many presidents of the United States were elevated to that office despite the grave doubts about them in the minds of their fellow citizens. Even as such men have risen to the office when given the opportunity, I am convinced that a similar rising to the occasion will occur if we open up college leadership posts to women and minorities. Recently we appointed a woman as treasurer and chief administrative services officer of the college, a rank equivalent to a vice-presidency. Women also hold such positions as dean of learning development (one of the three principal academic deanships), executive director of the Academic Affairs Council, Executive Assistant to the president, director of information services, and assistant treasurer. The other two principal academic affairs officers, at a level just below the vice-president, are black. (The Vice-president himself is an "inactive" Indian.) Each of the individuals whom we have employed is superbly qualified and doing an outstanding job. To make these appointments we had to be willing to look beyond conventional performance records. In short, we had to rise above our prejudices.

How does a student actually obtain an education at MMSC? He begins with admission. We have deliberately kept the admission forms simple. We seek only basic information (name, address, and so on) and whether or not the individual has completed two years of college or is seeking admission on an equivalency basis. As part of the admissions process, the student is interviewed and is provided with basic written materials about the college and its educational processes. Students may be admitted at any time. Currently we are admitting students at the rate of about fifty a month. This summer we will increase it to sixty a month. In a year we expect to increase it to a hundred per month. At the present time, all students who have completed two years of college (or more) are admitted. Those applying for an equivalency admission must complete additional forms and participate in a "self-assessment" process which includes in-depth interviews.

Once the student has been admitted, he joins an orientation group led by a full-time faculty member. Each group includes approximately ten students and meets for three weeks. They discuss the educational process at MMSC, engage in self-assessment in light of our competence areas, critique one another's self-evaluation, and bring together validating evidence to support their self-assessment. At the conclusion of the orientation period, most students are assigned to a permanent faculty adviser. Any student who in the judgment of his orientation leader has an inadequate understanding of MMSC will be assigned to another orientation group. During this orientation phase individual students may decide to drop out.

Students are assigned to permanent faculty advisers on the basis of mutual interests. Advisers may bring groups of their advisees together—in fact, this is encouraged, for students need the reinforcement of peer-group experiences. During the early phase of the relationship between adviser and advisee, the student concentrates on developing what we are now calling an "educational pact." Such a pact will include a statement of the student's educational goals or objectives, a statement of the strategies he intends to use to achieve these goals, and a statement of the assessment techniques and procedures which the college will utilize to determine that the student has in fact fulfilled the terms of his educational pact. The time needed to develop a pact varies. Some students are finding that they want to engage in individual or group teaching-learning situations with other faculty members before they complete the process of designing their educational program. This is permitted.

Once an educational pact has been drawn up and reviewed by the faculty adviser, it must also be reviewed by two students and two faculty members, each of whom must provide a written appraisal of the document. This latter appraisal becomes part of the document. All educational pacts are also reviewed by an officer designated by the vice-president. This review officer makes certain that each document is understandable and that all documents are consistent with any pertinent college policies or regulations. After an educational pact has been approved for a student, he can modify it, such modifications being subject to the same kind of review as was the original document.

Following the drafting of an educational pact, the student proceeds to implement the teaching-learning strategies contained in it. These may include both individual and group activities. The college emphasizes teaching students to use their work, their homes, and and their leisure-time activities as learning situations. In addition, the college seeks to bring into play the vast array of learning opportunities available in a major metropolitan area. The college relies heavily on internships, apprenticeships, participation in community projects, and other forms of "learning-by-doing." MMSC staff members arrange for such student experiences, usually under the supervision of community faculty members, which combine the practical with the theoretical.

In establishing this educational program, we have emphasized repeatedly that the college will not sponsor all the learning situations which students will use. We emphasize that it is not important where, when, how, or from whom students learn. What is important is that they learn. The college does sponsor certain kinds of learning activities. Some of these may look fairly conventional, in that they will be group activities conducted by faculty members. A basic characteristic of them, however, is that none is required in order to complete a degree. No record is kept of attendance or grades. The time frame for such activities is determined by the faculty member and the students, with the understanding that any particular student may drop out without any kind of penalty at any time. Students negotiate "competence contracts" with faculty members which set forth what both parties will contribute to particular teaching-learning situations. In a group-learning situation, therefore, different students may be working on different competencies with the particular faculty member. But students are free to implement their educational pacts with or without the use of such contracts and without reference to any college-sponsored programs.

The last phase of a student's relationship to MMSC is called the final assessment. When a student feels he is ready to receive his degree or has otherwise completed his educational pact, he notifies the college. The vice-president then establishes for him a Final Assessment Committee (FAC). The function of the FAC is to review a draft narrative transcript prepared by the student summarizing his educational accomplishments in the light of his educational pact. That narrative transcript incorporates all evaluations of the student by faculty members who have worked with him, as well as the student's response to such evaluations. The FAC may actually conduct the assessment of the student, if that is the way he wrote up his educational pact. On the other hand, the FAC may simply scrutinize the results of others' assessments of the student—review evaluations prepared by faculty, employers, peers, testing agencies, and so on. In the latter instance an FAC will rely on the original pact and the transcript to determine if in fact the student gained the competencies he set out to achieve. An FAC will conclude its work for successful degree candidates by a final editing of the narrative transcript, incorporating into it the committee's comprehensive written assessment of the student. If a student "fails" this final assessment, he may continue with his education until he is able to convince an FAC that he has achieved his educational goals.

The key to our educational program is assessment. We believe that the competence-assessment process—both initially and throughout the student's affiliation with the college, including the assessment which will culminate in his receiving a degree—should be individually structured to give the student a complete opportunity to demonstrate his real abilities. The function of assessment is not to fail students but to make sure they have the skills and knowledge, the values and attitudes, and the understanding—in short, the competencies—which are appropriate to their educational, career, and life goals.

To provide the type of higher education envisioned, the college operates on a calendar which differs significantly from the typical academic calendar. College programs are offered at times and in places which are convenient to the students we seek to serve, most of whom will be carrying on other (usually full-time) activities in addition to their studies. The college therefore offers its programs from early morning to late night, weekdays and weekends, year-round. It should never be necessary for a student to take any portion of his program during the regular work day, for example, in order to receive a degree. Full-time faculty are employed on a twelve-month contract rather than the traditional nine- or ten-month contract. There are no terms: quarters, semesters, trimesters. Students enter throughout the year. Group-learning experiences are scheduled informally around the needs of those involved and the characteristics of the material being covered.

In general, the college sets no absolute time limits for students to complete their programs. Students who enter with two years of college already completed should be able to complete a degree in no more than eighteen calendar months. Very often, however, even "average" students will be able to complete their studies in less time if they chose to do so. The college is prepared to work with students who are persistent until they achieve the level of competence requisite for a degree. Some students will take significantly less time than the average to complete a baccalaureate degree, while others may move very slowly—which is as it should be.

Tuition is based on how many years of college work a given student has completed when he enters. The rate is basically the same as that in the other Minnesota state colleges, except we do not charge the $45 per year student activity fee. For students who have completed two years, the total financial obligation to the college presently is $650. For a student who has completed more than two years, the total amount is reduced proportionately to a minimum of $325. Special fees have been established for those students who desire to participate in college programs but who are not working toward baccalaureate degrees. Whatever fees such students pay may be applied toward the total amount due should they transfer into a degree program.

The legislature appropriated $300,000 to the State College Board to plan and operate the institution for the two years beginning July 1, 1971, and ending June 30, 1973. We are projecting a total enrollment by the end of the biennium of approximately 850 students. This number of students will generate approximately $250,000. The other sources of funding for the college include major grants from the Hill Family Foundation, the Carnegie Corporation, the U. S. Office of Education, and the Bush Foundation. The projected budget for the biennium is $1,100,000.

The officers and staff of MMSC are conscious—extremely conscious—of the difficulties inherent in our approach to higher education. The difficulties of competence assessment, educational and career advising, and the development of individualized "educational pacts" with our students must not, we believe, be permitted to inhibit the development of an educational process which validates formal education in demonstrable skills, attitudes, and understanding rather than credit hours, grade-point averages, intuition, or even gross annual income. We have already learned something of the logistical problems associated with any college which has no central campus and a dispersed faculty. Through our experiences with students, faculty, and the community at large, we have become completely committed to this way of doing higher education. We are especially convinced that a student can take charge of his own education and that the college exists to make this possibility a reality.

℈ 21 ℈

Evaluating College Teaching: The Rhetoric and the Research

John A. Centra

There are two major reasons for evaluating teaching: one is to help make decisions about whom to promote, and the other is to improve instruction. The two need not, of course, be mutually exclusive. Whether evaluation can lead to either goal is the basic question. There is more rhetoric than hard evidence offered to answer it in spite of a half-century of research on teaching. I do not mean that the research efforts have been totally fruitless; but the findings have not, for a variety of reasons, been put into practice.

It is not difficult to criticize current faculty promotion practices. At larger institutions where the educational goals include advancing knowledge as well as passing it on, there is little question that faculty members are rewarded primarily for their efforts with the former even though lip service is given to the latter. The ability to publish, however, is at best only modestly related to teaching effectiveness according to the findings of various studies.[1] At smaller institutions where teaching is the primary function, recent surveys tell us that the judgments of one or more administrators are most frequently relied on to assess teaching effectiveness. Those judgments are often based on hearsay or on very slight evidence.

Systematic efforts to evaluate teaching have most typically had as their goal the improvement of teaching, and one of the most common methods employed has been the use of student ratings. Who else, it is argued, is in a better position to tell an instructor how to improve his course than the student-consumer? Indeed it has practically become part of the rhetoric or folklore on teaching to expect that student ratings will enable the instructor to improve his teaching.

Underlying the use of student ratings are the assumptions that, first, the instructor values student judgment enough to change his procedures when called for and, second, that the instructor learns something about his teaching from students that he does not already know. Both assumptions are open to question.

In an attempt to investigate these assumptions, I recently undertook an experimental study supported by a grant from the Esso Education Foundation. Five diverse colleges which did not have a formal program of student ratings of teaching participated in the study. They included two state colleges, one of which had a predominantly black enrollment, a selective liberal arts college, a multipurpose college, and an urban community college. A total of some 470 faculty representing more than three-quarters of those teaching cooperated in the study; in fact, the cooperation of the institutions and their faculties could not have been much better.

---

[1] See, for example, D. P. Hoyt, *Instructional Effectiveness Interrelationships with Publication Record and Monetary Record.* Manhattan: Office of Educational Research, Research Report #10, Kansas State University, May 1970.

Within each institution, teachers were randomly assigned to one of three groups. The feedback group administered a student rating form at midsemester and received a summary of the results within a week, along with some comparison data to aid in interpretation. In research terms this is the "treatment" group, with the treatment being essentially what is done at most colleges which use student ratings for instructional improvement. The no-feedback group used the rating form at midsemester but did not receive a summary of results until the end of the semester. This would be the so-called control group. The posttest group used the rating form only at the end of the semester in order to determine whether the midsemester ratings had a sensitizing effect on teachers in the no-feedback group—whether simply using the form caused teachers to change, even without getting feedback.

In addition to using the rating form at midsemester, the feedback and no-feedback groups also administered the form at the end of the semester. Both midsemester and end-of-semester ratings were collected during fall semester of 1971. A single semester instead of two successive semesters was used for the study to enable the same students to provide both sets of ratings. Moreover, a suggestion sometimes made is that instructors should obtain feedback from students at midsemester so that students who provide the information might benefit from their own suggestions.

A twenty-three-item form eliciting instructional procedures or behavior that an instructor presumably could change was used in the study. Included were items that I had asked faculty members in an earlier study to identify as providing information they would like to have from students.[2] Among the areas included were those dealing with the organization of the course, the clarity of objectives and presentations, and the instructor's helpfulness or availability to students. Several of the items may be found, with slight variations, in a number of current student-rating instruments.

If student feedback improved instruction, we would expect the end-of-semester ratings of the feedback group to be better than those of either the no-feedback or the posttest group. They were not. In fact, the three groups were nearly identical in their scores for

[2] J. Centra, *The Student Instructional Report: Its Development and Uses.* SIR Report Number 1. Princeton, N. J.: Educational Testing Service, 1972.

each of the items, indicating that the group of instructors who received student feedback did not noticeably modify their teaching practices.

Was this also true for instructors in all disciplines, from both sexes, and with varying amounts of teaching experience? From the preliminary analyses now completed, the answer appears to be yes. One would certainly expect that instructors in their first or second year of teaching would change, since they are less likely to have established rigid teaching habits; but student feedback did not result in changes even for this less experienced group.

There was yet another possibility: that teachers who received the poorest student reports at midsemester had changed but that these changes were not reflected in the average scores for the entire group. In view of the well-known tendency for students' ratings of teaching to be highly skewed in a positive direction—that is, for students to rate instruction rather leniently—this too appeared to be a viable hypothesis. So we looked at instructors with the poorest ratings at midsemester to see if the end-of-semester ratings for those who had received student feedback had improved more than those of instructors from whom feedback had been withheld. They had not. Ratings did, however, improve for both the feedback and no-feedback groups, but this improvement could be explained by what statisticians refer to as regression effects—that is, the tendency for low or high scores to move in the direction of the average on a retest.

Do these findings mean that students' ratings of instruction are of little value in changing instruction? Perhaps. But there are also several alternative explanations to consider. It may be that a half-semester is too short a period of time for changes to take place or that, if they did take place, the student ratings were not sensitive to them. I am hoping to follow up a sample of instructors at the end of the current semester to see if teaching changes are reflected after the longer time period.

I should point out here that when studies like this one were conducted with elementary and secondary schoolteachers, slight changes did occur.[3] Why student ratings produced teaching changes

---

[3] See, for example, B. W. Tuckman and W. F. Oliver, "Effectiveness of Feedback to Teachers as a Function of Source." *Journal of Educational*

at the lower educational levels but not at the college level is not clear. It does not seem likely that college professors would value student opinion any less; on the contrary, one would think that the opinions of college students would have greater impact than the opinions of high school students or sixth-graders.

If the findings of this five-college study hold up under continued analyses of the data, then the assumption that college teachers do change after receiving feedback from their students must be seriously questioned. What this implies is that other methods must be relied on to improve instruction or that students' ratings may need to be given some additional "clout." At some colleges that clout is provided by using student ratings as one of the inputs into salary and promotion decisions; at others the ratings are made public in various ways, such as in student-produced publications (of varied quality, I might add). The effects of using systematic student ratings for decisions on faculty promotions are, to my knowledge, not yet completely known. While they may result in more justifiable decisions than are now generally being made, the possibility exists that such emphasis will also reduce risk-taking and creativity in the classroom. We undoubtedly need more evidence on this question.

Another possible way in which student ratings may have more impact is by providing a better interpretation of the feedback than is typically given to each instructor. This could include written or graphic material or even personal counseling; in any event, the emphasis would be on helping the instructor better understand his results and what he might consider doing about them.

A second aspect of this study was to find out how much instructors actually learn from students about their teaching. To what extent, in other words, do instructors describe or rate their teaching differently from the way students do? It may be that instructors failed to change after receiving student feedback simply because they were not learning anything they did not already know.

Items from the student form were reworded slightly for in-

Psychology, 1968, *59*(4), 297–301. Also, N. L. Gage, P. J. Rankel, and B. B. Chatterjee, "Changing Teaching Behavior through Feedback from Pupils: An Application of Equilibrium Theory." In W. W. Charters and N. L. Gage (Eds.), *Readings in the Social Psychology of Education*. Boston: Allyn & Bacon, 1963, pp. 173–181.

structor responses. Instructors were asked, for example, whether they thought they had made objectives clear, whether they were encouraging students to think for themselves, and so on. This information was collected at midsemester.

There was a significant difference between instructor and student responses to most of the items, and in each instance instructors tended to describe or rate their teaching in more positive terms. In particular, instructors and their students did not agree on the extent to which course objectives had been made clear and on whether there was agreement between objectives and what was taught. This discrepancy suggests that many teachers need to spend more time clarifying their course objectives and directing their teaching toward those goals. There was also considerable lack of agreement on whether students had been encouraged to think for themselves, on whether the instructor was actively helpful to students, and on whether students were free to ask questions or express their opinions. These items would suggest that many instructors are not interacting with students as successfully as they think they are.

For several of the items, however, the gap between student and faculty responses was not very pronounced. There were more common views, for example, on whether the instructor was well prepared for class, on whether students' interest in subject areas had been stimulated, and on whether students seem to be putting a good deal of effort into the course. But even on these items, about a fourth of the teachers viewed the course or their teaching much more positively than did their students.

Although there was a good deal of similarity between teachers' and students' views, there were also sufficient differences to warrant the collection of students' opinions. It is possible, in fact, that student feedback results in changes only by those teachers who see themselves much differently from the way the students see them —a possibility that I am pursuing with current analyses.

My comments thus far have focused on the college classroom as the major arena for teacher evaluation, but as we all realize, a teacher's effects extend beyond the classroom walls—or at least they should. Student learning is said to be the ultimate criterion of such effects; in fact, some have argued that we should forget about evaluating teaching and concentrate instead on changes in students.

Measure the amount students learn (or "value-added," in economic terms) is what the proponents say.

At first glance the method seems easy enough to apply: simply administer a so-called pretest to students at the beginning of the course and follow it with an end-of-course test usually referred to as the posttest. Both examinations, of course, must suitably measure course objectives. Of interest are the average gains in students' scores, and the good teachers, naturally, are the ones whose students demonstrate the largest gains. Advocates of the method would argue that these teachers ought to be rewarded just as researchers are rewarded for the number of publications they produce; both measures are, after all, quantifiable.

This method of evaluating teaching, which seems to be another outgrowth of the cult of accountability, involves a number of problems. First, faculty members within a department or course must agree on the objectives to be measured and then tests must be devised to assess these objectives adequately and in the proper proportions. This is no small problem, but let's assume it can be done. Now, how do we compare score gains between classes? Is a twenty-point gain in physics with good students comparable to a twenty-point gain with poor students? In spite of certain standardizing manipulations (such as standard score conversions), any conclusions regarding differences between score gains could be totally unwarranted simply because, as numerous experts have pointed out, there is no way of making proper allowances for uncontrolled pre-existing differences between students in each class.[4] That is why the random assignment of subjects is so crucial in experiments. In fact, test score gains are used frequently in research on teaching, but that is a different matter from using them as a regular part of the reward structure.

If gain scores are fed into the reward structure, we can also expect that instructors will begin teaching to the test, an abuse of testing that will neither aid the student nor the institution that seeks to reward good teaching. It must be remembered that tests represent only a sample—indeed a very small sample—of the subject

[4] F. M. Lord, "A Paradox in the Interpretation of Group Comparisons." *Psychological Bulletin,* 1967, 68, 21–38.

matter included in a course or field, and if instructors merely emphasize that limited domain, they may appear as if they have been effective when in fact they have short-changed their students.

But tests properly used can, indeed, be very beneficial; they play an important role both in giving the instructor periodic feedback on his students' progress and in providing a summative evaluation of each student at the end of the course. More instructors, no doubt, could also profit from knowing more about their students at the beginning of a course—information such as their expectations for the course as well as their knowledge of subject matter. So tests per se are not the problem; what I am cautioning against is the systematic use of test scores as the sole criterion for determining which teachers have been most effective.

How, then, can teaching be evaluated in a way that will lead to instructional improvement or more valid decisions on promotion? To begin with, we will probably never entirely eliminate subjective judgment in evaluating teaching. What we might best do, then, is to utilize as many sources as possible for those judgments and when possible combine them with whatever "objective" information is available. The use of multiple measures of outcomes or performance is a relatively simple but often disregarded notion in evaluation. Administrators (chairmen and deans), students, and faculty colleagues are, of course, the primary groups available to rate teachers, and there is some research evidence on how these three groups compare in their judgments. In two separate studies—the first appeared over fifteen years ago[5] and the second has not yet been published[6]— each of the three groups evaluated the overall teaching effectiveness of specific instructors with whom they were acquainted and there was substantial agreement among all three.

Specifically, the correlations were in the .60 to .70 range, indicating that while their judgments were not in complete agreement, they did share a common basis in making their ratings. What that common basis is we can not be sure, but one possibility is that

---

[5] A. H. Maslow and W. Zimmerman, "College Teaching Ability, Activity, and Personality." *Journal of Educational Psychology*, 1956, *47*, 185–189.

[6] M. J. Clark and R. Blackburn, "Assessment of Faculty Performance: Some Correlates between Self, Colleagues, Students, and Administrators."

they are sharing what Polanyi refers to as "tacit knowledge."[7] Tacit knowledge, he says, includes those unmeasurables that underlie an individual's competence and show up in the impressions he makes on others. Those so-called unmeasurables are exactly why subjective judgments will continue to be used in teacher evaluation.

But this is not to say that the actual subjective evaluations cannot be made more precise. In addition to using as many sources as possible to collect judgments on teaching, it would seem that something more than an overall rating needs to be employed and that more direct evidence of performance both in and out of the classroom is needed. In particular, if course or instructional improvement is the goal, something more than a single overall rating is necessary. In the first place, a single rating assumes a unitary dimension of teaching ability—and that we know to be unlikely; secondly, an overall judgment does not give a teacher the kind of specific information needed for improvement. My tennis game would stand little chance to improve if I were simply told I was "below average." But when one of my tennis colleagues points out my backhand grip and stance are not right, then I can do something about it—maybe.

We might thus try to encourage more faculty members to sit in on their colleagues' courses or in various ways to help one another improve their courses or teaching. For example, a practice that has had some success is to have each teacher orally present to appropriate colleagues a summary of how he plans to deal with a particular unit in his course; in this way instructional objectives and techniques are shared among the group. While the five-college study reported here did not provide any hard evidence that students had much effect on changing instruction, one's colleagues may have more impact. College professors do not hesitate to review critically each other's research and scholarly outputs; is it not possible to bring that same spirit of criticism to each other's teaching?

[7] M. Polanyi, *Tacit Dimension.* New York: Doubleday, 1966.

PART SIX

Autonomy
and Control

Many administrators argue that the advent of centralization has created a great danger for colleges and universities, the danger of losing their freedom to become better educational institutions than they now are. Other administrators as well as many scholars in the field of educational organization argue that universities can no longer afford complete autonomy—that it is, in any case, not possible—and point out that universities are nonetheless free, within limits, to make changes to improve themselves.

This issue of autonomy is the controversial topic to which the three authors of Part Six address themselves. Each author speaks to the question from a different perspective. James Miller shows why statewide controls are a necessity. Robert Harris, arguing the case by concentrating on vocational programs in community colleges, asserts that the control of external agencies has been harmful.

And Gary Quehl, describing patterns of control and autonomy in voluntary consortia, concludes that the autonomy-control issue is only a way of disguising the real problem by means of a myth.

In "Coordination Versus Centralized Control," Miller takes the view that when a state is responsible for higher education, only an agency with statewide responsibilities can identify needs accurately and initiate action effectively. Miller agrees that local control is appropriate and viable in some areas, but he argues that heavy state controls are, for the most part, necessary.

Harris' chapter, "External Agencies: Roadblocks to Career Education," might well be read in conjunction with the chapters on the community college which have appeared in the last several volumes of Current Issues. *Various authors have expressed the view that the community college has not been allowed to develop its own character and shape because of pressures from other quarters within the higher education establishment. Harris presents another set of data to support that conclusion. His evidence shows that the action of various agencies, both governmental and nongovernmental, "has unduly limited local programs by imposing rules and regulations that are sometimes arbitrary, restrictive, or discriminatory."*

Quehl, in "Autonomy and Control in Voluntary Consortia," asserts that voluntary consortia have not, on the whole, had substantial impact on the academic life of their member colleges. By analyzing why the "early promises for the cooperative movement have not been accomplished," he comes to the conclusion that the myth of local autonomy has been, to a considerable degree, responsible. Quehl then investigates the concept of autonomy and helps the reader to demythologize it. Quehl's fascinating analysis of the way the myth has been used to prevent institutional collaboration makes an important contribution to Part Six and to this volume.

JOSEPH AXELROD

22

Coordination Versus Centralized Control

James L. Miller, Jr.

Does statewide coordination of higher education bring about added effectiveness or added bureaucracy? The answer, clearly, is: "Both." Like most products of contemporary civilization, coordination has advantages which make it desirable and necessary and disadvantages which cause annoying frustrations and which also pose important issues that cannot be solved by going back to the old way. The simple fact is that in certain respects higher education has outgrown its shell—its shell being the independent, single-campus institution. I call it a shell because the essence of higher education is learning, and therefore the many alternative arrangements which aid learning are not the heart of the matter but simply the casings in which we house and nurture learning.

The forms we use to facilitate learning are dictated partially by environmental circumstances and partially by the choice of the learner himself, his family, or his society. Individual tutoring, for example, was a necessity in some rural settings, and it remains today the choice of some individuals. Institutionalized forms of group learning—schools—are cheaper, provide educational opportunity to larger numbers, make possible many kinds of experiences which are unavailable to the isolated individual, and enable society to monitor some of what is taught. (The latter, of course, has both positive and negative implications.) Americans remember nostalgically the one-room schoolhouse, but we tend to forget that during the first two centuries of American history the colleges also tended to be small and ungraded. When urbanization brought together larger numbers of people and more of them began attending school, subdivision into grades and subject-matter classes took place. Further subdivision has occurred at all levels until, most recently, many institutions have adopted multicampus arrangements. Students in Dallas County Community College have their choice of three campuses, and students in Chicago's community college system have a choice of seven or eight. Students enrolling in the University of California may wind up on any of nine campuses.

In some respects the University of California multicampus set-up is a very convenient "have-your-cake-and-eat-it-too" arrangement, especially for administrators. When discussion focuses on equality of educational opportunity, one can point to the fact that students on all nine campuses are equally enrolled in *the* University, but when the discussion shifts to undesirable rigidities inherent in centralized control one can point to the distinctiveness of many campuses within the University of California system. At times one feels like saying, "Come off it! They are either alike or they are different." They are partly both, of course. And therefore, with the important exception of the administrative hierarchy at the top, the California arrangement somewhat parallels that found in states which have chosen quite a different route to the expansion of educational opportunity—expansion through a system of separate institutions. For example, in Michigan the University of Michigan, Michigan State University, and Wayne State University are separate institutions which offer programs having both parallel and unique aspects; together they make higher education available to larger numbers of people than would be possible on any one of the individual campuses.

One important difference between the California system of three levels—the nine-campus university tier, the state college tier, and the junior college tier—and the looser system used in such states as Michigan, Illinois, or Georgia is that the latter do not separate institutions into rigid categories—tiers—but allow more of a continuum of institutional types. Though the organizational systems differ, the net effect is mass educational opportunity.

The concept of education for all inevitably results in lots of people and lots of institutions, calling for administrative coordination and controls both within and among institutions. There are various means to accomplish this coordination, but none of the alternatives includes not doing it at all. *Within* institutions we have grown quite accustomed to administrative controls and services; we argue only about the forms they should take. *Among* institutions we are beginning to accept the same principle. Interinstitutional coordination in the public sector has taken the form of state-level planning and coordination, and I anticipate that we will stick with that method.

Just for fun, though, let me suggest some other possible forms. Richard Peterson suggests in a provocative piece[1] that the most logical organization of postsecondary education would be based on metropolitan regions, with all public universities and colleges grouped into a single multicampus regional arrangement. He also proposes, as have some others, that the major graduate and research universities of the nation might be fully funded by the federal government and organized as a system of exclusively graduate institutions. Peterson's proposal would subdivide states into metropolitan areas. Another alternative to using the fifty states as our basic higher educational service areas would be to use multistate regions of the country—New England, the Midwest, the mountain states, the South, and so on. And, of course, yet another possibility

---

[1] R. Peterson, "The Regional University and Comprehensive College: Some Ideas." In R. R. Perry and W. F. Hull (Eds.), *The Organized Organization: The American University and Its Administration*. Toledo: The University of Toledo, 1971, pp. 73–95.

is to use the nation itself as the service area, turning over completely to the federal government responsibility for coordinating and administering postsecondary education. Finally, consider the alternatives of turning higher education entirely over to the private sector, either profit or nonprofit, on a contract basis. The contract might be between a governmental unit and a contracting institution, or it might be between an individual and an institution with some governmental unit providing part or all of the funds used by the individual. These alternatives—metropolitan regions, multistate regions, federal control, or private sector subcontracting—suggest various possibilities, but all of them have a common denominator: some form of direct or indirect governmental administrative supervision and coordination.

My own best guess is that American society will do in the future what it generally has done in the past—place its bets on adaptation and evolution. Existing social institutions (colleges and universities), existing political boundaries (states), and existing decision-making bodies (legislatures and institutional governing boards) all will adapt, voluntarily or involuntarily, to the changing conditions of mass postsecondary education. During that evolutionary process, there will be a tendency to drop deliberately only those existing institutions and arrangements which manifestly will not fit the new needs. Similarly, new institutions and new arrangements will be introduced only when there seems little alternative. Evolution, as these comments suggest, is not an altogether rational process. It frequently makes use of the old, even when that use involves warping the old into a shape that is distasteful to those who loved its old form and only partially satisfying to those who sense the need for new functions. Nevertheless, the cumulative effect of incremental changes will be great and the relative importance of many existing institutions, types of institutions, and arrangements for coordination and control will change.

Whatever form it takes, statewide planning is essential because without it some geographic sections of a state and, more importantly, some elements of the population will not be provided with services. Fifteen years ago the movement developed to blanket each state with a system of two-year comprehensive community colleges in order to provide all citizens with geographic proximity to educational opportunity. Most states now are well along in developing public community college systems, some of which are the result of deliberate planning. I qualify this assertion because in many cases state-level planning was introduced midway in the process—only after some localities had established the value of community colleges by starting their own, thereby creating a situation in which some but not all sections of the state were being served.

More recently we have become sensitive to the fact that in most states population is concentrated in metropolitan areas while the senior educational institutions are scattered almost randomly across the geographic expanse of a state. There are interesting historical, sociological, and political reasons for this distribution, but an exploration of them would divert us from our main topic. The simple fact is that once American society subscribed to the goal of universal higher educational opportunity for the young and to the further concept of providing continuing lifetime educational opportunities for all, it found that the locations of four-year and graduate institutions did not place them within reach of most people. States have moved to remedy that situation through the establishment of additional urban campuses and/or through the take-over and expansion of formerly municipal or private urban universities. We have not faced up to the enormity of the task, however. In large metropolitan areas, one or even two state-supported senior institutions will not meet the numerical demand. We must develop a counterpart of the multicampus urban community college, with a number of senior campuses scattered over the metropolitan area (or perhaps it should be a multicampus counterpart which concentrates on upper-division, graduate, and professional programs). The organization can be a multicampus structure or it can be separately administered institutions whose functions and responsibilities are coordinated from a state agency, but whichever pattern of administration is followed, the educational opportunities must be provided.

But the needs do not end even there. We are failing miserably in another, less recognized form of postsecondary educational service to metropolitan areas and that is in the *types* of programs and services offered. In most cases the senior institutions are simply copies of senior institutions found in nonmetropolitan areas except that they frequently suffer from what is referred to as the "problem" of a part-time, commuting student body and many of them also find it necessary to respond—with various degrees of discomfort—

to a student demand for course work which is disproportionately weighted toward the academically less honored vocational fields. And finally, many urban institutions have unusual problems with what we awkwardly refer to by various euphemisms for poorly prepared students.

If we are to have anything truly resembling universal postsecondary educational opportunity—genuine opportunity which extends beyond just the suburbs and the smaller cities—we must recognize the centrality of learning and apply it to the metropolitan areas in a manner which will genuinely flesh out the state system of postsecondary education. Accomplishing this goal will mean spreading institutions and quasi-institutions throughout urban areas, revising our value systems to introduce increased respect for occupationally useful programs, and *planned* development of systems of lifetime learning opportunities. It will also entail restructuring both our attitudes toward learning processes and our attitudes toward the learning facilitation responsibilities of various types of institutions; and, finally, it means extensive introduction of multiple forms of credit by examination and credit for other-than-classroom experiences.

What has all of this to do with state planning and coordination? Everything. Since the state is the area to be served, only an agency with statewide responsibilities can identify new needs of a statewide nature, identify geographic or programatic gaps in the system of state service, and initiate action to fill these needs. Only a statewide agency can speak knowledgeably and nonparochially to the state legislature, governor, and budget office concerning higher education's needs—both its continuing needs and its newly emerging ones. Only this agency can determine the present and projected total demand for postsecondary education in the state and rationally allocate among the state's institutions responsibilities for meeting these several needs.

In the jargon of state planners and coordinators, I am talking about the absolute necessity for a coordinating agency having authority to allocate major functional responsibilities among institutions, authority for budgetary review, and authority for program review (insofar as that makes operational the agency's ability to monitor the allocation of programs). And primarily I am talking about the agency's responsibilities for statewide (and metropolitan) long-range planning—which includes making plans, the advocacy functions related to funding those plans, and *monitoring* functions associated with implementing them. The state agency's responsibility for some control over capital construction programs ties into this picture, and so, perhaps, does the authority to discontinue programs already operating in institutions. However, the latter seems to me a somewhat useless power which serves principally to generate warfare. Its one advantage is that it might be used to block a program which was still new and had been "bootlegged" into the curriculum by an institution.

Obviously the extensive responsibilities I am proposing for the central coordinating agency (powers which already are legally held by many, if not most, agencies now existing in the fifty states) require that the agency itself have a first-rate staff, outstanding leadership, and a board which represents statewide interests and not those of individual existing institutions.

All of this appears to add up to a rather powerful state control over public higher education. But let me turn to the other side of the coin to suggest the logical limits of state agency authority and activity. Earlier I asserted that the central concern in education is learning and that the free-standing individual campus or institution is simply a convenient container for facilitating certain forms of learning—a container we have outgrown in some respects as universal higher educational opportunity has moved us into state systems.

The incorporation of free-standing institutions into state systems alters some aspects of the institutions' autonomy (particularly those Berdahl refers to as "procedural" autonomy). But institutions are, and will continue to be for some time, the principal means through which most education is provided. Individual institutions (and units within institutions) operate best when decision-making is kept as close as possible to the place where the decision must be implemented.

In short, the responsibilities I suggest for statewide agencies are restricted to those which by their nature can only be exercised by a statewide body. These responsibilities relate to statewide planning and coordination of programs and services which then must be implemented by institutions. A maximum amount of decentralization should be present. Institutional distinctiveness, initiative, and choice concerning ways to implement broad educational objectives assigned to the institution should be maximized. Institutions are a major source of innovative ideas and methods—a fact we tend to overlook now that lambasting institutions for conformity and imitation is so popular. State controls, heavy-handedly imposed, repress innovation and may thereby cut off both desirable diversity to meet present needs and the emergence of new models for the future. One method for achieving and maintaining this distinction between the state agency's planning-coordinating-monitoring function and the institutions' implementation function is to keep the staff of the agency small. This helps to preclude meddling in institutional affairs.

Let me summarize my position quite baldly. First, state systems of higher education exist. There now are in every state a fairly large number of colleges and universities which among them constitute, either formally or informally, a delivery system for mass higher education. Second, it is both necessary and desirable that these systems be effectively planned and that many facets of their operation be coordinated. Third, I do not concur with the proposition that these systems must be controlled by centralized administrative direction from the central offices of the system. State systems are needed. They aid educational effectiveness. Inevitably, they are somewhat bureaucratic, but they do not need to be oppressively so.

❦ 23 ❦

External Agencies: Roadblocks to Career Education

Robert G. Harris

❦❦❦❦❦❦❦❦❦❦❦❦

Vocational education in community colleges across the nation offers a great diversity in programs. Undeniably this variety has developed primarily because vocational education is preparing students for the increasing number of careers which require more than a high school education but less than a baccalaureate degree. Right now and in the foreseeable future such career areas offer by far the greatest number of employment opportunities. The growing diversity is also due to a liberal interpretation of vocational education in most community colleges. Many other institutions still reveal remnants of the manual arts mentality which essentially says that if hands aren't dirty or if there are no sparks flying or chips on the floor, vocational education is not happening. But community college people have recognized the wide range of vocations that must be served.

Another reason for diversity lies in the needs orientation of the community college. Its programs are based on the needs of the community and the individuals it serves. Programs such as law enforcement, retail marketing, electronics technology, nursing, data processing, dental hygiene, drafting technology, and fashion merchandising are found in many localities, reflecting the common needs shared by all communities. Yet we also find special programs designed for specific local circumstances.

In Rhinelander, Wisconsin, Nicolet College offers a program titled Timber Producers' Aide which prepares students for work as logging operators, pulp producers, sawmill operators, and many other jobs related to timber production. Colby Community College in Colby, Kansas, conducts a program in Feedyard Management which serves the needs of the cattle-raising community of western Kansas. No one should be surprised that at the Leadville campus of the Colorado Mountain College, a vocational program in Ski Area Management is quite popular. Others are marine biology in Maine and citrus orchard management in California.

There also are many examples of programs to meet the needs of individuals, such as those especially designed for Cuban refugees, migrant farm workers, and urban minorities. A substantial effort is being made to reach the educationally, culturally, and physically disadvantaged. As an example, in Johnson County Community College, located in suburban Kansas City, we are in the middle of a three-phase plan to produce a vocational program for the hearing-impaired or deaf student. At present, programs for the hearing-impaired in secretarial careers and data processing are under way. The need for this program was determined by an educational needs survey in the community college district prior to the opening of the college. An unusually high percentage of Johnson County residents were found either to be deaf or to have problems of hearing impairment. This occurrence was attributed to the fact that many people come to the county in order to attend the Kansas School for the

Deaf and, after completion of their studies, remain as permanent residents.

I used to believe that the development of vocational education programs in response to community needs was limited only by imagination and money, and mostly by money. However, during the past few years, I feel the action of external agencies, both governmental and nongovernmental, has unduly limited many programs by imposing rules and regulations that are sometimes arbitrary, restrictive, or discriminatory. To illustrate, the Federal Aviation Administration specifies that a college seeking approval of its ground-school program must have a classroom that meets the following conditions: at least eighty square feet of floor area for five students, plus at least fifteen square feet for each additional student; heat and ventilation in accordance with public health laws; enough light to allow a person with normal eyesight to study or read without eye strain. How do the physical dimensions and conditions of a ground-school classroom really affect the competence of the student pilot? Shouldn't the FAA be less concerned about the physical dimensions of the classroom and more concerned about measuring the flying ability of the candidate for license? As a second example, the Manual of Requirements for Kansas Schools of Nursing issued by the State Board of Nursing states that "the director shall have a private office and not more than two instructors should share an office." Such a requirement seems to have little impact on the quality of the nursing program.

Another example from Kansas concerns the certification of instructors of dental hygiene. The State Department of Education requires the instructor to complete twelve "approved" semester credit hours of instruction in vocational education. Does the fulfillment of this requirement really have an effect on the quality of the dental hygiene program? Shouldn't the Board be more concerned with developing methods to evaluate the competence of the graduate of a dental hygiene program? There are many other examples of restrictions on the local institution. These agencies seem to be more concerned with input than with output.

After describing the educational system, one should identify the roles of the local institution and the external agencies in the operation of the system. There must be a sharing of responsibility in all areas. The development of evaluative criteria should be a cooperative effort of the local institution and the external agencies. Since many educational programs require either the financial support or the sanction of external agencies, there must be a cooperative agreement between the two parties relative to these matters. The external agencies should collaborate with the local institution in developing procedures for distribution of funds, establishing standards for licensure or approval, and in assessing the societal needs of the larger community.

The local institution must bear the prime responsibility for determining local needs and for obtaining and maintaining the resources required for conducting the educational program. The external agencies should meet the needs of the larger community, administer the evaluative criteria to determine whether the vocational program actually produces qualified personnel for the vocation, and exercise the proper control through the distribution of funds or the approval process of certification or accreditation.

The imposition of restrictive conditions and regulations must be reexamined before many of the needs of our communities can be adequately served. There are indications of a new trend developing in the accreditation, certification, and approval procedures of several external agencies. This trend suggests increased concern with evaluating the outcome of education and, hopefully, less interference with the local institution in the functions of the input and the process of education. In the words of Norman Burns, executive secretary of the North Central Association of Colleges and Secondary Schools:

The time has come for a major change in the approach to institutional evaluation for accrediting purposes. The present approach, devised at an earlier time and under different circumstances than exist today, is based on the assumption that, if an institution possesses certain structural characteristics which are generally recognized as good, the probabilities are high that good education will take place. These characteristics, as you know, relate to such matters as provisions for institutional governance and administration, the instructional arrangements and qualifications of the faculty, the adequacy of the program of student services, the library and learning resource materials, and the physical facilities. . . .

The accrediting agency must devise procedures and evalua-

tive techniques appropriate to these new educational patterns. No longer able to rely heavily on its traditional measuring sticks of structure and form, it must develop new measures to certify to the quality of learning experiences which may be made available outside the traditional institutional arrangements of faculty, administration, library, and physical facilities.

The new approach will involve heavier reliance on direct measurement of educational outcomes than has characterized the past. Efforts along this line will be facilitated by the increasing availability of increasingly sophisticated instruments for direct measurement of outcomes.[1]

In Spring 1972 Johnson County Community College was invited to participate in the field testing of some recently developed instruments and procedures for the evaluation of vocational-technical education. These instruments and procedures were developed as part of a national study being conducted by the American Vocational Association with support from the U. S. Office of Education. Lane C. Ash, director of the study, discusses innovative features of the proposed evaluation:[2] First, to hold schools accountable for preparing students for gainful employment. Traditional accreditation has held schools accountable for preparing students for further education. Such an objective applied to vocational-technical education would divert it from its purpose. Second, product and process factors are clearly differentiated. Emphasis is on evaluation in terms of product (outcomes). Third, objectives are expected to be in measurable performance terms permitting evaluation of achievement. And fourth, the relationship between need, objectives, and outcomes is expressed and used as a basis for evaluation (the product needed, the product promised, and the product produced).

Community colleges are responding to the needs of communities and individuals in diverse and imaginative ways. But in order to continue this forward movement, local institutions must have the responsibility of meeting these needs and managing the resources to do so without undue interference from any external agencies—either public or private.

---

[1] Address delivered to the National League for Nursing, October 1971.

[2] Memorandum to the author, 1972.

24

Autonomy and Control in Voluntary Consortia

Gary H. Quehl

It is unlikely that any voluntary consortium will ever share a common standard for success with any other. Each is its own standard for success. This is the first principle, and it bears repeating. The range of objectives, programs, and organizational characteristics is probably greater among the nation's sixty-six voluntary consortia than among the 662 colleges and universities that constitute their collective membership.

Yet it is no secret that something is wrong, because awareness of common problems is so widespread. Although consortia are increasing both in absolute numbers and rate of growth, early promises for the cooperative movement have not been accomplished. Like many ideas proposed a decade ago, the concept of voluntary cooperation was simple and compelling: Because every college and university in the country possessed both strengths and weaknesses in certain areas of institutional life, each could benefit if groups of colleges would only voluntarily choose to organize and share their resources for mutual advantage. Perhaps our original expectations were unrealistic because our needs and optimism were so great.

Whatever the alleged reason, it is doubtful that the voluntary consortium has had a *substantial* impact on the academic life of the colleges it was designed to serve. Of course, generalization is difficult because the national range of programs is great. But it does appear that such activities as faculty and student exchange have been modest; the voluntary consolidation of small and expensive academic departments into single educational resources for the benefit of all member colleges has been rare; and the creation of educational innovation among member colleges has not been significant even for those consortia designed for that purpose. The consortium *has* contributed to the development of off-campus studies, but this very success has unwittingly drawn large amounts of tuition income away from member colleges, prompting even the most well-established consortium to reduce the scope of its commitment.

Exposure of the hidden agenda which founded almost every voluntary consortium has produced a similar conclusion: Institutional budgets have not been reduced through collaboration, major economies have not been achieved on a continuing basis, and money for operating expenses has not been raised in significant amounts from external sources. The creation of new programs and the growth of a central office staff have been more apparent. It appears that success has fallen short of promise even among those cluster college centers which are purported to represent an advanced state of the art.

In all of this experience, the compelling purpose that was envisioned for large numbers of colleges and universities in the late 1950s has somehow been missed or avoided. Rarely has the voluntary consortium been able to function as an effective organization for achieving significant *inner-directed* academic and administrative programs among member colleges. Those who believe deeply in the potential of voluntary cooperative arrangements want to know why, for the trend toward unity in American higher education is increasing, and it is here to stay. For better or for worse, colleges that were fiercely independent in an earlier age are now bound together through an elaborate network of interlocking associations that cut through all levels of American higher education. The college that deliberately chooses to avoid all collaborative ties and dependencies does so at its own risk—if indeed this can be accomplished at all—and the risks for the loner are considerable.

If the question is not whether colleges and universities will collaborate but how, then the need for concrete answers runs deep. For this reason, the search for an appropriate explanation as to why the voluntary consortium has not performed as expected is anything but a temporary issue. As I shall attempt to demonstrate, the stakes are very high and the implications are long-term.

As one becomes acquainted with the literature on collaboration in American higher education, he immediately learns that "institutional autonomy" is generally regarded as a major obstacle to achieving successful programming. The lesson is clear: Unless a college is willing to give up the isolation of independence to achieve a greater good, it should never talk about joining with others. Unless a college actually does give up something, it is impossible to talk about achieving anything important. The problem is not simply autonomy but what we mean by that concept.

Alexis de Tocqueville once wrote that human institutions are so imperfect by nature that they can often be destroyed merely by extending their underlying ideas to the extreme. In this country, a basic idea such as "autonomy" *is* an institution. Unfortunately, the architects of American higher education did not take de Tocqueville's good counsel, for the value of autonomy has tended to become wedded to the value of academic freedom. In short, the concept of autonomy has been endowed with such near-metaphysical qualities that it has lost its usefulness as an operational term. Robert O. Berdahl has recently done us all the good favor of untangling the two ideas in a way that elevates academic freedom to its rightful place and demythologizes autonomy. According to Berdahl, academic freedom is universal and absolute, but autonomy is parochial and relative; the specific powers of governments and their relations with institutions of higher learning vary from place to place and from time to time.[1] Independent colleges, for example, are essentially autonomous from state control, but certain of them have violated academic freedom in the history of their development. Likewise, as Sir Eric Ashby has observed, academic freedom thrived in nineteenth-century German universities, but these institutions lacked autonomy because they were under the direct control of the state.[2]

Berdahl's primary concern is the relationship between state agencies and public institutions of higher learning, but his recommendations should be heeded by independent colleges as well; the more independent colleges encourage state financial assistance, the more they should expect to be held accountable to the public interest as it is exercised through state planning and coordinating agencies. He warns those who have equated institutional autonomy with academic freedom and who refuse to yield any of either concept to the state. He suggests that this strategy is counterproductive because it invites politicians to act in a similar manner; they may refuse to distinguish between the two concepts and may encourage state powers that are legitimate in some areas of institutional autonomy to intrude willfully and disastrously into the area of academic freedom.[3] For this reason Berdahl invites attention to the distinction between substantive autonomy and procedural autonomy. The former involves the right of a college to establish its own goals, policies, and programs. The latter concerns the right of a college to choose the procedural techniques that are to be used in achieving its goals, policies, and programs. The central problem is to determine which infringements on substantive and procedural autonomy are necessary safeguards for the public interest, which are marginal, and which constitute fundamental threats to the essential ingredients of autonomy.[4]

While precise answers will always be elusive, there are at least two schools of thought on this problem. The implications of

[1] R. O. Berdahl, *Statewide Coordination of Higher Education*. Washington D.C.: American Council on Education, 1971, p. 9.

[2] E. Ashby, *Universities: British, Indian, African; A Study in the Ecology of Higher Education*. London: Weidenfeld and Nicolson, 1966, p. 290.

[3] Berdahl, p. 9.

[4] Berdahl p. 10.

each are exceedingly important to the future and the effectiveness of the voluntary consortium. Those who tend to regard institutional autonomy as the central problem tend to believe that the consortium has not accomplished much precisely because it is voluntary. Volunteerism merely encourages individual colleges to pursue their own interests while they pretend to play at the game of collaboration. That is, they simply are unwilling to give up anything, and they are accountable to no "public interest" except like-minded actors within the consortium; most members merely drift along, engaging in programs that are relatively safe, insofar as institutional autonomy and the commitment of resources are concerned. Thus, it is reasoned that the consortium will not accomplish much of anything until state governments decide to grant it at least quasi-statutory authority and empower it with sufficient sanctions to bind colleges together by region or institutional type for the purpose of sharing in and contributing to statewide planning and coordination. In this view, those who urge the continuation of the voluntary consortium are seen as perpetuating institutional particularism at a time when acute financial problems will not permit the excesses of unbridled autonomy. Continuation is seen as not only wasteful but negligent and not in the public interest, because state and, increasingly, independent colleges and universities receive funding from the public treasury.

The most vocal and active advocates of this position seem to be found in state education departments and other similar agencies in state governments. Taxpayer revolts, declining public confidence in the management of both public and independent colleges and universities, unnecessary proliferation and duplication of programs, and new social needs have all contributed to a fiscal crunch at the state level. These exigencies have aroused an urgent search for ways of obtaining a more effective approach to coordinated statewide planning and the allocation of public resources.

Recent developments in New York State offer an exceptionally good example of the growth of statutory—as opposed to voluntary—cooperation arrangements. It was announced in the fall of 1971 that all public and independent colleges and universities were being grouped into eight planning regions within the state. Most observers welcomed this new opportunity for interaction and communication between public and independent institutions, but many also expressed the belief that the regional boundaries were arbitrarily and rigidly imposed with little thought given to educational considerations beyond political expediency.

The current objective is to have representatives from all public and independent institutions within each region come together to share plans. Then they are to request statutory status as the planning council for that region from the board of regents. Once authorized by the regents as a legal body, it has been proposed that each regional board will review and recommend all major program plans, all capital construction plans, and all coordinated operating arrangements among the public and private colleges and universities in the region.[5]

Initially, the education department was careful to say that the development of each regional board would be voluntary, but now there is ample evidence that coercive action will be used against those colleges and universities which do not choose to participate in this kind of statutory arrangement; the withholding of finances and the refusal to register new degree offerings and major programs of study are seen as the state's most formidable sanctions.[6] In addition, the representatives of many independent colleges feel that the regional boards will have the ultimate effect of abrogating the authority of institutional boards and thereby reducing the substantive autonomy of faculties and administrations to control their own fate.

The intent to avoid excessive proliferation and duplication of programs and facilities within the state is meritorious, and independent colleges know they must participate in planning if they expect to receive public funds. However, some people believe that the concept of nonstatutory regional planning councils would be more attractive than regional boards, especially if many of the features of Great Britain's University Grants Committee were adopted. The UGC serves as a buffer between the individual institutions and the Chancellor of the Exchequer, funneling institutional plans up to the government and finances down to the individual

[5] Regents of the University of the State of New York, *Financing Higher Education Needs in the Decade Ahead: A Statement of Policy and Proposed Action*. Position Paper No. 13. Albany: The State Education Department, 1972, pp. 24–25.

[6] Regents, p. 25.

institutions, all ideally done without political interference on the part of the British government. Presumably, the public interest is served and institutional autonomy is preserved.

What is especially noteworthy about the New York plan is that the education department initially chose not to build on the strengths of existing voluntary consortia or to promote the develop- ment of new ones to serve the state's planning needs. Indeed, the department pointed to the ostensible ineffectiveness of voluntary associations as the basic rationale for launching the concept of statutory regional consortia.[7] This course of action was adopted despite the fact that the education department had done little to stimulate the consortium movement over the years, other than to support conferences and several publications on interinstitutional cooperation. And most of these activities were undertaken on behalf of the state by individual consortia within the state. In recent months, the department has begun to involve several voluntary con- sortia in the planning process. Many observers hope that each con- sortium that was selected to participate in regional planning can demonstrate there is more to resolving the problems of collaboration among colleges than co-opting their autonomy.

The second school of thought on the question of institutional autonomy and the voluntary consortium regards institutional au- tonomy as an occasional obstacle to progress, but they tend to view the preservation of autonomy as the essential ingredient for long- term success within the consortium movement. They are the first to admit that voluntary cooperation is a painfully slow and difficult process. But it is viewed as the most effective method for ultimately improving the number and quality of academic programs, the efficiency of administrative offices, and the achievement of long- term economies among participating colleges. Proponents argue that those who are disillusioned with the achievements of the volun- tary consortium are impatient, if not naive. As one commentator has suggested, many simply do not realize that the slow nature of change in American higher education does not suggest that shotgun weddings will be long-lasting or promising.[8] The rapid development

[7] T. E. Hollander, *Regional Arrangements for a More Effective System of Post-Secondary Education.* Albany: New York State Education Department, 1971, p. 1. (mimeographed)

[8] L. D. Patterson, *Consortia in American Higher Education.* Report

of centralized state systems of higher learning over the last several decades is regarded as a good case in point. Originally established because they made good social, educational, and fiscal sense, many have grown to deny basic autonomy to individual campuses and erode public confidence, often leaving individual colleges and state agencies in adversary positions. Too often the result has been a monolithic system that has routinized and dehumanized education, has stimulated the rise of unionism among faculty members, and has helped to push many states to the brink of bankruptcy.

For these reasons, it is argued that the most efficient kind of cooperation over the long run is nonstatutory or voluntary. The continuing purposes are to identify and sustain cooperative programs that will enable participating colleges to become more complete, to be able to survive the forces that work daily toward conformity and extinction, and thereby to preserve the ability of each member college to become more self-reliant. Given this view, the public interest in a democratic society cannot be better served. Many of those who share this position are professionals in the field of consortium work —the new consortium that is experiencing its initial round of good will and the established consortium that has passed through major surgery to continue under new agreements that make success more likely.

The nature of these ground rules leads us back to the long-term effectiveness of the voluntary consortium: Is it doomed by institutional autonomy? Earlier I said that a college must actually give up something if voluntary cooperation is to be successful. The issue is whether this giving up "of something" requires a diminution of substantive autonomy or whether it is possible to proceed with cooperative programs by giving up only an agreed-upon amount of procedural autonomy. Those who regard autonomy as the primary barrier to the success of a voluntary consortium will propose that only the cession of substantive autonomy to the consortium can make voluntary cooperation effective. And since colleges will not cede substantive autonomy voluntarily, this type of consortium is doomed by institutional autonomy. Those who view the preservation of institutional autonomy as the essential ingredient for successful

No. R-7. (ED 043800) Washington, D.C.: ERIC Clearinghouse, 1970, p. 3.

voluntary cooperation over the long run do not see the cession of substantive autonomy as being necessary or desirable. The willingness of each member college to recognize the claims of academic freedom and substantive autonomy for the other should reinforce each member's willingness to cede certain procedural rights to the consortium. This choosing to give something up is itself an autonomous act of considerable importance.

In this view, a diminution of institutional autonomy is not required beyond the commitment to specific programs and agreement on the procedural techniques needed to achieve them. A decision on the theoretical limits of substantive autonomy need only be one of principle, for all participants have assurances that partial cession will not result in abuse. Assurances are the board of trustees; the judgment of the chief administrative officer of the central office, who is responsible to the board; and the structures and decision-making processes within each member college that determine personnel policies, program commitments, and the allocation of resources.

So much for assurances to individual colleges, but what about others who seek assurances that the voluntary consortium is worth founding or continuing? We might begin to look at the older consortia for practical answers to "the autonomy" issue, for many are currently engaged in a process of evaluation and realignment of institutional membership. Several have emerged from this process with a smaller but vastly strengthened membership that is committed to the cooperative ideal in exciting new ways. Also, a few have folded.

To the uninitiated, it might therefore appear that the voluntary consortium movement is breaking up and that the major reason is institutional autonomy. To those who understand, however, it is clear that autonomy is just a convenient issue. Autonomy has tended to pass as an ideological issue whenever there is need to rationalize interpersonal problems that arise *among* cooperating colleges but that actually exist as standard fare *within* these institutions—lack of direct participation in decision-making among constituencies, competition for scarce resources, inadequate student advising, attitudes about status and prestige, insufficient faculty incentives and rewards. These, not autonomy, are examples of the real issues with which each consortium must deal.

To the extent that many of these problems can be dealt with on a consortium-wide basis, the likelihood of institutional change is greatly enhanced. And so is the probability of significant achievement in each voluntary consortium. To faculty members, students, and administrators who are interested in generating useful change but are unable to do so for all the well-known reasons, the voluntary consortium is a promising innovation that is relatively untested. The movement has hardly reached adolescence.

Epilogue

In his great treatise on esthetics, Art as Experience, *John Dewey declared that art and life must become one. There is no place for art museums in a truly creative society, Dewey argued. It should not surprise us that curators and others whose livelihoods depend on the continued existence of art museums have not reacted positively to Dewey's stand. Others, too, whose profits depend on the continued separation of art and life oppose Dewey's esthetic ideas.*

Dewey also believed that education and life must become one but he did not foresee the day when our society could be deschooled. Yet by the time Dewey's centennial arrived in 1959, it had already become technologically feasible to carry to their logical conclusion his ideas about education and life: only by substituting education for schooling—that is, only by deschooling our entire society—could creative learning be brought to the center of life for both young people and adults.

This ideal, never completely spelled out in Dewey's thought, has become the central concept in the educational philosophy of another radical thinker, Ivan Illich. In "The Deschooled Society," the chapter that closes this volume, Illich presents three theses: the possibility that real learning can ever take place in what we call schools is an illusion; the "disestablishment" of the schools in our society is inevitable; and the end of the illusion that we need schools should, in Illich's words, "fill us with hope."

Illich's ideas do not prove attractive to establishment educators, especially to a certain brand of educational reformer. And in the context of problems today, such reformers thrive. While the ills of the entire educational structure stand patently visible, pressures are strong to preserve our schools more or less as they are. These reformers have persuaded themselves—and have been successful in persuading most of the rest of us—that if we work from their blueprints, we can improve schools without having to change them very much. Illich compares their effort, sincere as it is, with the activity of the medieval alchemists, and he predicts for them about the same degree of success.

Many readers of this volume will believe that Illich's chapter is visionary. Some will even find its theses outrageous. But if so, perhaps they will also find the theme of this entire volume outrageous, for many of the chapters in it support and illustrate the notion that to meet the future needs of our society, colleges and universities will have to expand their campuses right into the family rooms of average homes. When that expansion takes place—and the process has already, in fact, begun—then Illich's ideal will also have begun to take concrete shape and to affect the daily lives of all of us.

JOSEPH AXELROD

25

The Deschooled Society

Ivan Illich

For generations we have tried to make the world a better place by providing more and more schooling, but so far the endeavor has failed. What we have learned instead is that forcing all children to climb an open-ended education ladder cannot enhance equality but must favor the individual who starts out earlier, healthier, or better prepared; that enforced instruction deadens for most people the will for independent learning; and that knowledge treated as a commodity, delivered in packages, and accepted as private property once it is acquired must always be scarce.

I believe that the disestablishment of the school has become inevitable and that this end of an illusion should fill us with hope.

But I also believe that the end of the "age of schooling" could usher in the epoch of the global schoolhouse that would be distinguishable only in name from a global madhouse or global prison in which education, correction, and adjustment become synonymous. I therefore believe that the breakdown of the school forces us to look beyond its imminent demise and to face fundamental alternatives in education. Either we can work for fearsome and new educational devices that teach about a world which progressively becomes more opaque and forbidding for man, or we can set the conditions for a new era in which technology would be used to make society more simple and transparent, so that all men can once again know the facts and use the tools that shape their lives. In short, we can disestablish schools or we can deschool culture.

In order to see clearly the alternatives we face, we must first distinguish learning from schooling, which means separating the humanistic goal of the teacher from the impact of the invariant structure of the school. This hidden structure constitutes a course of instruction that stays forever beyond the control of the teacher or of his school board. It conveys indelibly the message that only through schooling can an individual prepare himself for adulthood in society, that what is not taught in school is of little value, and that what is learned outside of school is not worth knowing. I call it the hidden curriculum of schooling because it constitutes the unalterable framework of the system, within which all changes in the curriculum are made.

The hidden curriculum is always the same regardless of school or place. It requires all children of a certain age to assemble in groups of about thirty, under the authority of a certified teacher, for some 500 or 1000 or more hours per year. It does not matter whether the curriculum is designed to teach the principles of Fascism, liberalism, Catholicism, socialism, or liberation, so long as the institution claims the authority to define which activities are legitimate "education." It does not matter whether the purpose of the school is to produce Soviet or United States citizens, mechanics, or doctors as long as you cannot be a legitimate citizen or doctor *unless* you are a graduate. It makes no difference whether all meetings occur in the same place so long as they are somehow understood as attendance: cane-cutting is work for cane-cutters, correction for prisoners, and part of the curriculum for students.

What is important in the hidden curriculum is that students learn that education is valuable when it is acquired in the school through a gradual process of consumption; that the degree of success the individual will enjoy in society depends on the amount of learning he consumes; and that learning *about* the world is more valuable than learning *from* the world. The imposition of this hidden curriculum within an educational program distinguishes schooling from other forms of planned education. All the world's school systems have common characteristics in relation to their institutional output, and these are the result of the common hidden curriculum of all schools.

Educational reformers who accept the idea that schools have failed fall into three groups. The most respectable are certainly the great masters of alchemy who promise better schools—alchemists being those who sought to refine base elements by leading their distilled spirits through twelve stages of successive enlightenment, so that for their own good and for all the world's benefit they might be transmuted into gold. The most seductive reformers are those popular magicians who promise to make every kitchen into an alchemic lab. The most sinister are the new Masons of the Universe who want to transform the entire world into one huge temple of learning.

Notable among today's masters of alchemy are certain research directors employed or sponsored by the large foundations who believe that schools, if they could somehow be improved, could also become economically more feasible than those that are now in trouble, and simultaneously could sell a larger package of services. Those who are concerned mainly with the curriculum claim that it is outdated or irrelevant. So the curriculum is filled with new packaged courses on African Culture, North American Imperialism, Women's Lib, Pollution, or the Consumer Society. Passive learning is wrong—it is indeed—so we graciously allow students to decide what and how they want to be taught. Schools are prison houses. Therefore principals are authorized to approve teach-outs, moving the school desks to a roped-off Harlem street. Sensitivity training becomes fashionable. So we import group therapy into the classroom. School, which was supposed to teach everybody everything, now becomes all things to all children.

Other critics emphasize that schools make inefficient use of modern science. Some would administer drugs to make it easier for the instructor to change the child's behavior. Others would transform school into a stadium for educational gaming. Still others would electrify the classroom. If they are simplistic disciples of McLuhan, they replace blackboards and textbooks with multimedia happenings; if they follow Skinner, they claim to be able to modify behavior more efficiently than old-fashioned classroom practitioners can.

Most of these changes have, of course, some good effects. The experimental schools have fewer truants. Parents do have a greater feeling of participation in a decentralized district. Pupils, assigned by their teacher to an apprenticeship, do often turn out to be more competent than those who stay in the classroom. Some children do improve their knowledge of Spanish in the language lab because they prefer playing with the knobs of a tape recorder to conversation with their Puerto Rican peers. Yet all these improvements operate within predictably narrow limits, since they leave the hidden curriculum of school intact.

Some reformers would like to shake loose from the hidden curriculum of public schools, but they rarely succeed. Free schools that lead to further free schools produce a mirage of freedom, even though the chain of attendance is often interrupted by long stretches of loafing. Attendance through seduction inculcates the need for educational treatment more persuasively than does the reluctant attendance enforced by a truant officer. Permissive teachers in a padded classroom can easily render their pupils impotent to survive once they leave. Learning in these schools often remains nothing more than the acquisition of socially valued skills defined, in this instance, by the consensus of a commune rather than by the decree of a school board. New presbyter is but old priest writ large.

Free schools, to be truly free, must meet two conditions: first, they must be run in a way to prevent the introduction of the hidden curriculum of graded attendance and certified students studying at the feet of certified teachers. And more importantly, they must provide a framework in which all participants, staff and pupils, can free themselves from the hidden foundations of a schooled society. The first condition is frequently stated in the aims of a free school. The second condition is only rarely recognized and is difficult to state as the goal of a free school.

An ideal free school tries to provide education and at the same time tries to prevent that education from being used to establish or justify a class structure, from becoming a rationale for measuring the pupil against some abstract scale, and from repressing, controlling, and cutting him down to size. But as long as the free school tries to provide "general education," it cannot move beyond the hidden assumptions of school. Among these assumptions is that which impels us to treat all people as if they were newcomers who had to go through a naturalization process. Only certified consumers of knowledge are admitted to citizenship. Another assumption is that man is born immature and must "mature" before he can fit into civilized society. Man must be guided away from his natural environment and pass through a social womb in which he hardens sufficiently to fit into everyday life. Free schools can perform this function often better than schools of a less seductive kind.

Free educational establishments share with less-free establishments another characteristic. They depersonalize the responsibility for "education." They place an institution *in loco parentis*. They perpetuate the idea that "teaching," if done outside the family, ought to be done by an agency, for which the individual teacher is but an agent. In a schooled society even the family is reduced to an "agency of acculturation." Educational agencies which employ teachers to perform the corporate intent of their board are instruments for the depersonalization of intimate relations.

A revolution against those forms of privilege and power which are based on claims to professional knowledge must start with a transformation of consciousness about the nature of learning. This means, above all, a shift of responsibility for teaching and learning. Knowledge can be defined as a commodity only as long as it is viewed as the result of institutional enterprise or as the fulfillment of institutional objectives. Only when a man recovers the sense of personal responsibility for what he learns and teaches can the spell be broken and the alienation of learning from living be overcome.

The recovery of the power to learn or to teach means that the teacher who takes the risk of interfering in somebody else's private affairs also assumes responsibility for the results. Similarly, the student who exposes himself to the influence of a teacher must take responsibility for his own education. For such purposes educational institutions—if they are needed at all—ideally take the form of facility centers where one can get a roof of the right size over his head, access to a piano or a kiln, and to records, books, or slides. Schools, TV stations, theaters, and the like are designed primarily for use by professionals. Deschooling society means above all the denial of professional status for the second-oldest profession, namely teaching. The certification of teachers now constitutes an undue restriction on the right to free speech; the corporate structure and professional pretensions of journalism an undue restriction on the right to free press. Compulsory attendance rules interfere with free assembly. The deschooling of society is nothing less than a cultural mutation by which a people recovers the effective use of its Constitutional freedoms: learning and teaching by men who know they are born free rather than treated to freedom. Most people learn most of the time when they do whatever they enjoy; most people are curious and want to give meaning to whatever they come in contact with; and most people are capable of personal intimate intercourse with others unless they are stupefied by inhuman work or turned off by schooling.

The fact that people in rich countries do not learn much on their own constitutes no proof to the contrary. Rather it is a consequence of life in an environment from which, paradoxically, they cannot learn much, precisely because it is so highly programmed. They are constantly frustrated by the structure of contemporary society in which the facts on which decisions can be made have become more elusive. They live in an environment in which tools that can be used for creative purposes have become luxuries, an environment in which the channels of communication serve a few to talk to many.

A modern myth would make us believe that the sense of impotence with which most men live today is a consequence of technology that cannot but create huge systems. But it is not technology that makes systems huge, tools immensely powerful, channels of communication one-directional. Quite the contrary: Properly controlled, technology could provide each man with the ability to understand his environment better, to shape it powerfully with his own hands, and to permit him full intercommunication to a degree never before possible. Such an alternative use of technology constitutes the central alternative in education.

If a person is to grow up he needs, first of all, access to

things, to places, and to processes, to events, and to records. He needs to see, to touch, to tinker with, to grasp whatever there is in a meaningful setting. This access is now largely denied. When knowledge became a commodity, it acquired the protections of private property, and thus a principle designed to guard personal intimacy became a rationale for declaring facts off-limits for people without proper credentials. In schools teachers keep knowledge to themselves unless it fits into the day's program. The media inform, but exclude those things they regard as unfit to print. Information is locked into special languages, and specialized teachers live off its retranslation. Patents are protected by corporations, secrets are guarded by bureaucracies, and the power to keep others out of private preserves—be they cockpits, law offices, junkyards, or clinics —is jealously guarded by professions, institutions, and nations. Neither the political nor the professional structure of our societies, East and West, could withstand the elimination of the power to keep entire classes of people from facts that could serve them. The access to facts that I advocate goes far beyond truth in labeling. Access must be built into reality, while all we ask of advertising is a guarantee that it does not mislead. Access to reality constitutes a fundamental alternative in education to a system that only purports to teach *about* it.

Abolishing the right to corporate secrecy—even when professional opinion holds that this secrecy serves the common good— is, as shall presently appear, a much more radical political goal than the traditional demand for public ownership or control of the tools of production. The socialization of tools without the effective socialization of know-how in their use tends to put the knowledge-capitalist into the position formerly held by the financier. The technocrat's only claim to power is the stock he holds in some class of scarce and secret knowledge, and the best means to protect its value is a large and capital-intensive organization that renders access to know-how formidable and forbidding.

It does not take much time for the interested learner to acquire almost any skill that he wants to use. We tend to forget this in a society where professional teachers monopolize entrance into all fields and thereby stamp teaching by uncertified individuals as quackery. There are few mechanical skills used in industry or research that are as demanding, complex, and dangerous as driving a car, a skill that most people acquire quickly from a peer. Not all people are suited for advanced logic, yet those who are make rapid progress if they are challenged to play mathematical games at an early stage. One out of twenty kids in Cuernavaca can beat me at Wiff 'n' Proof after a couple of weeks' training. In four months all but a small percentage of motivated adults at our Center for Intercultural Documentation learn Spanish well enough to conduct academic business in the new language.

A first step toward opening up access to skills would be to provide various incentives for skilled individuals to share their knowledge. Inevitably, this would run counter to the interests of guilds and professions and unions. Yet multiple apprenticeship is attractive. It provides everybody with an opportunity to learn something about almost anything. There is no reason why a person should not combine the ability to drive a car, repair telephones and toilets, act as a midwife, and function as an architectural draftsman. Special interest groups and their disciplined consumers would, of course, claim that the public needs the protection of a professional guarantee. But this argument is now steadily being challenged by consumer protection associations. We have to take much more seriously the objection that economists raise to the radical socialization of skills: that "progress" will be impeded if knowledge—patents, skills, and all the rest—is democratized. Their arguments can be faced only if we demonstrate to them the growth rate of futile diseconomies generated by any existing educational system.

Access to people willing to share their skills is no guarantee of learning. Such access is restricted not only by the monopoly of educational programs over learning and of unions over licensing but also by a technology of scarcity. The skills that count today are know-how in the use of tools that were designed to be scarce. These tools produce goods or render services that everybody wants but only a few can enjoy and which only a limited number of people know how to use. Only a few privileged individuals out of the total number of people who have a given disease ever benefit from the results of sophisticated medical technology, and even fewer doctors develop the skill to use it.

The same results of medical research have, however, also been employed to create a basic tool kit that permits army and navy medics, with only a few months of training, to obtain results under battlefield conditions that would have been beyond the expectations of full-fledged doctors during World War II. On an even simpler level any peasant girl could learn how to diagnose and treat most infections if medical scientists prepared dosages and instructions specifically for a given geographic area.

All these examples illustrate the fact that educational considerations alone suffice to demand a radical reduction of the professional structure that now impedes the mutual relationship between the scientist and the majority of people who want access to science. If this demand were heeded, all men could learn to use yesterday's tools, rendered more effective and durable by modern science, to create tomorrow's world.

Unfortunately, precisely the contrary trend prevails at present. I know a coastal area in South America where most people support themselves by fishing from small boats. The outboard motor is certainly the tool that has changed most dramatically the lives of these coastal fishermen. But in the area I have surveyed, half of all outboard motors that were purchased between 1945 and 1950 are still kept running by constant tinkering, while half the motors purchased in 1965 no longer run because they were not built to be repaired. Technological progress provides the majority of people with gadgets they cannot afford and deprives them of the simpler tools they need.

Metals, plastics, and ferro cement used in building have greatly improved since the 1940s and ought to provide more people with the opportunity to create their own homes. But in the United States, while in 1948 more than 30 per cent of all one-family homes were owner-built, by the end of the 1960s the percentage of those who acted as their own contractors had dropped to less than 20 per cent.

The lowering of the skill level through so-called economic development becomes even more visible in Latin America. Here most people still build their own homes from floor to roof. Often they use mud in the form of adobe and thatchwork of unsurpassed utility in the moist, hot, and windy climate. In other places they make their dwellings out of cardboard, oildrums, and other industrial refuse. Instead of providing people with simple tools and highly standardized, durable, and easily repaired components, all governments have gone in for the mass production of low-cost buildings.

It is clear that not one single country can afford to provide satisfactory modern dwelling units for the majority of its people. Yet everywhere this policy makes it progressively more difficult for the majority to acquire the knowledge and skills they need to build better houses for themselves.

The first step, then, toward opening up access to skills is to provide incentives for skilled individuals to share their knowledge. Secondly, every postindustrial society must possess a basic tool kit which by its very nature counteracts technocratic control. For educational reasons we must work toward a society in which scientific knowledge is incorporated in tools and components that can be used meaningfully in units small enough to be within the reach of all. Only such tools can socialize access to skills. Only such tools favor temporary associations among those who want to use them for specific occasions. Only such tools allow specific goals to emerge in the process of their use, as any tinkerer knows. Only the combination of guaranteed access to facts and of limited power in most tools renders it possible to envisage a subsistence economy capable of incorporating the fruits of modern science. The development of such a scientific subsistence economy is unquestionably to the advantage of the overwhelming majority of people in poor countries. It is also the only alternative to progressive pollution, exploitation, and opaqueness in rich countries. But, as we have seen, the dethroning of the GNP cannot be achieved without simultaneously subverting GNE (Gross National Education—usually conceived as manpower capitalization). An egalitarian economy cannot exist in a society in which the right to produce is conferred by schools.

The feasibility of a modern subsistence economy does not depend on new scientific inventions. It depends primarily on the ability of a society to agree on fundamental, self-chosen antibureaucratic and antitechnocratic restraints. These restraints can take many forms, but they will not work unless they touch the basic dimensions of life. The substance of these voluntary social restraints would be very simple matters that can be fully understood and judged by any prudent man. All such restraints would be chosen to promote stable and equal enjoyment of scientific know-how. The French say that it takes a thousand years to educate a peasant to deal with a cow. It would not take two generations to help all people in Latin America or Africa to use and repair outboard motors, simple cars, pumps, medicine kits, and ferro cement machines if their design does not change every few years. And since a joyful life is one of constant meaningful intercourse with others in a meaningful environment, equal enjoyment does translate into equal education.

At present a consensus on austerity is difficult to imagine. The reason usually given for the impotence of the majority is stated in terms of political or economic class. What is not usually understood is that the new class structure of a schooled society is even more powerfully controlled by vested interests. No doubt an imperialist and capitalist organization of society provides the social structure within which a minority can have disproportionate influence over the effective opinion of the majority. But in a technocratic society the power of a minority of knowledge capitalists can prevent the formation of true public opinion through control of scientific know-how and the media of communication. Constitutional guarantees of free speech, free press, and free assembly were meant to ensure government by the people. Modern electronics, photo-offset presses, time-sharing computers, and telephones have in principle provided the hardware that could give an entirely new meaning to these freedoms. Unfortunately these things are used in modern media to increase the power of knowledge bankers to funnel their program-packages through international chains to more people, instead of being used to increase true networks that provide equal opportunity for the encounter among the members of the majority.

Deschooling the culture and social structure requires the use of technology to make participatory politics possible. Only on the basis of a majority coalition can limits to secrecy and growing power be determined without dictatorship. We need a new environment in which growing up can be classless, or we will get a brave new world in which Big Brother educates us all.

Index